KT-478-553

*Economic Theory and Policy
in the UK*

ECONOMIC THEORY AND POLICY IN THE UK

An Outline and Assessment of the
Controversies

Rod Cross

Martin Robertson · Oxford

© Rod Cross 1982

First published in 1982 by Martin Robertson & Company Ltd.,
108 Cowley Road, Oxford OX4 1JF.

All rights reserved. No part of this publication may be
reproduced, stored in a retrieval system, or transmitted, in
any form or by any means, electronic, mechanical, photo-
copying, recording or otherwise, without the prior written
permission of the copyright holder.

Except in the United States of America, this book is sold
subject to the condition that it shall not, by way of trade or
otherwise be lent, re-sold, hired out, or otherwise circulated
without the publisher's prior consent in any form of binding
or cover other than that in which it is published and without
a similar condition including this condition being imposed on
the subsequent purchaser.

British Library Cataloguing in Publication Data

Cross, Rod
   Economic theory and policy in the UK.
   1. Great Britain – Economic policy – 1945 –
   I. Title
   330.9'41'0858   HC256.6

   ISBN 0-85520-408-7
   ISBN 0-85520-407-9 Pbk

Typeset in 10 on 12pt IBM Press Roman by Unicus Graphics, Horsham
Printed and bound in Great Britain at
The Camelot Press Ltd, Southampton

To my late father

Contents

Preface

This book was written in August 1981 and at least in part reflects the preoccupations of this time. Many of the themes discussed, however, are likely to be relevant to the whole of the 1980s, and perhaps longer in view of the tendency of current policy debates to repeat the themes of past policy debates. I would like to thank my ex-colleagues David Laidler and Bernard Corry for unwittingly having helped me to understand some of economic thought. I would also like to thank Keith Shaw for being the inspiration behind the enterprise as a whole; and my colleagues Antoni Chawluk and David Cobham for many helpful discussions of the issues covered in this book. I am indebted to Anne Stewart who prepared the bibliography and assisted the enterprise in many other ways. My thanks are also due to Betty Niven who typed the manuscript. None of the above are responsible for the errors and confusion that remain.

Rod Cross
St Andrews
September 1981

1 Introduction

> The worst readers are those who proceed like plundering soldiers:
> they pick up a few things they can use, soil and confuse the rest, and
> blaspheme the whole. (Friedrich Nietzsche, *Mixed Opinions and
> Maxims*, 1879)

This book attempts to explain and assess the main controversies regarding the conduct of macroeconomic policy in the UK. The aim is to
make it easier for the beginner or layman to understand the issues
involved in such controversies. We hope that in presenting a summary
of the issues on which economists are divided we have not proceeded
like the plundering soldiers in the quotation above.

The point of departure for many of the controversies regarding
economic policy in the 1980s has been the policy innovations introduced by the Conservative government which came to power in May
1979. This new economic strategy was

> based on four principles: first, the strengthening of incentives, parti-
> cularly through tax cuts, allowing people to keep more of their
> earnings in their own hands, so that hard work, ability and success
> are rewarded; second, greater freedom of choice by reducing the
> state's role and enlarging that of the individual; third, the reduction
> of the borrowing requirement of the public sector to a level which
> leaves room for the rest of the economy to prosper; and fourth,
> through firm monetary and fiscal discipline, bringing inflation under
> control and ensuring that those taking part in collective bargaining
> are obliged to live with the consequences of their actions.[1]

This strategy marked the culmination of the retreat from demand
management policies evident since the mid-1970s; marked the beginning

of a supply side strategy for managing the economy; and marked a return to restrictive fiscal and monetary policies rationalized by arguments similar to those used by the authorities in the 1920s and 1930s.

In the 2 years after this strategy was initiated unemployment rose from 1.3 million to nearly 3 million; the rate of inflation rose from 13.4 per cent in 1979 to 18 per cent in 1980 before falling back to around 12 per cent in 1981; industrial output fell by 15 per cent over the 2 years; the effective exchange rate for sterling rose from 88.1 in June 1979 to 102.5 in February 1981 before falling back to 95.4 in June 1981; and the UK experienced the most severe cyclical downswing in economic activity experienced since the interwar period. It is absurd to blame the government for everything that has happened in the UK economy over the last 2 years, but it is equally absurd not to attribute a good part of what has happened to the government's economic strategy. As far as the rest of the 1980s is concerned the government's view is that the economy will recover from the present severe recession under its own steam on the basis of current policies. The argument here is that the rate of inflation will fall sufficiently to allow the limits for money spending implied by the Medium Term Financial Strategy to permit a recovery in real spending in the UK economy. Once such a turnround occurs, the argument goes, the policies to stimulate the supply side of the economy will come into their own. Such a prognosis reflects what can be called a *New Classical Macroeconomics* view of the economy.

The government's economic strategy has encountered severe criticism from those who see the current strategy as a recipe for a severe depression in the UK economy during the 1980s. Many of the government's own supporters have called for a U-turn in economic policy, recommending activist measures to expand aggregate demand. More radical policies have been suggested under the banner of the Alternative Economic Strategy (AES) espoused by sections of the Labour party and other socialist groups.[2] Significant differences exist amongst the left regarding the constituents of the AES,[3] and the following is merely a list of the elements included in at least one version of the AES: increased public spending; relaxation of monetary policy; import controls; nationalization of the banking system and certain large companies; industrial democracy in work-places; controls on capital movements; direction of the investment funds of the large institutional investors; prices and/or incomes policies; planning agreements between the government and private sector; a shorter working week; national minimum wages and maximum salaries; and a wealth tax.

In between the radical strategy of the present government and the radical strategy involved in the AES come a wide variety of economic strategies which could be pursued. It is completely wrong to assert that an economic strategy must be based on demand management or supply management alone. Indeed it can be argued that only strategies which involve the management in tandem of the supply and demand sides of the economy will permit the achievement of policy objectives.

The rest of this book is concerned with explaining and assessing the controversies surrounding macroeconomic policy strategies for the UK economy. Section I details the different views of the way the economy works which are involved in the main research programmes in macroeconomics, and outlines the programmes of political action which are suggested. Section II considers the nature of unemployment, inflation, economic growth and business cycles as objectives of economic policy. Section III outlines the main policy instruments available to the authorities to pursue such objectives: fiscal policy, monetary policy, wage and price controls, import controls and exchange rate policies. During the course of the book we will offer our own appraisal of the controversies and suggest certain courses of policy action. The view taken here is that a hysteresis-augmented version of *Orthodox Monetarism* best explains the workings of the UK economy – see the discussion in Chapters 8 and 12-19. Our appraisals and suggestions are open to the maxim coined by Mandy Rice-Davies: 'Well, he would say that, wouldn't he?'

Section 1

Research programmes in macroeconomics

2 Arguments in macroeconomics

'Do you want an Argument or Abuse?' (Monty Python)

Economists often wash their differences regarding the appropriate conduct of macroeconomic policy in public. On 30 March 1981, for example, several national newspapers in the UK published the following statement, signed by 364 academic economists:

We, who are all present or retired members of the economics staffs of British universities, are convinced that: (a) there is no basis in economic theory or supporting evidence for the Government's belief that by deflating demand they will bring inflation permanently under control and hereby induce an automatic recovery in output and employment; (b) present policies will deepen the depression, erode the industrial base of our economy and threaten its social and political stability; (c) there are alternative policies; and (d) the time has come to reject monetarist policies and consider urgently which alternative offers the best hope of sustained economic recovery.

On the same day HM Treasury issued a statement 'totally disagreeing' with the statement of the 364. On the following day the Prime Minister and First Lord of HM Treasury, Mrs Thatcher, told the House of Commons that 'I rather thought those 364 did themselves more damage than anyone else'. Of the reasons why certain academic economists did not sign the statement, the following is fairly representative:

The first clause is wrong – there are theories which would support the government's policies. Moreover the statement is weak because it is wholly negative. Finally, although the present policies should not

7

have been adopted, and have incurred very heavy costs, it would make no sense to reverse them now. What could be gained? A couple of hundred thousand off the unemployment rate?[1]

Sources of disagreement

Although such disputes are given almost daily coverage in the media, it is not usually clear why such differences exist. Is it simply because academic economists like to argue? Or is it because economists have a vested interest in particular macroeconomic policies? Or because the values of academic economists differ as to relative costs of unemployment, inflation and low economic growth? Or do the differences derive from different conceptions as to the way the economy works? Or from different diagnoses of the current state of the economy? At this juncture it is worth pointing out that, despite pejorative aphorisms such as 'with five economists you will get at least six different opinions', 'lay all the economists in the world end to end and you will not reach a conclusion', other academic disciplines are characterized by somewhat similar disagreements. What differentiates economics, and especially macroeconomics, from other disciplines is that debates at the 'frontiers of knowledge' tend to take place very much in the public eye as well as in learned journals. One of the more obvious reasons for this is that the controversies touch on issues of direct relevance to everyday life. Everyone is an amateur economist in a sense in which everyone is not an amateur physicist.

Methodological considerations

To try and disentangle the reasons why academic economists often disagree with each other regarding the appropriate conduct of macroeconomic policy it is useful to look at some methodological considerations. A first and familiar consideration is the Humean guillotine between 'is' and 'ought' statements, or between 'positive' and 'normative' economics. Statements about what 'ought' to be done as far as macroeconomic policy is concerned cannot be derived from statements or hypotheses about the way the economy 'is' structured alone: values regarding political or moral matters need to be introduced in order to derive 'ought' statements. Similarly statements about the way the economy 'is' structured cannot be derived from statements about the way the economy 'ought' to be structured. Providing that we are careful in our use of language – words such as 'bastard', 'drunk' and 'unemployed' often carry both descriptive and evaluative meaning – it is possible to preserve the Humean guillotine between 'is' and 'ought' statements.[2]

Given this distinction, differences between academic economists regarding the conduct of macroeconomic policy can be traced either to differences in their values as to how economies 'should' be structured, or differences as to how economies 'are' structured. Whilst on the surface it would appear that economists differ markedly in the relative importance they attach to such items as having single- rather than double-digit rates of inflation;[3] the distress associated with high un-employment;[4] or the benefits to be derived from a higher rate of economic growth;[5] such differences often prove on closer examination to derive from disagreements about the way economies *are* structured. Thus, different views as to the priority to be attached to policies to reduce the rate of inflation often derive from different estimates of the costs of living with say a 15 per cent as opposed to a 5 per cent rate of inflation; different views as to the importance of taking macroeconomic policy measures to reduce unemployment often reflect different theoretical positions regarding the extent to which unemployment is caused by microeconomic factors, such as real wages or unemployment benefits being 'too high', as opposed to macroeconomic factors, such as aggregate demand being 'too low'; even differences concerning such as the importance of achieving a higher rate of economic growth turn in part on differences regarding the efficiency of resource allocation systems in discouraging any 'bads' which arise from economic growth.

The view taken in this chapter is that the main source of disagreement amongst academic economists arises from 'is' questions rather than 'ought' questions. No doubt there are differences in moral and political judgements amongst academic macroeconomists, but we would argue that such differences do not loom large in relation to the disagreements which concern the way economies *do* work as opposed to how they *should* work.

So far we have only considered the reasons for disagreement amongst *academic* economists. Surely once we come to consider politicians and other amateur economists, disagreements over values or 'ought' questions come to play a dominant role? Even here, however, it is plausible to argue that disagreements over 'is' questions play at least as important a role. The following concluding remarks from Maynard Keynes' *General Theory* make precisely this point:

Is the fulfilment of these ideas a visionary hope? Have they insufficient roots in the motives which govern the evolution of political society? The ideas of economists and political philosophers, both when they are right and when they are wrong, are more powerful than is commonly understood. Indeed the world is ruled by little else. Practical men, who believe themselves to be quite exempt from intellectual influences, are usually the slaves of some defunct economist. Madmen in authority, who hear voices in the air, are distilling their frenzy from some academic scribbler of a few years back. I am sure that the power of vested interests is vastly exaggerated compared with the gradual encroachment of ideas. Not, indeed, immediately, but after a certain interval; for in the field of economic and political philosophy there are not many who are influenced by new theories after they are twenty-five or thirty years of age, so that the ideas which civil servants and politicians and even agitators apply to current events are not likely to be the newest. But, sooner or later, it is ideas, not vested interests, which are dangerous for good or evil.[6]

Appraising economic theories

Given our argument that the main disagreements amongst macroeconomists arise from differences in view as to the way economies work, are there rational grounds we can state for preferring one theoretical conception, as to the way economies work, to another? The orthodox answer to this question among economists is that 'positive' economic theory is concerned with the derivation of testable hypotheses about the economic world and with attempts to falsify such hypotheses.[7] This is the *falsificationist* methodological position outlined by the philosopher Karl Popper. As far as the *appraisal* of competing theories in macroeconomics is concerned, this methodological position would have us proceed as follows.

In advance of testing – this is *prior appraisal* – we should prefer one theory T to another theory T' if T makes more falsifiable claims about the economic world than T', that is if T makes more precise claims about a wider range of economic phenomena than T'. After testing our theories – this is *posterior appraisal* – we are instructed to prefer T to T' if (1) T has more *true* consequences or predictions regarding the economic world than T' *and* if (2) T has fewer *false* consequences or predictions regarding the economic world than T'.[8]

Several problems arise with the application of such a method of appraisal in macroeconomics. First, there is the problem that much of the observational evidence which we use to test theories is itself subject to dispute – this is the case in other disciplines as well as in economics. How are we, for example, to distinguish between refutations of a theory which arise from 'false' observations of unemployment based on a 'bad' theory as to how to measure unemployment, and refutations which arise from 'true' observations based on a 'good' theory as to how to measure unemployment?

Second, there is the problem that theories are often *incommensurate* in the sense that they talk about different things. Theories can not only have (1) *true* consequences and (2) *false* consequences regarding economic phenomena, but also (3) can be completely *silent* as to the economic phenomena in which we are interested. How are we then to trade proficiency as far as (1) *true* consequences or predictions are concerned, with deficiencies as far as (2) *false* consequences or predictions or (3) *silence*, or no consequences or predictions, are concerned? The problem here is one of comparing like with like in macroeconomics. Keynesian and monetarist theories, to take a purely hypothetical example, might have similar *true* consequences or predictions regarding output and unemployment, but the Keynesian theory might be *silent*, i.e. have no consequences or predictions, regarding the rate of inflation, whereas the monetarist theory might have *false* consequences or predictions regarding the rate of inflation. Our appraisal of the relative merits of the Keynesian and monetarist theories would then depend on whether we prefer a theory which is *silent* about the rate of inflation to one that has *false* consequences or predictions regarding the rate of inflation.

Third, it is not obvious that the econometric methods conventionally used to test economic hypotheses provide us with much revealing information about the merits of competing theories in macroeconomics. Many supposed tests of hypotheses using econometric methods amount to little more than a description of macroeconomic data during a particular estimation period. What usually happens is that the investigator searches the data for the quantitative specification of an hypothesis which best 'fits' the particular period of economic history used for estimation purposes. Often little can be said about the statistical significance of quantitative specifications of hypotheses derived from such data searches, and the goodness of 'fit' of such specifications during their estimation period often proves to be a poor guide to their predictive performance outside the sample period.[9] Given that most hypotheses in macroeconomics talk only about the *qualitative* or sign (up or down) effects of one economic phenomenon on another, it is not obvious that the precisely *quantified* versions of hypotheses in macroeconomics derived from econometric estimation can be used justifiably to represent the underlying *qualitative* hypotheses. There is much leeway for holding on to an underlying *qualitative* hypothesis in the face of false consequences or predictions being encountered by a surrogate *quantitative* version of the hypothesis. Such considerations suggest that macroeconomists would be well advised to place greater weight on testing the *qualitative* consequences or predictions of their hypotheses. It is wrong to think that we can appraise only the *quantitative* consequences or predictions of hypotheses.

The Duhem-Quine thesis

A final and arguably most important problem with the *falsificationist* method of appraising the relative merits of theories in macroeconomics is its failure to take into account the conjointness of hypothesis testing. Consider the following hypothesis, H_0: the rate of inflation is determined by the prior rate of monetary expansion. In order to test the consequences or predictions of this hypothesis we inevitably need to introduce other hypotheses in order to produce statements about the economic world which are clear enough for us to be able to say whether they are true or false. The following are some of the *auxiliary* hypotheses which will usually have to be invoked *conjointly* with H_0 in order to give H_0 testable consequences regarding the rate of inflation. First, a set of hypotheses H_A which specify how variables *co-determined* with the rate of inflation, such as the level of output or unemployment, are determined. Second, a set of hypotheses H_B which specify how to *measure* the variables such as the rate of inflation, rate of monetary expansion or level of unemployment mentioned in the theory. Third, hypotheses H_C which specify the *time lags* involved in the economic relationships postulated. Fourth, hypotheses H_D which distinguish *endogenous* from *exogenous* variables so as to be able to identify the H_0 hypothesis over the observations available. Fifth, a set of hypotheses H_E which specify the behaviour of the economic system *as a whole*, the H_0 relationship forming part of the interactive economic system specified. Sixth, H_F hypotheses which postulate how *statistical inferences* are to be drawn from the available observations. Seventh, H_G ceteris paribus hypotheses which state which things are to be held equal in order that the H_0 relationship be observed. Finally, but by no means exhaustively, we have a set of hypotheses H_H which specify the *boundary conditions* for the theory, that is the range of economic phenomena which are commensurate with the H_0 hypothesis.

Given this large number of sets of *auxiliary* hypotheses $H_A, H_B, \ldots, H_H$ which are being tested *conjointly* with H_0, all that we can say if a particular test statement regarding the H_0 hypothesis turns out to have false consequences or predictions is that at least one of the hypotheses H_0, $H_A, H_B, H_C, \ldots, H_H$ is false. *Prima facie* it could be any of the H_A, H_B, $H_C, \ldots, H_H$ hypotheses which are responsible for the false consequences or predictions rather than H_0. There will not usually be any sure method of finding out which of the constituent hypotheses is responsible for the false consequences or predictions.

This state of affairs is summarized in the *Duhem-Quine thesis* which states that *it is not possible to falsify single hypotheses*. The *weak* version of the Duhem-Quine (DQ) thesis, which derives from the French physicist Pierre Duhem (1906), reasons that *we can never be sure* that saving auxiliary hypotheses do not exist which could rescue our target hypotheses, such as H_0, from refutation. The *strong* version of the DQ thesis, derived from the early work of the American philosopher Willard van Orman Quine (1951), argues that we can *always* save target hypotheses from refutation by sufficiently rearranging our auxiliary hypotheses and statements.[10] The *conjointness* of hypothesis testing emphasized in the DQ thesis helps to explain why controversies in macroeconomics often concern whole groupings of hypotheses, or schools of thought, rather than single hypotheses. The question of how to appraise the relative merits of such groupings of hypotheses, or schools of thought, then arises. This problem was one of the major concerns of the philosopher Imre Lakatos.

Lakatos

Lakatos sees hypotheses as being grouped together in structured wholes in the form of *research programmes*. Adherents to a research programme share a common set of *heuristics*, or methods of solving problems. The method by which they do *not* solve problems is termed the *negative heuristic*. The latter serves to define a set of basic propositions or *hard-core* hypotheses which are seen as being fundamental to the way adherents to the research programme think about and explain, in this context, the behaviour of economic systems. Thus members of a research programme may believe that private sector behaviour is such that mixed capitalist economies tend to return quickly to equilibria characterized by 'full' employment, stable inflation rates and maximum economic growth under their own steam provided that governments abstain from discretionary or activist policies of macroeconomic management. According to the Lakatos characterization, members of such a research programme would not challenge or re-think such *hard-core* propositions regarding the way mixed capitalist economies work in the face of difficulties in explaining the evidence as to how such economies actually behave. Instead the *positive heuristic* aspect of their research programme would direct their attention to the amendment of less fundamental, or *protective belt*, hypotheses in order to explain the evidence. If, for example, the level of unemployment were to rise in a manner not predicted by the research programme, members of the research programme would amend their *protective belt* hypotheses dealing with such things as the effects of unemployment insurance benefits on 'voluntary unemployment'[11] in order to explain the rise in unemployment, rather than question their *hard-core* propositions regarding the overall workings of mixed capitalist economic systems.

To appraise the merits of rival *research programmes*, the Lakatos method proceeds by comparing the content of corroborated consequences or predictions in the rival research programmes: a programme with more corroborated predictions is to be preferred to one with less. Over time research programmes will be challenged by new evidence regarding macroeconomic phenomena thrown up by contemporary history or derived from looking at other countries or earlier historical time periods. If the hypotheses in a research programme are amended in such a way as to increase the testable consequences or predictions of the research programme, and if such additional consequences or predictions are corroborated, the research programme is termed *progressive*. If the research programme is amended in such a way as to reduce its range of predictions or testable consequences, or if the number of corroborated predictions or consequences falls, the research programme is termed *degenerate*.[12]

We would argue that the above Lakatos appraisal criteria offer a useful way of comparing the relative merits of different macroeconomic theories. There are still difficulties in comparing like with like, given that certain macroeconomic theories give false predictions regarding certain macroeconomic phenomena, whereas other theories are simply silent as regards such phenomena. Despite such problems, we would argue that the Lakatos method of appraisal offers a sensible way of approaching the appraisal problem raised by the DQ thesis. In the discussion of particular schools of thought in macroeconomics in the rest of this section, we will *implicitly* employ Lakatos' appraisal criteria.

3 The schools of thought

> And what rough beast, its hour come round at last,
> Slouches towards Bethlehem to be born?
> (W. B. Yeats, *The Second Coming*)

So far we have argued that different theoretical conceptions about the way economies work account for much of the disagreement amongst macroeconomists regarding the appropriate conduct of macroeconomic policy; and that we can only test and appraise such different theoretical conceptions as systems of theories or research programmes rather than as individual hypotheses. The task of the coming chapters is to outline some of the main research programmes in macroeconomics and the courses of macroeconomic policy action which such research programmes tend to suggest. Before proceeding to this task it is worthwhile to point out some of the complications which arise in relating the ideas contained in academic research programmes to the actual conduct of macroeconomic policy.

Policy action and economic theory

First of all academic research programmes in macroeconomics will usually be of interest to policy-makers only if they *suggest* (rather than *imply*) a specific programme of political action, that is if they suggest a specific agenda of policy measures.[1] Thus, in terms of the Lakatos appraisal criteria discussed in the last chapter, we can think of research programmes as not only having consequences or content regarding the explanation of macroeconomic phenomena, but also as having content with regard to the macroeconomic policy measures which they suggest. Thus it is possible to think of a research programme which has a high content of corroborated consequences or predictions regarding the

15

explanation of macroeconomic phenomena, but which has little content regarding the specific policy measures it suggests. Such a research programme might be preferred on academic grounds to other research programmes, but policy-makers may prefer a more *degenerate* – in the academic sense – research programme which provides a wider or more interesting programme of political action. Thus the research programmes which provide a 'better' explanation of macroeconomic phenomena need not necessarily be those adopted by policy-makers. It is possible to argue that 'revolutions' in macroeconomics only occur when a research programme not only supersedes its rivals in terms of its corroborated consequences and predictions but also offers a more interesting programme of political action. The 'revolution' associated with the publication of Keynes' *General Theory* can be explained in such terms. All this means that we should not necessarily expect academic appraisal criteria regarding theories to accord with political appraisal criteria. A research programme in the 1980s which successfully explained the massive increase in UK unemployment since the late 1960s would not be of much interest to policy-makers unless it were to suggest a feasible set of policy measures to reduce unemployment.

Secondly, it would be naive to think that policy-makers are likely to commit themselves lock, stock and barrel to particular research programmes. They are more likely to behave like jackdaws, and pick out the elements in research programmes which provide them with a rationale for the policy actions they wish to take, discarding the elements which they do not find amenable. This means that policy-makers are likely to base their policy measures on the suggestions which arise from more than one research programme. Such pragmatic or opportunist use of academic theories as to how economies work can lead to considerable confusion in public debates about the merits and demerits of macroeconomic research programmes. The economic doctrines used by the Conservative government of 1979–84 are a good case in point. This administration has been labelled 'monetarist' in the media and elsewhere, where 'monetarism' is used to indicate anything from '... support for Latin American dictatorships employing torture ... to ... the hardships deliberately imposed on peoples by governments to punish them for laziness or poor productivity'.[2] The general public no doubt have some vague idea that 'monetarism' also concerns some 'technical' relationship between the money supply and inflation, but would find it hard to recognize a description of the academic research programme – such as given later in this book – which gave birth to the term 'monetarism'. The bastards bred by such illegitimacies in the breeding of programmes of political action are not conducive to rational public debate of the merits and demerits of the underlying economic theories as to how economies work. As we shall see, the macroeconomic policies pursued by the 1979-84 Conservative government would be better labelled 'New Classical Macroeconomics' rather than 'monetarist'.

Thirdly, adherents to academic research programmes would stress, with a greater or lesser emphasis, the contingency or uncertainty surrounding their claims about the way economies actually work. If we follow the logic of our methodological position through, all we as academic economists can claim for our theoretical positions is that they have so far proved to have fewer false consequences or predictions than other theoretical positions. The absence of certainty in the world at large applies equally as well to theoretical conceptions as to the way the world works. We know what we do not know. This means that decisions regarding macroeconomic policy inevitably have to take place under conditions of uncertainty as to which theory or research programme 'best' explains the workings of economic systems. Given this we would be wise to discount macroeconomic policy advice emanating from those who claim to know with certainty how economic systems work.

It is a vulgar and harmful misconception to believe that there are policy prescriptions which are certain to have the desired effects. We do not expect such certainty of doctors – why of economists? We simply do not know enough and perhaps we cannot know enough.[3]

Fourthly, macroeconomic policy measures are not only undertaken in the face of uncertainty as to the way the economy works, but also in the face of uncertainty as to the current state – and even recent history – of the economy. Thus, for example, expansionary fiscal measures were undertaken in the Spring Budget of 1972 at least in part on the understanding that the level of unemployment had shown no sign of falling away from the then post-1945 high – in excess of 1 million unemployed – which had been reached during the 1971-72 Winter. Hindsight allows us to say that unemployment was already falling by the time the Spring Budget of 1972 measures were announced, let alone before such measures came to take effect. The point is that policy-makers were not aware of this at the time, and could not have known with certainty that this was the case. Our knowledge of the current state of the economy is fraught with uncertainty, and such uncertainty will inevitably influence our views as to the most appropriate set of macroeconomic policy measures.

Finally, it would be misleading to think that we can neatly classify all macroeconomists as adhering to one or other of the research programmes which we will discuss. Not only do the hypotheses which make up research programmes change over time in response to logical or empirical challenge, but so also does the set of economists who adhere to a particular research programme. Some economists will be like 'floating voters', uncommitted to any particular research programme. Others will be against particular research programmes but not 'for' any particular alternative. Yet others will be eclectic in their ideas. The number of economists who have a strong commitment to a particular research programme is possibly rather small. Such economists, however, tend to have an influence which belies their numerical strength. It is for this reason that we will centre our discussion around the specific research programmes.

Identifying research programmes

The problem here is one of identifying *recognizable* research programmes. To draw a distinction merely between monetarists and Keynesians would be too *simpliste*. To list the ideas of influential economists one by one would be too tedious. The procedure adopted here for identifying research programmes follows on from the discussion of Lakatos in the previous chapter, and identifies research programmes by way of the basic *positive heuristic*, or method of solving problems, used in the research programme. We would argue that it is possible to trace the often complex networks of propositions or hypotheses which constitute research programmes back to such basic *positive heuristics*. The research programmes selected for discussion, along with their basic *positive heuristics*, are as follows:

(a) *Orthodox Keynesian:* 'explain fluctuations in output and employment by analysing fluctuations in the aggregate demand for output';
(b) *Disequilibrium Keynesian:* 'explain fluctuations in output and employment by analysing trading sequences taking place at disequilibrium prices';
(c) *Fundamental Keynesian:* 'explain fluctuations in output and employment with reference to fluctuations in expectations formed

in the face of intractable uncertainty regarding the future state of the economy';

(d) *New Cambridge Keynesian:* 'amend the propositions of orthodox Keynesianism to take account of the effects of financial assets on expenditure';

(e) *Orthodox Monetarist:* 'explain sustained variations in the rate of inflation by sustained prior variations in the rate of monetary expansion';

(f) *New Classical Macroeconomics:* 'analyse economies as being in a state of continuous market-clearing equilibrium with output and employment fluctuations reflecting errors in the rationally formed expectations of economic agents regarding prices';

(g) *Supply Side Macroeconomics:* 'explain variations in output and employment by reference to the factors which determine aggregate supply'.

4 Orthodox Keynesianism

'Explain fluctuations in output and employment by analysing fluctuations in the aggregate demand for output.'

Outline

The thrust of Keynes' *General Theory* (1936) was towards demonstrating that private sector behaviour in capitalist economies would not in general tend to generate temporary equilibrium positions for the economy which would be characterized by 'full' employment. Keynes' ideas have had a strong influence on most if not all of the research programmes to be discussed in later chapters – the New Classical Macroeconomics and Supply Side Macroeconomics can be seen as reactions *against* Keynes' ideas. Keynes' ideas also suggested a programme for political action: governments should intervene in capitalist economies to create a level of aggregate demand which would be sufficient to stimulate output levels which would lead to 'full' employment of the labour force. The novelty of the programme of political action suggested by Keynes' *General Theory* has been overestimated. Most of the 'classical' economists, including A. C. Pigou, whose ideas were rebutted by Keynes, also advocated public works programmes and the like at various times during the 1920s and 1930s.[1] The 'revolution' associated with Keynes' *General Theory* is more to be found in his theoretical analysis of *effective demand*, though such analysis did provide a firmer footing for political measures to stimulate aggregate demand than was provided by the alternative 'classical' theories of output and employment.

In the UK the main vehicle for the interpretation and development of Keynes' ideas up until the late 1960s was the Orthodox Keynesian

research programme. The ideas contained in this research programme
'... went cantering briskly through the fifties and early sixties; faltered
sometime in the middle sixties ... stumbled into the seventies ...';[2] and
staggered into the eighties. The central hypothesis or proposition used
in this research programme is that the level of aggregate output in an
economy is determined by the level of aggregate demand: *output is
demand-determined*; that is: $AD \rightarrow Y$, where AD is the level of aggregate demand and Y is the level of output. Figure 4.1 illustrates this
theory of output determination using the familiar income–expenditure
model. The equilibrium condition is $AD = Y$.

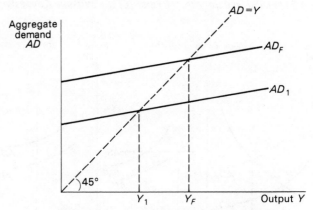

Figure 4.1. Aggregate demand and output

The second popular illustration of orthodox Keynesian theory is
given in the *IS–LM* model which has two equilibrium conditions,
$AD = Y$ (*IS* curve) and $M^S = M^D$ (*LM* curve), where M^S is the money
stock and M^D is the demand for money, thus introducing monetary
factors into the theory of income determination. In the UK the orthodox Keynesian research programme has not taken monetary factors to
have an important role in the determination of aggregate output.[3]
Figure 4.2 illustrates the general *IS–LM* model of income determination – Figure 4.2(a); and the extreme UK orthodox Keynesian cases
where monetary factors have a purely passive role in output determination – Figure 4.2(b) and (c). The latter cases will arise when aggregate
demand is completely insensitive to interest rates, and thus we have a
vertical *IS* curve (Figure 4.2(b)); or when either there is a liquidity

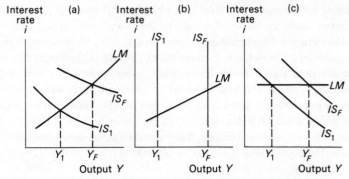

Figure 4.2. (a) The general case; (b) and (c) the extreme Keynesian cases

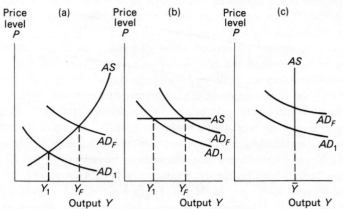

Figure 4.3. (a) The general case; (b) the extreme Keynesian case; (c) the extreme classical case

trap[4] or the authorities fix interest rates,[5] thus making the *LM* curves horizontal (Figure 4.2(c)).

A third popular vehicle for expressing the ideas of the orthodox Keynesian research programme is the aggregate demand and aggregate supply framework of analysis. Figure 4.3(a) illustrates the general case where both aggregate supply and demand help determine the level of output; Figure 4.3(b) illustrates the extreme UK Orthodox Keynesian case where aggregate supply is perfectly elastic with respect to the price level and so aggregate demand determines output; and Figure 4.3(c) illustrates the extreme Classical case where aggregate supply is perfectly inelastic, and so aggregate supply determines output.

The analysis illustrated in Figures 4.1, 4.2(b), 4.2(c) and 4.3(b) encapsulates quite well the thinking underlying the Orthodox Keynesian research programme in the UK. Output is determined by the level of *aggregate demand*, and both *monetary factors* and factors determining *aggregate supply* are given little or no role in determining the level of output and other variables such as employment which are at least partly determined by output. The fact that *monetary factors* are de-emphasized means that *fiscal policy* is assigned a key role in ensuring the creation of a level of aggregate demand, AD_F or IS_F, sufficient to yield a full employment level of output, Y_F.[6] The lack of emphasis on the role of *aggregate supply* factors in output determination means that *microeconomic* policy measures to influence such things as labour supply, productivity and the efficient functioning of markets are *not* assigned a key role by this research programme.

The theoretical conception underlying this research programme is one of disembodied and homogeneous flows of expenditure demand, income and output. Little or no attempt is made to trace such flows back to the choice decisions made by individual economic agents, and as such the theory can aptly be described as deriving from an 'hydraulic' conception of the workings of economic systems.[7] The main defence of this interpretation of the ideas contained in Keynes' *General Theory* is that Keynes himself did not disassociate himself from the *IS-LM* characterization of his theory. Writing to John Hicks, who invented the *IS-LM* apparatus,[8] on 31 March 1937, Keynes said, regarding the *IS-LM* model: 'I found it very interesting and really have next to nothing to say by way of criticism'.[9] Even if we accept the *IS-LM* characterization of Keynes' theory – see the arguments for not doing this by Disequilibrium and Fundamental Keynesians discussed later in this book – this does not mean that we have to accept that Keynes shared the de-emphasis of *monetary* and *aggregate supply* factors in income determination which is a characteristic of UK Orthodox Keynesian economists.

Appraisal

The Orthodox Keynesian research programme developed content or predictions primarily by investigating the factors determining the components of aggregate demand such as consumption, investment, government spending, taxes, imports, exports and stocks. In the 1950s and 1960s academics and those working in bastions of Orthodox Keynesianism such as HM Treasury and the National Institute of Economic and Social Research, produced many, apparently corroboratory, econometric studies of the determinants of the components of aggregate demand. As we shall see in our chapter on Fiscal Policy (Chapter 15), however, government attempts to use government expenditure and taxation policy as instruments to achieve output targets met with less success. Orthodox Keynesian economists have adopted a defensive reaction to the lack of corroboration of their predictions as to the effects of fiscal policy, saying, for example, that the policy measures were 'mistimed', or that balance of payments constraints in the 1950s and 1960s, and inflation constraints in the 1970s, have accounted for the failure of aggregate output to react in the manner predicted to fiscal policy-engendered changes in aggregate demand. The poor empirical performance of the predictions of this research programme, and the defensive amendments which have reduced the empirical content or predictions of the programme, indicate *degeneracy*, to use the Lakatos term of appraisal.

In the late 1950s and early 1960s the Orthodox Keynesian research programme was initially successful in extending its content or predictions to cover the rate of inflation. This was done by introducing the *Phillips curve*,[10] which describes an inverse curvilinear relationship between the level of unemployment and the rate of change of money wage rates. This relationship is illustrated in Figure 4.4. Given that output is one of the main determinants of employment, and that unemployment is inversely related to employment, the Phillips curve can be used to link the Orthodox Keynesian theory of output determination to a theory of wage inflation. Given further a theory that prices are set by adding a profit mark-up to costs, the main component of which is wages, this means that the Phillips curve can also be used to yield a theory of price inflation. Observations of unemployment and inflation rates in the 1950s and early 1960s, in other countries as well as in the UK, seemed to corroborate the relationship postulated in the Phillips curve. As far as political action was concerned this was taken to mean that governments were faced with a trade-off between unemployment and inflation: they could either operate their economies at low levels of unemployment at the cost of having a higher rate of inflation, or settle for the lower inflation rates which would be engendered by higher unemployment rates.

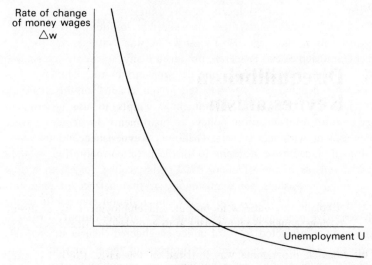

Rate of change
of money wages
$\triangle$w

Unemployment U

Figure 4.4

Observations of the rate of inflation since the middle 1960s, however, have been far higher than those predicted by the Phillips relationship. Inflation rates have shown no sign of falling at levels of unemployment far in excess of those experienced in the 1950s and 1960s. Thus there has been empirical degeneration in this theory. The reaction amongst Orthodox Keynesian economists has been to postulate that the inflation rate is determined by trade union, 'sociological' or other factors determined outwith the scope of the theory, thus reducing the empirical content or predictions of the theory and implying theoretical degeneration.[11]

5 Disequilibrium Keynesianism

'Explain fluctuations in output and employment by analysing trading sequences taking place at disequilibrium prices.'

This research programme was initiated in the early 1960s by Axel Leijonhufvud[1] and Robert Clower,[2] and motivated by concern that Orthodox Keynesian economics did not incorporate central features of 'the economics of Keynes'. The argument is that the theoretical conceptions of Keynes relate to the choices made by individual economic agents when *relative prices* are not at their equilibrium values, and thus economic agents trade at disequilibrium prices. The 'hydraulic' conceptions of Orthodox Keynesian economics, such as contained in the income–expenditure and *IS–LM* models, do not analyse formally individual choices made in the face of disequilibrium prices. Thus, it is claimed, Keynesian orthodoxy does not do justice to the revolutionary nature of Keynes' analytical system in rebutting the 'classical' Walrasian conception of economic systems as being sufficiently well coordinated to ensure that trade takes place at equilibrium prices.[3] The argument for seeing Keynes' theoretical contribution in this light is that it is otherwise difficult to make logical sense of Keynes' ideas. 'Keynes either had [disequilibrium trading] at the back of his mind, or most of the *General Theory* is theoretical nonsense.'[4]

Analysis

The reasons why disequilibrium trading on individual markets is likely to lead to the unemployment of economic resources are illustrated in Figure 5.1.[5] In Figure 5.1(a) the shaded area represents the prices buyers would wish to pay for the resources being traded if trade is taking place

26

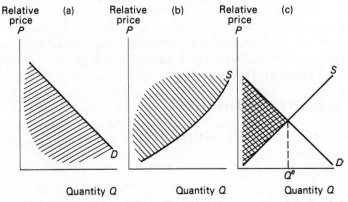

Figure 5.1. (a) Bliss zone of buyers; (b) bliss zone of sellers; (c) inter-section of bliss zones

at disequilibrium prices and thus they are not necessarily on their demand schedules:[6] buyers would obviously prefer lower than equilibrium prices. The shaded area in Figure 5.1(b) illustrates the selling prices which would be preferred by sellers if disequilibrium trading takes place;[7] sellers would obviously prefer higher than equilibrium prices. Figure 5.1(c) illustrates the intersection of these two shaded areas or 'bliss zones'. Given that trade is voluntary and thus neither buyers nor sellers can force their preferences on the other side of the market, the price–quantity outcomes to emerge from disequilibrium trading will lie inside this intersection of bliss zones. Thus the quantity actually traded is going to fall short of the equilibrium quantity Q^e which would have been traded if the market, and the economy of which the market forms a part, had been sufficiently well co-ordinated to ensure the establishment of equilibrium prices.

In this manner the *Disequilibrium Keynesian* research programme traces shortfalls in output and employment from full employment levels back to co-ordination failures in the economic system as a whole. The symptom of such co-ordination failures will be that trade takes place at disequilibrium prices. Policy measures to increase aggregate demand may help to increase output and employment, but will only be sufficient to generate 'full' or equilibrium output and employment if they also serve to establish equilibrium prices. This suggests that *micro-economic* policy measures designed to make markets function more smoothly by removing any barriers to the establishment of equilibrium prices will need to be used as well as aggregate demand policy measures in order to achieve 'full' or equilibrium output and employment.

The analysis of output and employment fluctuations which proceeds from such considerations is illustrated in Figure 5.2. In Figure 5.2(a) we consider the implications for aggregate output if trading takes place at either output prices which are too high, P^+, or too low, P^-, in relation to the equilibrium price P^e. Given voluntary trading, such disequilibrium prices will lead to at most the output level Y_1 being bought and sold rather than full employment output Y_F. Moving to the labour market, Figure 5.2(b), E_1 indicates the amount of labour firms will

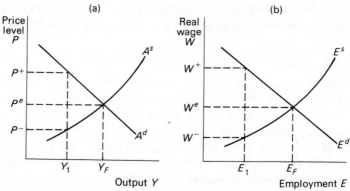

Figure 5.2. (a) Output market; (b) labour market

employ in order to produce the constrained output level Y_1. Thus unemployment indicated by the distance E_1-E_F has arisen from the disequilibrium in the output market, and could be accompanied equally as well by an equilibrium real wage, W^e, or real wages being too low, W^-, as by real wages being too high, W^+, the latter being the orthodox 'classical' explanation for the existence of unemployment. To put flesh on to Figure 5.2 we could think of the situation in which the price of UK output is too high, P^+, as relating to periods in which the UK foreign exchange rate was over-valued, as in 1925 when the authorities returned to the pre-1914–18 war gold standard parity for sterling, or in 1980 when the sterling exchange rate at one point reached $2.56 per pound sterling. In such situations a reduction in real wages would not by itself lead to a reduction in unemployment, and indeed real wages might already be too low, W^-, in relation to the equilibrium level, W^e.

The above analysis can be turned round to investigate what happens in the output market in response to an initial disequilibrium in the labour market. Figure 5.3(a) illustrates a labour market in which unemployment, measured again by the distance E_1-E_F, exists because the wage rate is either too high, W^+, or too low, W^-, in relation to the equilibrium wage rate W^e. In Figure 5.3(b) the level of output Y_1 which will correspond to the employment level E_1 is illustrated. Thus disequilibrium in the labour market can generate disequilibrium in the output market, and shortfalls from 'full' employment output can occur even when the price of output is at its market-clearing value P^e.

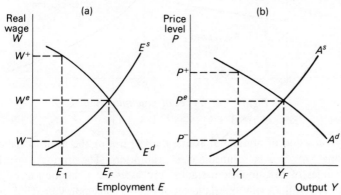

Figure 5.3. (a) Labour market; (b) output market

The above analysis does not do full justice to the interactions in the economic system which will arise from disequilibrium trading. Unemployment in the labour market, for example, will affect the demand for output in a manner which will depend on whether real wages are too high, W^+, or too low, W^-. Thus the aggregate demand for output will be higher, for any given employment level, if the real wage rate is W^+, and so labour income is E_1W^+, than if the real wage rate is W^- and labour income is E_1W^-. Similarly labour supply will be higher, at any given output level, if the price level for output is P^+, and thus households' budget constraints are tighter because their money assets are worth less in real terms than if the price level for output is P^-, and thus the money assets of households are worth more in real terms. This is because the assets owned by households provide an alternative source to labour income for the finance of consumption, and thus the higher

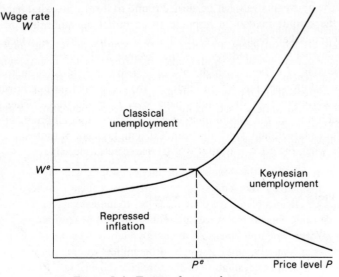

Figure 5.4. Types of unemployment

the real value of household assets, the less urgent the need for labour income to finance immediate consumption. The various possible outcomes of disequilibrium trading processes are illustrated in Figure 5.4.[8] The 'full' or equilibrium levels of output and employment will only emerge if trading takes place at the equilibrium relative prices, represented in this Figure by wage rate W^e and price level P^e. At non-equilibrium prices unemployment will occur. Such unemployment may be accompanied by an excess supply of both labour and goods – *Keynesian unemployment*; excess supply of labour accompanied by excess demand for goods – *'classical' unemployment*; or by excess demand for both labour and goods – *repressed inflation*. Thus there are many juxtapositions of 'wrong' relative prices, and of excess supplies and demands, which can be invoked to account for the unemployment of resources.

Political action

As far as political action is concerned, the Disequilibrium Keynesian research programme suggests policy measures to correct for relative prices being out of line as well as the measures to remedy deficiencies in aggregate demand suggested by Orthodox Keynesianism. There is a clear warning that aggregate demand policies on their own are not likely to be sufficient to generate 'full' employment. The direction which policy measures should take to correct for the unemployment consequences of prices being out of line depends on the diagnosis of the sources of unemployment. If unemployment is diagnosed to be of the *classical* variety – see Figure 5.4 – the recommendation would be that real wages be reduced by such measures as income policies designed to have money wages grow at a rate less than the rate of inflation. Here there is the problem raised by Keynes: 'the precise question at issue is whether the reduction in money wages will or will not be accompanied by the same aggregate effective demand as before ...'.[9] Thus a judicious blend of policy measures to increase aggregate demand at the same time as real wages are reduced would be required to correct for *classical* unemployment. If unemployment is diagnosed to be of the Keynesian variety, the research programme would suggest policy measures such as devaluation of the foreign exchange rate to correct for output prices being too high. Again a judicious mixture of policies to influence relative prices with measures to increase aggregate demand would be required in order to achieve 'full' employment. Similarly if unemployment is of the type which accompanies *repressed inflation*, a mixture of policy measures to increase output prices at the same time as reducing aggregate demand would be required.

Appraisal

Thus the Disequilibrium Keynesian research programme explains variations in output and employment by variations in relative prices and/or aggregate demand. Here the content, or predictions given, is heavily contingent on initial conditions describing the state of the economy. In order that the research programme be used to explain fluctuations in actual output and employment it is first necessary to specify to what extent unemployment arises from output prices and wage rates being out of line, and to what extent from aggregate demand being too low. In situations in which the relative price of UK output rises dramatically, as in the foreign exchange rate appreciations of 1920-25 and 1980, or when UK real wages rise dramatically, as in 1979-80, it might be reasonably easy to diagnose in what manner relative prices are out of line, and thus we will be able to state confidently the initial conditions necessary for the research programme to have refutable content or predictions regarding output and employment. Otherwise it will be difficult to diagnose whether or not relative prices are out of line, and in what direction. There have not been enough detailed attempts at describing the relative price history of the UK or other Western industrial economies[10] for us to be able to appraise the empirical performance of the Disequilibrium Keynesian research programme. What we can say here is that without a detailed statement of the direction in which relative prices are out of line the research programme does not have refutable content or give refutable predictions. It is interesting that the main empirical applications have been to Soviet-type economies where relative prices are fixed by the State and are not usually given an important role to play in resource allocation.

A problem with the Disequilibrium Keynesian research programme derives from the very fact that its analytical procedures are based on the analysis of markets in which prices do not move to clear the markets. This means not only that the research programme is not geared towards explaining what happens in markets characterized by flexible prices, for example most financial markets, but also that the programme does not have content or predictions regarding the rate of inflation. The ideas contained in Disequilibrium Keynesianism would need to be extended to provide a theory of changes in prices in order to have content regarding the rate of inflation. As the research programme stands, relative prices are postulated to influence quantities traded without the quantities traded in turn being allowed to influence relative prices.

6 Fundamental Keynesianism

'Explain fluctuations in output and employment with reference to fluctuations in expectations formed in the face of intractable uncertainty regarding the future state of the economy.'

Outline

This research programme makes the most thoroughgoing claims for the revolutionary nature of Keynes' departure from 'classical' economic ideas. The argument is that Keynes rejected the choice-theoretic foundations of 'classical' economics and the notions of equilibrium derived from such foundations. His reasons for doing so are most clearly stated in an article written in 1937 in response to reviewers of the *General Theory*:

I accuse the classical economic theory of being ... one of these pretty, polite techniques which tries to deal with the present by abstracting from the fact that we know little about the future. ... The hypothesis of a calculable future leads to a wrong interpretation of the principles of behaviour which the need for action compels us to adopt, and to an underestimation of the concealed factors of utter doubt, precariousness, hope and fear. ... My theory can be summed up by saying that, given the psychology of the public, the level of output and employment ... depends on the amount of investment. ... More comprehensively aggregate output depends on the propensity to hoard, on the policy of the monetary authority as it affects the quantity of money, on the state of confidence concerning the prospective yield on capital assets, on the propensity to spend, and on the social factors which influence the level of the money wage. But of these several factors it is those which determine the rate of investment which are the most unreliable, since it is they which are influenced by our views of the future about which we know so little.[1]

If we accept this characterization, Keynes comes to be seen as denying the relevance of the orthodox economic theory of choice with its clearly specified objectives and constraints. Instead the basis of economic choice would be seen to lie

... in vague, uncertain and shifting expectations of future events and circumstances: expectations that have no firm foundations in circumstances, but that take their cues from the beliefs of others, and that will be sustained by hopes, undermined by fears and continually buffeted by 'the news'.[2]

Given such factors at work in influencing economic behaviour, it is argued that the use of equilibrium notions to describe the reconciliation of individual economic choices is not justified.[3] Thus the Orthodox and Disequilibrium Keynesian research programmes are seen as illegitimate progeny of Keynes which do not express Keynes' 'fundamental' points of departure from 'classical' economics.

Many of the founders of the Fundamentalist Keynesian research programme, such as Joan Robinson, Nicholas Kaldor and G. L. S. Shackle, were contemporaries of Keynes at Cambridge. Even so, it is not obvious that Keynes agreed with their interpretation of his ideas. As we saw in Chapter 4, Keynes said he had 'next to nothing to say by way of criticism' of the *IS-LM* characterization of his ideas, and even Joan Robinson tells us that '... Keynes himself began the reconstruction of the orthodox scheme he had shattered ...'.[4] There are several aspects of Keynes' *General Theory*, such as the treatment of the demand for labour, and several passages in the book, such as Chapter 23, which are not consistent with a 'fundamentalist' interpretation of his ideas.

The Fundamentalist Keynesian research programme does not offer a determinate theory of how the economy functions at the aggregate level, and does not give any definite predictions about the way policy measures will affect the economy. The circumstances in which economic actors make decisions are seen to be such as to deny the use of stable behavioural relationships or of equilibrium analysis. This state of affairs is described in Figure 6.1, which is based on a picture which hangs in

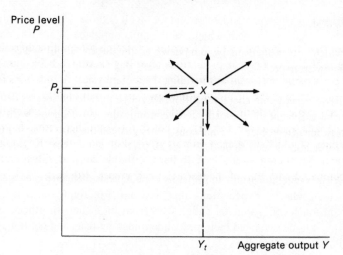

Figure 6.1. A non-diagram

the Tate Gallery. The point X describes the current position of the economy. The direction in which output and the price level moves will be heavily contingent on vague, uncertain and shifting expectations of future events about which economic theory has little or nothing to say.

Political action

The stance of the research programme towards political action is ambivalent. On the one hand there seems to be vast scope for political action to improve the workings of capitalist economies. On the other hand the very uncertainties surrounding private sector decision-taking which account for the malfunctioning of capitalist economies will also have to be coped with by political decision-takers. The research programme suggests that economic behaviour is not sufficiently predictable for governments to have reliable foundations on which to base macro-economic policies designed to stimulate private sector behaviour. Furthermore it is not entirely obvious that having the State take over responsibility for economic decisions will improve the functioning of the economy. Increasing the role of the State in economic decision-taking, desirable or undesirable as it might be for other reasons, will not in itself remove the intractable uncertainties which, it is claimed, pervade economic activity.

Appraisal

Given that the Fundamentalist Keynesian research programme does not have refutable content or predictions regarding economic behaviour, it can perhaps be best seen as providing the metaphysical foundations for the emergence in the future of some new way of analysing the workings of economic systems.[5] The criticisms levied by Fundamentalist Keynesians against the theoretical constructs of other research programmes would have greater import if the Fundamentalist Keynesian research programme were itself to have refutable content which could be compared with that of the research programmes criticized.

7 New Cambridge Keynesianism

'Amend the propositions of orthodox Keynesianism to take account of the effects of financial assets on expenditure.'

New Cambridge Keynesianism is the name which has been given to the ideas which have emerged from the Cambridge Economic Policy Group since the early 1970s. The point of departure from Orthodox Keynesianism was '... the realisation as to how unsatisfactory was the treatment of financial stocks and flows in the "vulgar" Keynesian position generally taught in the 1950's and 1960's'.[1] The New Cambridge research programme emerged at a time when the empirical content or predictions of Orthodox Keynesianism had come to be found wanting in the face of the lack of success of aggregate demand policy measures in achieving the desired stimulation of output and employment. The Director of the Cambridge Economic Policy Group (CEPG), Wynne Godley, worked in HM Treasury from 1956 to 1970, having been Deputy Director of the Economic Section from 1967 to 1970, and in a co-authored submission to the House of Commons Expenditure Committee in 1974 had the following to say on the record of Orthodox Keynesian aggregate demand policy measures:

The record of demand management in the last twenty years has been extremely poor. Throughout this whole period fiscal policy has been operated in alternating directions to produce periods of strong demand expansion, followed by reversals of policy in crisis conditions. ... The sharp reversals of policy indicate that the outcome of previous phases of policy was not acceptable ... some of the outcomes of policy were not properly foreseen....[2]

37

The New Cambridge research programme retains the Orthodox Keynesian focus on *aggregate demand* as being the main determinant of output and employment, with *aggregate supply* and *monetary* factors being assigned passive roles in the determination of output and employment. A US Keynesian economist has commented on

> ... how many aspects [of New Cambridge] have already been jettisoned here [in the US], often after a great controversy: the completely passive supply side, the fixed interest rate, the interest-inelastic investment demand, the trivialisation of monetary policy, and so on. ...[3]

The 'New' part of the New Cambridge research programme is its specification of private sector expenditure as depending on the private sector's stock of financial assets as well as on disposable income. Orthodox Keynesianism does not analyse the effects of financial assets on private sector expenditure, and in following through the logic of a theory which postulates that the private sector has a stable relationship between expenditure and financial assets New Cambridge produces some novel predictions about the workings of economic systems.

Analysis

The analysis of New Cambridge in linking private sector expenditure to private sector financial asset (PSFA) holdings runs as follows. By identity,

$$C_t + I_t \equiv Y_{D_t} - \Delta \mathrm{PSFA}_t \qquad (1)$$

where C_t and I_t are the consumption and investment components of private spending, Y_{D_t} is private sector disposable income and $\Delta \mathrm{PSFA}_t$ is the change in the stock of private sector financial assets. If $\Delta \mathrm{PSFA}_t$ is positive this indicates that the private sector is spending less than its current disposable income and so the private sector is accumulating financial assets; if $\Delta \mathrm{PSFA}_t$ is negative this indicates that spending is more than current income and so financial asset holdings are being run down.

The next step is to postulate that the private sector holds a stock of financial assets which is directly proportional to private sector disposable income. In symbols

$$\text{PSFA}_t = (1-x)\,Y_{D_t} \tag{2}$$

where $(1-x)$ is the factor of proportionality between financial assets and disposable income. This relationship implies that the private sector will increase its holdings of financial assets by a fraction $(1-x)$ of any increase in private sector disposable income.

Putting the steps involved in (1) and (2) together implies that:

$$C_t + I_t = xY_{D_t} + (1-x)\,Y_{D_{t-1}} \tag{3}$$

or that the private sector has a propensity to consume of unity out of the current *and* last year's disposable income.[4] The relationship (3) contrasts sharply with the Orthodox Keynesian relationship:

$$C_t = a + bY_{D_t} \tag{4}$$

and

$$I_t = \bar{I} + c\Delta Y_{D_t} \tag{5}$$

where (4) is the Keynesian consumption function and (5) is the Keynesian accelerator theory of investment. The relationships (4) and (5) together imply:

$$C_t + I_t = a + \bar{I} + (b+c)\,Y_{D_t} - cY_{D_{t-1}} \tag{6}$$

and where the propensity to consume out of this *and* last year's disposable income, $(b+c) - c = b$, would be less than the unity postulated by New Cambridge.

The New Cambridge research programme argues that the private sector expenditure relationship (3) has profound implications for the theory of output determination and the conduct of macroeconomic policy. To see this consider the familiar income–expenditure model equilibrium condition for aggregate output

$$I + G + X = S + T + M \tag{7}$$

where *injections* are on the left-hand side, *withdrawals* on the right-hand side, and G is government spending, X is exports, T is taxation receipts and M imports. Re-arrange (7) as follows:

$$(G - T) = (S - I) + (M - X) \tag{8}$$

or

$$\Delta(G - T) = \Delta(S - I) + \Delta(M - X) \tag{9}$$

where $(G - T)$ is the government fiscal deficit, $(S - I)$ is the private sector surplus, $(M - X)$ is the balance of payments deficit, that is the surplus accruing to those overseas, and Δ indicates the change in such deficits and surpluses. The private sector surplus $(S - I)$ is then taken to be reflected in an accumulation of *financial* assets:

$$S - I \equiv \Delta\text{PSFA} \tag{10}$$

with private sector holdings of *real* assets being omitted from the analysis. Using relationship (2), this means that

$$S - I \equiv \Delta\text{PSFA} = (1 - x)\Delta Y_D \tag{11}$$

Thus if ΔPSFA is indeed a stable proportion of ΔY_D, as hypothesized in relationship (2), we can say as an approximation that

$$\Delta(S - I) \simeq 0 \tag{12}$$

This means that in (9) we have

$$\Delta(G - T) \simeq \Delta(M - X) \tag{13}$$

and thus that changes in government fiscal deficits will be reflected in changes in balance of payments deficits. This in turn means that government fiscal policies designed to stimulate the demand for *domestic* output by expansionary fiscal policies will in the main succeed only in stimulating the demand for *foreign* output. The main domestic consequence of an expansionary fiscal policy would thus be a balance of payment deficit rather than an increase in domestic output and employment.

A second, though less fundamental, departure from Orthodox Keynesianism comes with the New Cambridge theory of inflation. The theory begins by postulating the existence of a target real wage which workers seek to achieve. This target real wage is determined exogenously to the theory, and provides an exogenous determinant of the rate of price inflation similar to that involved in the trades union or 'sociological' factors invoked by Orthodox Keynesianism. To achieve the target real wage workers are postulated to seek increases in money wages which will not only compensate them for past tax charges and the recent rate of price inflation, but also permit the desired increase in real disposable wages. *Ex post*, workers may not achieve their desired target real wage if this is not feasible given available resources. Any frustration of such desires for real wage increases would be accompanied by an increase in the rate of price inflation, with workers achieving higher money wage settlements only at the cost of a higher rate of price inflation. The rate of price inflation is derived from the rate of money wage inflation by postulating that firms determine prices by adding a profit mark-up to 'normal' costs, the main determinant of which will be money wages. Thus the New Cambridge theory of the rate of inflation is derived from the view that '... in the U.K. the general movement of money wages is governed by institutional bargaining which is virtually independent of market forces'.[5] One exception to this is that New Cambridge theory turns the orthodox Phillips curve on its head: '... under the CEPG assumptions a lower rate of unemployment (given the balance of payments and terms of trade) would normally be associated with a slower rate of inflation'[6] – see Figure 7.1. This is

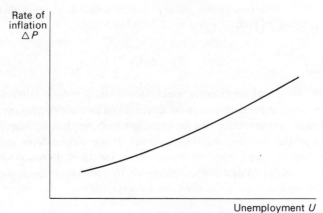

Figure 7.1. New Cambridge Phillips relationship

because lower rates of unemployment are associated with higher levels of output which allow desired increases in real target wages to be achieved without the inflationary consequences which would ensue were such desires to be frustrated.

Political action

The New Cambridge research programme has been geared towards suggesting specific programmes of political action. 'Our views have often emerged in a disorderly way, usually in the service of intervening, under a time constraint, in the public discussion of policy issues'.[7] The main determinant of output and employment in the research programme is aggregate demand, but an expansionary fiscal policy, as we have seen, will serve mainly to stimulate *foreign* output and employment through a balance of payments deficit engendered by the fiscal deficit. To allow expansionary fiscal policies to expand *domestic* output and employment New Cambridge advocate the imposition of *import controls*. Such controls would take the form of tariffs placed on all manufactured imports, and would, it is alleged, allow the UK to import the same *level* of manufactured imports as before controls were imposed because UK output would be higher as a result of the domestic containment of the expansionary effects of fiscal policy. This, the principal policy recommendation of New Cambridge, has been extensively criticized[8] and such criticisms will be discussed later in this book. Further policy recommendations given by New Cambridge range from the advocacy of sustained rather than 'fine-tuning' fiscal policies through to more explicitly political measures such as withdrawal from the EEC.[9]

Appraisal

Most of the novel predictions which flow from the New Cambridge research programme derive from its specification of the determinants of private sector expenditure; see relationship (3) above. To our American Keynesian this '... unusual specification of aggregate private sector expenditure ... [was] the one feature that should elicit the greatest interest on the [US] side of the Atlantic'.[10] This private sector expenditure relationship

$$C_t + I_t = xY_{D_t} + (1-x)Y_{D_t} \tag{3}$$

also implies that:

$$C_t + I_t = xY_{D_t} + \text{PSFA}_{t-1} \tag{13}$$

given that from (2):

$$\text{PSFA}_{t-1} = (1-x)Y_{D_{t-1}}$$

Expressed in this way the hypothesis is that in a particular period the private sector spends *all* of its inherited stock of financial assets and saves a fraction $(1-x)$ of its current disposable income. This implies a wealth or financial asset effect on spending far in excess of that picked up in studies of consumer and investment spending.[11] Furthermore, empirical studies indicate that the private sector spending hypothesis postulated in (3) above is not empirically stable.[12] Given the nature of national income accounting identities we would expect some relationship between private sector spending and disposable income. This relationship, however, does not seem to be one characterized by the unitary propensity to consume out of this and last year's disposable income postulated by New Cambridge.

Further problems arise if we look at issues which the New Cambridge analysis ignores. A first point is that New Cambridge does not contain an account of how private sector *real* assets fit into the picture. Private sector wealth consists of such *real* assets as well as *financial* assets. In terms of the orthodox theory of choice we would expect the private sector to substitute real for financial assets in its wealth holdings if the returns on real assets increase, and vice-versa. The 'hydraulic' conception of the workings of economic systems, in which relative prices and market forces have little or no influence on behaviour, similarly ignores the influence we would expect interest rates to have on the private sector's choice between assets as a whole and current expenditure. On the basis of choice theory we would be surprised to observe a fixed ratio between private sector financial assets and spending. A second point is that New Cambridge predictions regarding the effects of fiscal deficits on balance of payments deficits relate only to the *current* account of the balance of payments, and not to the *capital* account. Flows on the *capital* account of the balance of payments have often been more responsible for balance of payments deficits or exchange rate changes, and the associated policy problems, than have *current* account flows. Thus again we are only given part of the story by New

Cambridge. Such gaps in the empirical content or predictions of the New Cambridge research programme have the unfortunate effect of permitting members of the research programme to invoke *ad hoc* hypotheses to explain away empirical evidence which the research programme has difficulty in explaining. Thus while New Cambridge has succeeded in *progressively* amending the Orthodox Keynesian research programme by adding an hypothesis about the relationship between private sector expenditure and financial asset holdings, there are gaps in the analysis as well as severe doubts as to whether the private sector expenditure hypothesis holds empirically.

8 Orthodox monetarism

'Explain sustained variations in the rate of inflation by sustained prior variations in the rate of monetary expansion.'

The term 'monetarism' was coined by Karl Brunner in 1968[1] to refer to the set of ideas which claims that changes in the stock of money are the major source of changes in nominal income. Changes in nominal income can be decomposed into changes in real output and changes in the price level. Given that monetarism also claims that equilibrium real output will not be affected by changes in the stock of money,[2] and that economies will on average tend to experience equilibrium output,[3] this means that changes in the stock of money will determine changes in the price level. In terms of rates of change, this means that the rate of monetary expansion determines the rate of inflation. This *Orthodox Monetarist* research programme was initiated by Milton Friedman[4] in the mid-1950s, and in having its attention centred on nominal income and the rate of inflation it stands in marked contrast to the *Keynesian* research programmes discussed earlier in this book which centre their attention on explaining the level of output.

Analysis

We can think of three phases in the development of Orthodox Monetarism. In the first phase, from the mid-1950s to mid-1960s, the 'classical' quantity theory of money was reformulated as a theory of the demand for money. The quantity theory of money is derived from the famous equation of exchange:

$$MV \equiv PT \tag{1}$$

45

The quantity theory postulates that the velocity of circulation of money V, and the volume of transactions in the economy T, are approximately constant. This implies that exogenous shifts in the money stock M will lead to directly proportional changes in the price level P. Friedman, in his 1956 paper,[5] reformulated this theory as a theory of the demand for money. Using many aspects of the monetary theory developed by Keynes in his *General Theory*,[6] Friedman postulated that, as an *empirical proposition*, the demand for money was a stable function of a limited number of explanatory variables. A simplified form of this function is:

$$M^d = f(Y, i) P \qquad (2)$$

where Y is real output and i is 'the' rate of interest proxy for a set of differentials between the rate of return on money and the rates of return on other assets. A linear version of (2) expressed in terms of rates of change is

$$\Delta M^d = m\Delta Y - l\Delta i + \Delta P \qquad (3)$$

where ΔM^d is the rate of change of the demand for money, ΔY is the rate of change of output, Δi is the rate of change of the interest rate, ΔP the rate of inflation, and m and l represent respectively the income and interest rate elasticity of the demand for money. Now if the rate of increase of the money supply ΔM^s is determined independently of the factors determining ΔM^d, the extreme case of which will arise when the rate of monetary expansion is completely exogenous $\Delta M^s = \Delta \bar{M}^s$, the market clearing or equilibrium condition $\Delta \bar{M}^s = \Delta M^d$ implies

$$\Delta \bar{M}^s = m\Delta Y - l\Delta i + \Delta P \qquad (4)$$

Orthodox Monetarism then postulates that in the short run ΔY and Δi change in response to changes in the rate of monetary expansion, but that in the long run $\Delta Y = \Delta Y^*$ where ΔY^* is the 'natural' or equilibrium rate of output growth determined by exogenous factors such as productivity or factor supply growth, and that $\Delta i = 0$ - otherwise shifts between money and other assets would occur. Thus in long-run equilibrium we have the quantity theory of money result:

$$\Delta \bar{M}^s - m\Delta Y^* = \Delta P \qquad (5)$$

that is that the rate of monetary expansion determines the rate of inflation. In the short run we have the prediction that variations in the rate of monetary expansion generate variations in the rate of output growth and changes in interest rates.

The second phase in the development of the Orthodox Monetarist research programme started just after the mid-1960s. This involved the formulation of a more precise theory as to how the effects of variations in the rate of monetary expansion ΔM^s are divided up between variations in the rate of output growth ΔY and variations in the rate of inflation ΔP. The theory here amended the orthodox Phillips curve analysis – see Chapter 4 of this book – to take account of *inflation expectations* and the *natural rate of unemployment*. In contrast to the orthodox statement of the inverse Phillips relationship between the inflation rate ΔP and the unemployment rate U

$$\Delta P = g(U) \tag{6}$$

the theory is that

$$\Delta P = h(U - U^*) + \Delta P^e \tag{7}$$

where U^* is the natural rate of unemployment, ΔP^e is the expected rate of inflation, and h is a negative parameter describing the effect of excess demand $(U - U^*)$ on the rate of inflation.[7] The natural rate of unemployment is taken to be determined by *microeconomic* factors which will not be affected by ΔM^s or other macroeconomic policy variables, and the theory is that if unemployment is held below its natural rate U^*, the rate of inflation will increase, and if unemployment is held above the natural rate U^* the rate of inflation will fall. This is illustrated in Figure 8.1. At points to the left of U^* where $U < U^*$, the rate of inflation will increase because the economy is in a state of excess demand; this will lead to a higher rate of inflation than was expected; that is, $\Delta P > \Delta P^e$; thus people will revise upwards their expectations of the rate of inflation; and this in turn will lead to a higher actual rate of inflation. So long as U is held below U^* the economy will be in a state of excess demand, and the rate of inflation will increase. At points to the right of U^*, where $U > U^*$, the rate of inflation will fall because the economy is in a state of excess supply; this will lead to a lower rate of inflation than was expected; that is, $\Delta P < \Delta P^e$; thus people will revise downwards their expectations of the

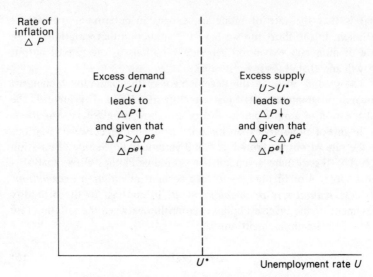

Figure 8.1. The natural rate of unemployment

rate of inflation; and this in turn will lead to a lower actual rate of inflation. So long as U is held above U^* the economy will be in a state of excess supply, and the rate of inflation will fall. Only when unemployment is at the natural rate U^* will the rate of inflation remain constant.

This analysis of the relationship between unemployment and inflation can be linked to output by postulating that corresponding to the natural rate of unemployment U^* is a natural level of output Y^*, again determined by factors other than ΔM^s or other macroeconomic policy variables. The following relationship is sometimes known as *Okun's Law*

$$U - U^* = s(Y - Y^*) \qquad s < 0 \qquad (8)$$

where $U - U^*$ is the gap between the actual and natural rate of unemployment and $Y - Y^*$ is the gap between the actual and natural level of output. Combining (8) with (7) we have

$$\Delta P = hs(Y - Y^*) + \Delta P^e \qquad (9)$$

and thus a relationship between the rate of inflation and the gap between the actual and natural level of output. The analysis is similar to before, with Y^* replacing U^*: when $Y > Y^*$ the rate of inflation will increase; when $Y < Y^*$ the rate of inflation will fall. The introduction of inflation expectations and the natural rate of unemployment or natural level of output into the Phillips relationship allows Orthodox Monetarism to spell out more clearly the channels by which changes in the rate of monetary expansion have short-run effects on output and employment and long-run effects on the rate of inflation. In the absence of the unstable cases where the rate of inflation either always increases or always decreases, the economy will tend to experience the natural rate of unemployment U^* and the natural level of output Y^*. Thus, providing the unstable cases do not arise,[8] in the long-run equilibrium, where $U = U^*$ and $\Delta P = \Delta P^e$, we have the quantity theory of money result that the effects of monetary expansion will be felt purely on the rate of inflation. Thus in direct contrast to the Keynesian research programmes discussed earlier in this book, Orthodox Monetarism predicts that the rate of monetary expansion – and other factors affecting aggregate demand – will not have any influence on the equilibrium levels of output and employment. Such equilibrium or natural levels of output and employment will be determined by the largely *microeconomic* factors which determine *aggregate supply*.

The third phase in the development of Orthodox Monetarism started around 1970 when a version of the 'classical' *monetary theory of the balance of payments and exchange rates* was incorporated into the analysis.[9] When foreign exchange rates are fixed, as under the Bretton Woods system which lasted from the immediate post-1945 period up until 1971, the theory concerns the balance of payments. The analysis starts from the observation that if the authorities have fixed the price of their money issue by fixing the foreign exchange rate, they, like monopolists elsewhere, lose control over the quantity of money. The commitment of the authorities to maintain a fixed exchange rate means that they will have to be prepared to buy sterling in exchange for foreign currencies to cover any balance of payments deficit, and sell sterling to cover any balance of payments surplus. This means that an increase in the domestic money supply can arise through the balance of payments intervention policies of the authorities as well as from purely domestic sources. In symbols this means that

$$\Delta M^s = \Delta C + \Delta R \tag{10}$$

where ΔC is the domestic source of monetary expansion, or *domestic credit expansion* (DCE); ΔR is the surplus on the balance of payments, as reflected in the increase in foreign exchange reserves arising from the authorities selling sterling in the face of a balance of payments surplus. If ΔR is negative this indicates a deficit in the balance of payments, and a fall in foreign exchange reserves as the authorities buy up the excess supply of sterling corresponding to the balance of payments deficit.

All this means that in a fixed exchange rate economy the authorities will be able to control only the domestic source of monetary expansion, but not the total increase in the money stock. Using the market-clearing equilibrium condition

$$\Delta M^s = \Delta M^d$$

implies

$$\Delta C + \Delta R = \Delta M^d \qquad (11)$$

or

$$\Delta R = \Delta M^d - \Delta C \qquad (12)$$

Thus the prediction is that a balance of payments surplus $\Delta R > 0$ will arise when domestic credit expansion is less than the increase in the demand for money; that is when $\Delta C < \Delta M^d$. Similarly a balance of payments deficit will arise when domestic credit expansion is greater than the increase in the demand for money, i.e. when $\Delta C > \Delta M^d$.

The next step in the analysis invokes the *law of one price* to postulate that in equilibrium the prices of goods in the UK change at the same rate as goods prices in the rest of the world. If this were not the case, there would be a tendency for purchases of goods to be re-directed towards countries where goods prices are increasing at a lower rate. In equilibrium such *arbitrage* activities are postulated to tie the UK rate of inflation to that in the rest of the world; that is, $\Delta P = \Delta P_w$ where ΔP_w is the inflation rate in the rest of the world. Similarly in the face of *arbitrage* activities on capital markets UK interest rates are postulated to be tied to those in the rest of the world; that is, $\Delta i = \Delta i_w$ where Δi_w is the change in the rest of the world interest rate. In equilibrium $\Delta i = \Delta i_w$, otherwise shifts between money and other assets would occur. Given also that in equilibrium UK output is postulated to increase at its *natural* rate ΔY^*, this means that the change in the UK demand for money will be

$$\Delta M^d = m\Delta Y^* - l\Delta i_w + \Delta P_w \qquad (13)$$

where ΔY^*, Δi_w and ΔP_w are all determined independently of the rate of domestic credit expansion ΔC. Substituting (13) into (12) we have

$$\Delta R = (m\Delta Y^* - l\Delta i_w + \Delta P_w) - \Delta C \qquad (14)$$

and thus UK domestic monetary expansion ΔC will have only the power to influence the balance of payments ΔR, and *not* the UK rate of inflation, interest rates, or the rate of output growth.

If foreign exchange rates are *flexible*, as has been the case in the UK for most of the period since 1971, the theory concerns the determination of the foreign exchange rate. In a pure system of foreign exchange rates the authorities do not intervene on the foreign exchange rate market, and so $\Delta R = 0$. The analysis for this case is based on similar foundations to the analysis of fixed exchange rates, but this time it is the foreign exchange rate which moves to reflect any difference between domestic credit expansion ΔC and the increase in the demand for money ΔM^d. The *law of one price* propositions now relate to prices denominated in foreign currency, with the UK exchange rate *appreciating* if the domestic rate of inflation ΔP is *lower* than the rest of the world inflation rate ΔP_w; and depreciating if ΔP is higher than ΔP_w. In an equilibrium where $\Delta Y^* = \Delta Y_w^*$, i.e. UK output is growing at the same rate as in the rest of the world, this means that

$$\Delta ER = \Delta P_w - \Delta P \qquad (15)$$

with the UK exchange rate ER appreciating, $\Delta ER > 0$, if $\Delta P_w > \Delta P$; and the exchange rate depreciating, $\Delta ER < 0$, if $\Delta P > \Delta P_w$. In terms of rates of monetary expansion the theory implies that[10]

$$\Delta ER = \Delta M_w^s - \Delta M^s \qquad (16)$$

with the UK exchange rate ER appreciating, $\Delta ER > 0$, if the rate of monetary expansion in the rest of the world, ΔM_w^s, is greater than the rate of monetary expansion in the UK, ΔM^s; and the exchange rate depreciating, $\Delta R < 0$, if $\Delta M > \Delta M_w$. Thus by allowing the foreign exchange rate to float and be determined by market forces, the authorities regain control over the domestic rate of monetary expansion. Such control also means that the authorities regain control over the UK rate of inflation, with the foreign exchange rate depreciating or appreciating to reflect any difference between the UK rate of monetary expansion and rate of inflation and the rest of the world rate of monetary expansion and rate of inflation.

Political action

The Orthodox Monetarist research programme's view of how the economy works has radically different implications for political action from those suggested by the Keynesian research programmes discussed earlier in this book. One implication is that in the long run *aggregate demand* policy measures will not have any effect on output, employment and unemployment.[11] In the long run economies will experience their *natural* levels of output, employment and unemployment which will be determined by *aggregate supply* factors. Thus *microeconomic* policy measures to increase aggregate supply, by such as measures to improve the efficiency with which markets function or stimulate the supply of factors of production, are suggested to achieve long-run output, employment and unemployment targets. In the short run changes in the rate of monetary expansion and other *aggregate demand* policy measures are postulated to affect output and employment, but the time lags before such policy measures take effect are seen to be too long or too variable for the policy-makers to be able to use such measures successfully to achieve desired output, employment and unemployment targets. Given such long and variable time lags for aggregate demand policy measures to take effect, the recommendation is that policy-makers refrain from using aggregate demand policies to achieve short-run output, employment and unemployment targets. Rather the recommendation is that policy-makers follow *rules* for such as the rate of monetary expansion to avoid having their own policies provide a source of instability to the economy as a whole. Such *rules*, it is argued, should be changed only *gradually* if policy-makers seek to achieve such as a reduction in the rate of inflation, in order to minimize the disruptive effects of changes in policy.

As far as the rate of inflation is concerned, if the foreign exchange rate is fixed Orthodox Monetarism sees the UK rate of inflation as being determined by the factors outside the control of UK policy-makers which determine the world rate of inflation. UK policy measures will only be able to influence the balance of payments. If the foreign exchange rate if flexible, the UK rate of inflation will be determined by the UK rate of monetary expansion, so to reduce the rate of inflation the policy-makers would need to reduce the rate of monetary expansion. In both cases prices and incomes policies will not have, it is argued, a lasting effect on the rate of inflation because they do influence the world rate of monetary expansion (the fixed exchange rate case) or the UK rate of monetary expansion (the flexible exchange rate case) which determine the UK rate of inflation.

Appraisal

Appraised as a research programme, Orthodox Monetarism developed in a both *theoretically* and *empirically progressive* manner for most of the period from the mid-1950s to the early 1970s. By the early 1970s it had succeeded in generating more corroborated empirical content or predictions than its rivals. The content created in the first phase of reformulating the *quantity theory of money* around the hypothesis of an empirically stable demand for money function was found to be corroborated by studies of the demand for money function[12] and of the relationship between the money stock and nominal income.[13] The additional content created in the second phase of incorporating an *inflation expectations* and *natural rate of unemployment* augmented version of the Phillips curve was similarly corroborated in that Orthodox Monetarism could explain why both the UK rate of inflation and unemployment rate increased in the late 1960s and early 1970s. The natural rate of unemployment in the UK was seen as rising after the mid-1960s in response to an increase in voluntary unemployment arising from higher unemployment benefits – see Chapter 12 on Unemployment. The UK rate of inflation was seen as rising in response to the increase in the world rate of inflation arising from the increase in the world money supply, the latter arising from the extra dollars created by the US to finance the escalation of its involvement in the Vietnam war. Similarly the new content created in the third phase of incorporating the *monetary theory of the balance of payments* into Orthodox Monetarism was corroborated in that novel predictions such as the convergence of inflation rates under the Bretton Woods system were found to hold empirically.[14] Thus the story of Orthodox Monetarism from the mid-1950s to the early 1970s is one of the original empirical content with regard to money income and the rate of inflation being extended to cover the actual and natural rates of unemployment, actual and natural levels of output and the balance of payments or exchange rate. Most of this additional empirical content was corroborated, thus signifying a *progressive* research programme.

Since the early 1970s, however, signs of *degeneracy* have appeared in Orthodox Monetarism. As far as empirical performance is concerned, the unusually high holdings of money in the UK in 1972–74 and 1980 have cast doubt on the hypothesis of an empirically stable demand for money function; the quadrupling of the UK unemployment rate during 1975–81 is far in excess of the rise which can be explained by factors so far invoked by monetarists to explain the natural rate of unemployment;[15] similarly, the sharp depreciation of the sterling exchange rate in 1976, and the appreciation in 1980 are not easily reconcilable with the monetary theory of exchange rates. On the theoretical side, *degeneracy* can be seen in the reaction of monetarists to such anomalous observations. The tendency has been to invoke exogenous factors not explained by the research programme to account for the lack of corroboration of its predictions. Thus 'structural change', 'mismanagement of monetary policy' and 'increased uncertainty' have been invoked to explain the high money holdings of 1972–74 and 1980; 'oil price shocks', 'real wages being too high' and 'the emergence of new industrial economies in the Third World' have been invoked to explain the rise in UK unemployment from 1975 to 1981; and similar *ad hoc* explanations involving 'confidence' and 'North Sea oil effects' have been used to explain the sterling exchange rate movements in 1976 and 1980. Such *ad hoc* amendments have reduced the empirical content of Orthodox Monetarism and constitute *theoretical degeneration*.

When appraising research programmes, however, the emphasis should be on *comparison* of empirical content. It would not be wise to discard a particular research programme unless there are alternative research programmes which have more empirical content which has been corroborated. Although Orthodox Monetarism has *degenerated* during the course of the 1970s, it is by no means obvious that the alternative research programmes offer more corroborated empirical content. Orthodox Monetarism still explains quite well the broad path of the UK rate of inflation, and explains some of the exchange rate movements which have occurred in the UK since 1971, and some of the massive rise in UK unemployment since the mid-1960s. It is not obvious that the 'lack of aggregate demand' and 'disequilibrium trading' explanations of unemployment provided by the Keynesian research programmes discussed earlier in this book provide a 'better' explanation of what has happened to UK output and unemployment since the mid-1960s than does the natural rate of unemployment theory used by Orthodox Monetarism. Even if this were to be the case, the silence or lack of empirical corroboration of Keynesian research programme predictions regarding such as the rate of inflation and exchange rates would make it less than obvious that such research programmes provide a 'better' explanation of the workings of the UK economy as a whole.[16]

The most unsatisfactory aspect of the Orthodox Monetarist research programme is its specification of the natural or equilibrium levels of output and unemployment as being completely independent of aggregate demand. On the theoretical side we would expect that economies would recover only slowly from shocks to aggregate demand such as those associated with UK anti-inflation policies in 1973/74 and 1979/81. Firms that are made bankrupt during such shocks cannot be immediately replaced once demand recovers. People made unemployed cannot be immediately taken out of cold storage and re-employed once demand recovers – indeed, as we shall see in Chapter 12 on Unemployment, the probability that people re-gain employment once they have been unemployed for longer than 6 months is very low. For such reasons we would expect the aggregate demand history of the economy to affect the natural levels of output and unemployment.[17] Thus the natural rate of unemployment would be seen as rising after the shocks of 1973/74 and 1979/81, increasing the rate of unemployment which is consistent with an unchanging rate of inflation. Similarly the natural level of output would fall. Such an amendment of the natural rate theory would remove from monetarism the prediction that long-run output and employment are independent of the money stock and aggregate demand. On the empirical side, however, such an amendment would allow monetarism to more easily explain the massive rise in UK unemployment from 1975 to 1981. The inability of monetarism as it stands to explain satisfactorily this massive increase in unemployment is a major indictment.

9   New classical macroeconomics

> 'Analyse economies as being in a state of continuous market clearing equilibrium with output and employment fluctuations reflecting errors in the rationally formed expectations of economic agents regarding prices.'

The foundations of this research programme were laid in 1972 by Robert Lucas[1] and mark a revival of the 'classical' economics view of the economic system as being in a more or less continuous state of economic equilibrium in which all markets clear. Thus this research programme not only stands in marked contrast to the Keynesian research programmes discussed earlier in this book, but also in marked contrast to Orthodox Monetarism which sees economies as being in a state of natural rate equilibrium only in the long run, the short run being characterized by disequilibrium trading. *New Classical Macroeconomics* retains the monetary explanation of inflation contained in Orthodox Monetarism but departs radically in its theory of output and employment fluctuations. The implications for political action are radically different in that it is predicted that economic policy measures which are anticipated by the private sector will have no effect on output and employment.

Analysis

The first plank in New Classical Macroeconomics is the *rational expectations* hypothesis.[2] This postulates that the expectations which economic agents form about the variables in which they are interested, such as the rate of inflation, will:

(a) make *efficient* use of all publicly available information about the factors which determine the variable about which expectations are formed – thus if it is believed that the rate of monetary expansion determines the rate of inflation economic agents will make efficient use of information regarding the rate of monetary expansion when forming expectations about the rate of inflation;

(b) form expectations which will not be systematically wrong over time, that is, will be *unbiased* – this means that although economic agents will make errors in their expectations about economic variables they will on average have correct expectations; and

(c) the errors in expectations will be *serially uncorrelated* over time – that is the error made in the expectation for a particular time period will not depend on the errors made in previous time periods.

The *rational expectations* hypothesis can be illustrated by contrasting it with the *error-learning expectations* hypothesis commonly used in Orthodox Monetarism to explain inflation expectations. The *error-learning* hypothesis can be expressed as

$$\Delta P_t^e = \Delta P_{t-1}^e + \lambda \left[\Delta P_t - \Delta P_{t-1}^e \right] \qquad (1)$$

that is the expected rate of inflation formed in this year ΔP_t^e will equal the expected rate of inflation formed last year plus a proportion $0 < \lambda < 1$ of the error made in last year's expectation of this year's actual rate of inflation, $\Delta P_t - \Delta P_{t-1}^e$. Thus economic agents are postulated to learn from experience of the errors they make in forming expectations regarding inflation. Such a method of forming expectations will not usually be consistent with (a), (b) and (c) above: regarding (a) *information* about such as the rate of monetary expansion is not used; regarding (b) in such cases as ever-increasing inflation expectations will be *biased*, in this case downwards; regarding (c) the error made in the current period's expectations will usually depend systematically on *previous errors* in expectations.

In contrast the *rational expectations* hypothesis postulates that economic agents will derive their expectations from the 'best' theory of what, in this case, determines the rate of inflation. If the 'best' theory is the equilibrium version of the monetarist explanation of the rate of inflation:

$$\Delta P_t = \Delta M_t^s - m \Delta Y_t^* \qquad (2)$$

– see equation (5) of Chapter 8 of this book – then the *rational* expectation of the rate of inflation would be

$$\Delta P_t^e = E\left[\Delta P_t \mid \Phi_t\right] = \Delta M_t^s - m\Delta Y_t^* \tag{3}$$

where $E\left[\Delta P_t \mid \Phi_t\right]$ stands for the mathematically expected value of ΔP_t formed on the basis on the information publicly available at time t, Φ_t. It is argued that such expectations will satisfy (a), (b) and (c) above and be *rational* in the sense that they make best use of the information available. It is not argued that economic agents all have direct information about the economic theory summarized in (2) above. Rather it is postulated that there will be profits to be made from using such information, and that market pressures and information indirectly acquired, for example, through the media, will lead economic agents to adopt implicitly such criteria when forming expectations. An important assumption used by the New Classical Macroeconomics is that the most recent information available to economic agents when forming expectations relates to one period ago. Thus, in the context of the example cited above, information about the last period's but not the current rate of monetary expansion would be used when forming inflation expectations. This means that the current rate of monetary expansion can lead to the actual rate of inflation being different to that expected.

The second plank in the New Classical Macroeconomics is the postulate that a unique *competitive equilibrium* exists and that all markets in the economy continuously clear to establish this equilibrium. 'In short, the long-time controversy about the degree of price inflexibility in the economy and its consequences is resolved by assuming ... perfect price flexibility.'[3] Robert Lucas illustrated the importance of this line of reasoning as follows.

How will a monkey that has not been fed for a day react to a banana tossed into its cage? I take it we have sufficient previously established knowledge about the behaviour of monkeys to make this prediction with some confidence. Now alter the question to: How will five monkeys that have not been fed for a day react to one banana thrown into their cage? This is an entirely different question, on which the knowledge of preferences (each monkey wants as much of the banana as he can get) and technology (banana consumption in total cannot exceed unity) gives us scarcely a beginning. We clearly need to know something about the way a group of monkeys interacts, in addition to their individual preferences, in order to have any hope of progress on this complicated question. . . . The ingredient omitted so far is, of course, *competition*. Let us take our banana, cut it into five pieces, give each of the five monkeys one piece, and impose on them the rule they may interact only by exchanging banana pieces for back-scratching, at some fixed rate. . . . Now in this situation, and given sufficient information as to how individual monkeys are willing to trade-off back-scratching and banana eating, we can predict the outcome of this interaction (equilibrium price and quantities exchanged) . . . it is the hypothesis of competitive equilibrium which permits group behaviour to be predicted from knowledge of individual preferences and technology.[4]

Thus competitive forces are seen to be strong and untrammelled enough to establish a continuous series of equilibrium states in the economy, and macroeconomic outcomes are interpreted in this light.

The third plank in New Classical Macroeconomics is its *business cycle* theory which postulates that fluctuations in output and employment arise from the errors economic agents make in forecasting prices. In the old 'classical' macroeconomics firms and workers would foresee a proportionate rise in all output prices and money wage rates in response to an increase in aggregate demand and thus would not increase their supplies of output and labour, implying that aggregate demand variations will have no 'real' effects. In the New Classical Macroeconomics firms and workers are postulated to mistake money price for *relative price* changes and so react by changing their supplies of output and labour. Firms experiencing a higher money price for their output are postulated to mistake this for an increase in the relative price of their own output, and respond by producing more output. Workers seeing their money wage rates rise are postulated to mistake this for an increase in either their real wage or their money wage relative to that received by other workers, and respond by increasing their labour supply. Thus output and employment increase in response to increases in aggregate demand which raise money prices, this being the upswing phase of the business cycle - see Figure 9.1. The downswing of the trade cycle arises from a reverse process. The fall in actual money prices compared to expected prices is interpreted by individual firms to signal a decline in their *relative* output prices, and interpreted by individual workers to signal a decline in their *real* or *relative* wage rates. Thus output and employment decline - see Figure 9.1.

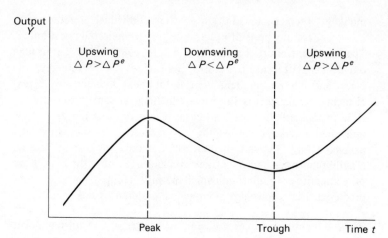

Figure 9.1. The business cycle

This theory of the business cycle amounts to a reinterpretation of the *natural rate* and *inflation expectations* augmented version of the Phillips curve – see Chapter 8 – as an *aggregate supply* equation.[5] The Orthodox Monetarist interpretation of the Phillips curve was summarized in equation (9) of Chapter 8:

$$\Delta P = hs(Y - Y^*) + \Delta P^e \qquad (4)$$

This is re-written in New Classical Macroeconomics as what is known as a Lucas supply curve:

$$hs(Y - Y^*) = \Delta P - \Delta P^e \qquad (5)$$

or

$$y = \frac{1}{hs}[\Delta P - \Delta P^e] \qquad (6)$$

where $y = Y - Y^*$, the deviation of actual output from its natural equilibrium level. Thus output fluctuates around its equilibrium value in response to errors in expectations regarding the rate of inflation. Only when inflation expectations are exactly correct, i.e. when $\Delta P^e = \Delta P$, will equilibrium output be realized.

Political action

The main implication of New Classical Macroeconomics for political action is almost an implication for political inaction, given the implied severe limitations of the government's influence over the 'real' economy. Given that economic agents are seen as taking all publicly available information into account when forming their rational expectations, and given that macroeconomic policy measures which are announced in advance will form part of such publicly available information, the implication is that macroeconomic policy measures which are announced in advance of taking effect will have no effect on output and employment. To see this think of what happens when the policy-makers announce a fixed target rate of monetary expansion $\Delta \bar{M}$, but that the actual rate of monetary expansion is

$$\Delta M^s = \Delta \bar{M} + \delta \tag{7}$$

where δ is the difference between the target and actual rate of monetary expansion, or the unanticipated component of monetary expansion. Given the equilibrium change in the demand for money

$$\Delta M^d = m\Delta Y^* + \Delta P \tag{8}$$

the market clearing condition $\Delta M^s = \Delta M^d$ implies

$$\Delta P = \Delta \bar{M} - m\Delta Y^* + \delta \tag{9}$$

The *rational* expectation of the rate of inflation will be

$$\Delta P^e = E\left[\Delta P_t \mid \Phi_t\right] = \Delta \bar{M} - m\Delta Y^* \tag{10}$$

given that the δ component of monetary expansion cannot be anticipated. Subtracting (10) from (9) gives

$$\Delta P - \Delta P^e = \delta \tag{11}$$

that is only the unanticipated component of monetary expansion will create an error in inflation expectations. Substituting (11) into (6) gives

$$y = \frac{\delta}{hs} \tag{12}$$

and thus output will only deviate from its equilibrium value in response to the *unanticipated* component of monetary expansion δ, and *not* respond to the *anticipated* component of monetary expansion $\Delta\bar{M}$.

All this means that policy-makers will not be able to exert any systematic influence on output, employment or unemployment by way of announced macroeconomic policy measures.[6] It will only be the unintended or unannounced changes in macroeconomic policy which will have effects on output, employment and unemployment. This implies, for example, that if the authorities announce a reduction in the rate of monetary expansion the private sector will immediately revise downwards their expectations regarding the rate of inflation, and that in so far as the authorities achieve their target rate of monetary expansion, a reduction of the rate of inflation can be achieved without the output and unemployment costs which Orthodox Monetarism would predict to arise from such a policy.[7] Thus as far as reducing the rate of inflation is concerned, the authorities might as well go for the 'big bang' policy of dramatically reducing the rate of monetary expansion in view of the absence of output and unemployment costs with such policies.

The other main policy implications arise from the postulate that the output, employment and unemployment levels actually experienced will on average be the equilibrium or natural rate levels determined by aggregate supply. Thus if unemployment rises dramatically and output falls dramatically, as in 1979–81, this is seen as reflecting the equilibrium supply decisions of workers and firms. To achieve a reduction in unemployment or an increase in output policy-makers are recommended to pursue *microeconomic policy* measures to increase *aggregate supply*. The UK New Classical Macroeconomics school at Liverpool University, for example, advocate measures to reduce trades union power and to reduce unemployment benefits in order to stimulate output and employment.[8]

Appraisal

Appraisal of the New Classical Macroeconomics can be conducted by analysing the three main planks in the research programme, and the implications of the research programme as a whole. Concerning the first plank, the *rational expectations* hypothesis, such problems as the costs of acquiring information about theories as to how the economy works, uncertainty about which is the best theory, and overlapping wage contracts which imply that expectational errors in one period will depend systematically on previous errors, mean that the extreme version of the hypothesis is not likely to hold.[9] As far as the second plank is concerned, the hypothesis of a *market-clearing competitive equilibrium*, there appear to be too many markets in the economy characterized by fixed rather than flexible prices for this proposition to hold.[10] As far as the third plank, or *business cycle* theory, is concerned, the short-run elasticity of supply of labour does not appear to be high enough to corroborate the hypothesis that employment fluctuations arise predominantly from supply decisions arising from errors in expectations.[11] Thus severe doubt can be cast on the basic postulates underlying the New Classical Macroeconomics.[12]

Turning to the implications of the research programme, New Classical Macroeconomics has certainly generated substantial empirical content with its prediction that only unanticipated policy measures will affect output, employment and unemployment. Some of these predictions appear to have been corroborated, both in the US[13] and the UK.[14] Although such apparent corroborations of the empirical content of New Classical Macroeconomics signify a *progressive* research programme in its early stages, the doubts surrounding the underlying postulates of the research programme have not yet been dispelled. Until the empirical content arising from such postulates has been subjected to more scrutiny it would not be wise to rely too heavily on the policy implications which can be drawn from the research programme. In particular the research programme would need to offer more convincing *aggregate supply* explanations of output, employment and unemployment movements than have so far been offered. The challenge here is to explain such as the high unemployment levels in the UK in the 1920s, 1930s, 1970s and 1980s as reflecting changes in aggregate supply. The explanations offered so far are not convincing.[15] A further unsatisfactory feature of this research programme is the hypothesis used to explain the persistence of deviations from equilibrium output over the business cycle. Here it is postulated that aggregate output depends systematically on its own lagged value as well as on expectational errors. This is an *ad hoc* hypothesis which has 'no relation to rational expectations and so far as I can see very thin intrinsic justification'.[16]

10 Supply side macroeconomics

'Explain variations in output and employment by reference to the factors which determine aggregate supply.'

The main point made in this research programme is that aggregate output, employment and unemployment will be determined predominantly by the *microeconomic* factors which determine *aggregate supply*. The extreme version of this line of reasoning is that *aggregate supply* is completely inelastic with respect to aggregate demand. Thus output and employment are *supply-determined*, in direct contrast to Orthodox Keynesianism where output and employment are *demand-determined*. This position is illustrated in Figure 10.1 where aggregate output can only be increased from Y_1 to Y_2 only by shifts in aggregate supply from AS_1 to AS_2. The effect of this line of thought is to return to the 'classical' economics proposition that supply determines output. The *microeconomic* theorizing underlying *Supply Side Macroeconomics* thus provides New Classical Macroeconomics with a theory of what determines equilibrium and hence actual output and employment. Orthodox Monetarism makes use of such theorizing to explain only the long-run or natural equilibrium levels of output and employment. Keynesian research programmes make use of such theorizing only to determine the full employment levels of output and employment which economies could achieve if they were sufficiently well co-ordinated to generate 'full' employment, which by hypothesis they are not.

There are many microeconomic factors which *Supply Side Macroeconomics* could use to explain changes in aggregate output and employment. In the UK the following are some of the main factors which have been called into play to account for variations in output and employment.

64

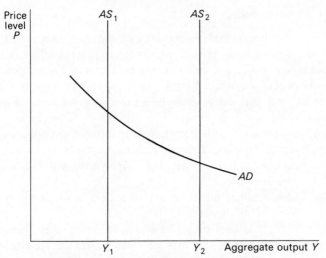

Figure 10.1. Supply-determined output

Balance between public and private sector

Here it is argued that the private sector is more efficient than the public sector in organizing economic activity, and hence that if the proportion of the public sector in total economic activity increases, productivity levels and hence output will fall.[1] Such reasoning has been developed into a theory of the poor growth performance of the UK economy.[2] This theory has been convincingly refuted.[3] There are severe problems in comparing the performance of public sector with private sector organizations, given that the activities which go on in the two sectors are often so qualitatively different as to defy comparison. Such attempts as have been made to compare the efficiency of public with private sector organizations do not suggest that there is any clear-cut presumption of greater efficiency on either side.[4] The chairman of a nationalized industry which is characterized allegedly by chronic over-staffing, for example, can usually point to several people in the private sector television team which is interviewing him whose productive function is less than obvious. Even if it were the case that the private sector is more efficient, it is not necessarily the case that a 'privatization' of economic activities would be desirable, given the social implications. It is a mistake to think that productive efficiency and profits are the sole objectives of economic organizations and their activities.[5]

Taxation and incentives

The argument here is that income taxes, expenditure taxes and national insurance contributions provide a disincentive to work effort and thus reduce labour supply and aggregate output. This would mean that those in work would work less hard if the marginal tax take were to be increased, and that there would be an incentive for more people to become unemployed, or remain unemployed for longer spells, in the face of post-tax wages falling in relation to untaxed social security and unemployment benefits. Thus an increase in the marginal tax take would not only reduce output and employment but also increase unemployment.

The microeconomic theorizing behind such claims is that the *substitution* effect of an increase in taxes – which reduces the marginal benefit of work as opposed to leisure or unemployment – dominates the *income* effect of the tax increase – which increases the amount of work which is required to yield a given real income after tax. Microeconomic studies of income and substitution effects, however, suggest that if anything the balance of effects is the other way round, that is the *income* effect dominates the *substitution* effect: '... we must be suspicious of categorical statements ... that an increase in the average rate of taxation in the U.K. would seriously discourage the supply of labour. Such evidence as there is, albeit scanty, points the other way ...'.[6] Here it must be remembered that income is but one of several factors such as the working environment which we would expect to influence labour supply and work effort decisions; and that many workers have no control over the length of their working week. One area in which the disincentive effects of taxation do appear to have a strong effect on labour supply behaviour is in the employment/unemployment decision for those on low incomes. In the 'poverty trap' case involving people who would earn only low wages if in employment, the extremely high marginal tax rates – often in excess of 100 per cent – experienced if people move from unemployment to low-paid jobs do seem to be a major disincentive to taking up employment.[7]

Macroeconomic studies of the disincentive effects of taxation have largely taken the form of estimating *Laffer curves*. Such a curve is illustrated in Figure 10.2. Figure 10.2(a) illustrates the Laffer curve proposition that the government's total tax revenue will not only be zero at a zero tax rate, but also be zero if the tax rate is 100 per cent. The reason for the latter is that it is postulated that no-one would work, and thus no-one would have income which could be taxed, if all

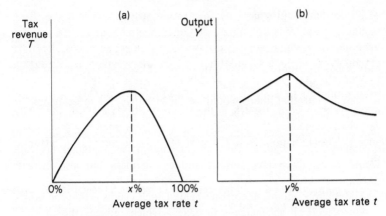

Figure 10.2. (a) Laffer curve; (b) output and tax rates

of income were to be taxed. Such polar positions are used to infer that in between 0 per cent and 100 per cent tax rates there will be some tax rate x per cent above which total tax revenue will fall. The implications of the Laffer curve for aggregate output are illustrated in Figure 10.2(b), where output is postulated to fall as the average tax rate increases beyond a certain rate y per cent. Such a Laffer curve has been estimated for the UK and the author infers that '... cutting the tax rate from its current level of 40 per cent to 35 per cent would raise GDP by about 15 per cent ...'.[8] This study has been extensively criticized,[9] and the empirical evidence does not support the view that the disincentive effects summarized in the Laffer curve are anywhere near to having been reached in the UK: '... the evidence runs strongly against the argument that tax rates in Britain, or any other country, are at levels such that the maximum available tax revenue is close to being obtained.[10] Thus the evidence does not support the Supply Side Macroeconomics claim that tax cuts would be self-financing because they would encourage people to work harder and produce more output, and so increase the total income to be taxed.

Unemployment and social security benefits

The argument here is that the existence of unemployment insurance and social security benefits leads people to choose longer spells of unemployment than otherwise would have been the case. Thus increases in benefit rates will lead to increases in unemployment and lower levels of output and employment because people will choose longer spells of unemployment. It is also argued that unemployment and social security benefits, by providing a backstop source of income, automatically make certain low-paid jobs so unattractive that they cannot be filled, thus further reducing the aggregate supply of output. Empirical evidence has been produced to show that much if not most of the high unemployment experienced in the UK in the 1920s, 1930s, late 1960s and 1970s can be explained by the liberality of provision of unemployment insurance.[11] The Liverpool New Classical Macroeconomics group estimate that

> ...a combination of a 15 per cent cut in real social scecurity benefits to the employable (and a 15 per cent reduction in the trade union mark up over non-union wages)... spread over three years from 1982 to 1984, would reduce permanent unemployment in the U.K. by around $1\frac{1}{4}$ millions by the mid-1980s.[12]

As we shall see in more detail in Chapter 12 on Unemployment, such claims that unemployment benefits have a large effect on unemployment are exaggerated. One of the main faults with such evidence is that some 'notional' maximum rate of unemployment benefit which could be received by, say, a married man with two children who has been unemployed for less than 6 months, is wrongly applied to explain unemployment amongst people who are not in such circumstances.[13] Single people would not receive such benefits; those unemployed for more than 6 months would not receive earnings-related benefits; and those unemployed for longer than a year do not receive unemployment benefit at all – only social security benefits. Such people constitute a large proportion of the unemployed, and their behaviour cannot be explained by factors which apply only to a supposedly 'representative' unemployed person. More sophisticated studies of the effects of unemployment on unemployment indicate a smaller influence than that claimed by Supply Side Macroeconomics.[14] Furthermore any such widespread voluntary unemployment arising from the effects of unemployment insurance would fly not only in the face of the active measures which are often taken to disqualify suspected 'malingerers' from receipt of benefit,[15] but also in the face of social attitudes which discourage people from unemployment.[16] Thus while some component of observed fluctuations in output, employment and unemployment can be attributed to the effects of the unemployment insurance system, this component is not as large as alleged. As far as the massive rise in UK unemployment since the mid-1960s is concerned, the thesis is largely irrelevant because rates of unemployment benefit compared to wages have fallen during much of this period.[17]

Trade unions

The hypothesis here is that trade unions, by forcing up the real wages of their members, reduce aggregate supply by lowering output and employment and increasing unemployment compared to what would have been the case in the absence of trade unions. Estimates of the size of the effect of trade unions on aggregate supply are derived from estimates of how much trade unions manage to increase real wages in the unionized sector compared to the non-union sector.[18] Estimates of the latter trade union mark-up can vary widely according to the analytical assumptions used. The New Classical Macroeconomics group at Liverpool take this mark-up to be 12-25 per cent in the UK and estimate that 'this raises permanent unemployment by 0.4-0.8 millions...' and recommend that '... there must be further legislation to curtail and over a period eliminate the ability of unions to raise relative wages and enforce restrictive practices ...'.[19]

The problem with this theory is that orthodox microeconomic theory would lead us to believe that the activities of trade unions lead to less employment in the unionized sector but more employment in the non-unionized sector, with labour displaced in the unionized sector finding employment in the non-unionized sector. Supply Side Macroeconomics does not give a clear explanation for why output and employment should not increase in the non-unionized sector to compensate for the lower output and employment in the unionized sector. The analysis is conducted as though the whole economy were unionized, whereas less than 60 per cent of the UK workforce is unionized. Furthermore the power of trade unions to raise the relative wages of their members is of a once-off variety. Thus trade union factors can only be used to explain sustained *changes* in aggregate supply if there are sustained *changes* in trade union membership. No doubt the activities of trade unions in the UK do have some effect in reducing aggregate supply, but it is not obvious that this is as high as that alleged. Furthermore it is by no means obvious that the relatively high proportion of the UK labour force which is unionized has led money and real wages to be more inflexible in the UK compared to other countries.

The black economy

The argument here is that the high rates of taxation or disqualification from benefit which apply to economic activities which are declared to the tax and social security authorities encourage the pursuit of economic activities which are not declared either to the tax or social security authorities. Such activities collectively constitute the 'black economy'. Supply Side Macroeconomists tend to argue that the black economy constitutes a high proportion of total economic activity in the UK and that official output, employment and unemployment figures are distorted by not including black economy activities.

> Official government statistics reveal that the past decade has been characterised by declining rates of growth in real output and productivity, accompanied by unemployment levels which had been thought to be fatal for any government presiding over them. Concurrently inflation rates have soared ... the widening gap between the predictions of our traditional theories and our measured observations of economic activity induce concern and frustration amongst professional economists, politicians and citizens. Before we race lemming-like towards the unchartered sea of 'supply side' economics, perhaps we should consider more seriously a jestful adage often heard in the corridors of 'Chicago School' economists: 'If the facts don't fit the theory, check the facts'.[20]

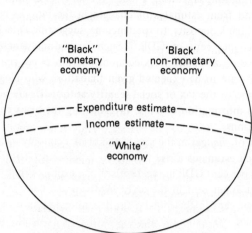

Figure 10.3. The black economy

The way the black economy relates to the economy observed in official statistics – the 'white' economy – is illustrated in Figure 10.3.[21] In the face of income which is not declared to the tax and social security authorities, the expenditure estimate of national income will exceed the income estimate. Outside this observable 'white' economy will come income created by transactions involving money – the black monetary economy – and transactions where no money changes hands – the black non-monetary economy.

Thus black economy considerations would lead us to believe that output and employment are higher than suggested in official statistics, and that unemployment is lower. Our interest is likely to be, however, in *changes* in the size of the black economy. If it could be shown, for example, that from 1975 to 1981 the size of the black economy has increased markedly, then this would mean that economic theories in general, and Supply Side Macroeconomics more particularly, would experience less difficulty in explaining the stagnant UK output and employment levels and the massive rise in UK unemployment observed in official statistics during this period. The problem is then one of estimating the size and changes in the *unobserved* black economy. Such estimates have been derived from the difference between expenditure and income estimates of national income, suggesting a black economy of around 4 per cent of GDP;[22] from Inland Revenue estimates of tax evasion, suggesting a black economy of around $7\frac{1}{2}$ per cent of GNP;[23] from comparing Family Expenditure Survey with Inland Revenue income information, suggesting a black economy of around $2\frac{1}{2}$ per cent of GDP;[24] and from estimates of changes in the ratio of currency, or currency and bank deposits, to total income, suggesting a black economy of around 15 per cent of GDP.[25] Such large discrepancies between estimates of the size of the black economy – from $2\frac{1}{2}$ per cent to 15 per cent of GDP – are to be expected given that those who illegally fail to declare income to the tax or social security authorities are not likely to disclose such information to those investigating the black economy for academic reasons.

Estimates of *changes* in the size of the black economy vary from one method which estimates a rise from 1 to 2 per cent GDP in the 1960s to around 4 per cent GDP in the 1970s;[26] one estimate that the rise was from around 2 per cent in the early 1960s, to 10 per cent in the late 1960s, 23 per cent in the mid-1970s, declining to around 15 per cent in 1980;[27] and one estimate which sees the black economy falling in size from 24 per cent in the early 1960s, 16 per cent in the early 1970s to 7 per cent in 1979.[28] The estimate which sees the size of the black economy rising from the mid-1960s to the mid-1970s would be compatible with the Supply Side Macroeconomics argument that the 'real' economy does not present as much of a puzzle for economic theory to explain as official statistics suggest. Even here, however, the estimated fall in the relative size of the black economy in the late 1970s is incompatible with the argument that the massive rise in unemployment from 1975 to 1981 is in part an illusion created by official statistics. Furthermore one of the estimates outlined above suggests that the relative size of the black economy has declined consistently since the 1960s. Thus while the black economy is no doubt a well-established feature of the UK economy, estimates of *changes* in its size by no means support the Supply Side Macroeconomics claim that the decline in the *observed* UK 'real' economy in the 1970s can be explained in large part by compensating changes in the *unobserved* UK 'real' economy. Given such discrepancies between estimates of the size and changes in the UK black economy, it is wise to treat cynically 'supply side' explanations of the performance of the UK 'real' economy in the 1970s which rely heavily on a postulated increase in the size of the black economy.

Legislation

Supply Side Macroeconomics often points to the effects of government legislation in discouraging the supply side of the economy. Minimum wage and other employment legislation such as that contained in the Redundancy Payments Act of 1965, the Industrial Relations Act of 1972, and the Employment Protection Act of 1975 have been enacted with social goals in mind. Such legislation has also, however, had the side-effect of raising the costs to employers of hiring, employing and/or firing workers. Similarly industrial legislation in the form of health and safety provisions and so on has the side-effect of similarly raising employers' labour costs. Thus we would expect that the enactment of such legislation would be followed by a decline in UK output and employment and a rise in unemployment. The question here is one of how important such side-effects are on output and employment. Empirical estimates suggest significant effects arising from the Acts of Parliament specifically referred to above.[29] The order of magnitude of such effects, however, is not large enough to explain more than a small proportion of the massive changes which have occurred in the UK 'real' economy in the 1970s. Thus again 'supply side' factors seem to be able to explain some of what has happened to UK output, employment and unemployment since the mid-1960s, but by no means the whole part.

Other factors

Finally Supply Side Macroeconomics has pointed to a whole range of other factors at work on the supply side of the UK economy which have served to reduce output and employment and increase unemployment in recent years. The following list is by no means exhaustive: housing policies such as rent controls in the private sector which have served to reduce labour mobility; the emergence of new industrial nations in the Third World which has rendered uncompetitive several sectors of UK industry; the oil price increases of 1973/74 and 1979/80 which have made oil-using machinery in UK industry obsolete; and the effects of incomes policies in distorting wage differentials and so making it more difficult for firms to fill certain job vacancies.[30] The return to the 'classical' economics stress on the *supply side* determinants of output and employment is not quite complete because so far the weather has not been called into play to account for what has been happening to output, employment and unemployment in the UK economy. Perhaps in due course the sun-spot theory of the trade cycle will be revived.

On balance it would seem that Supply Side Macroeconomics has successfully corrected for the tendency to think in terms of *aggregate demand* as being the sole determinant of aggregate output, as encouraged by Keynesian research programmes. So far, however, theories put forward to provide an *aggregate supply* explanation of aggregate output either do not stand up to close examination, do not explain more than a small proportion of aggregate output changes or constitute *ad hoc* explanations put forward after the event. To provide a more complete story of what determines aggregate output and related variables in the UK economy it is necessary to invoke not only the demand side of the economist's pair of scissors but also problems that arise from the failure of supply and demand to be co-ordinated synergetically.

Section II

Objectives of macroeconomic policy

11 Formulation of macroeconomic policy

> It is a vulgar and harmful misconception to believe that there are policy prescriptions which are certain to have the desired effects. We do not expect such certainty of doctors – why of economists? We simply do not know enough and perhaps we cannot know enough. (Frank Hahn, *The Times*, April 1981.)

There are several objectives with which UK governments have been concerned when framing their macroeconomic policies. In this section we will discuss unemployment, inflation, economic growth and business cycles as policy objectives. Governments, of course, have had many other objectives than these in mind when formulating macro-economic policies. Thus at various times governments have attempted to reduce regional imbalances in the UK, change the distribution of wealth or income, increase the provision of public goods and services, reduce the size of the public sector in economic activity, change the power in society of groups such as employers or trade unions, and so on. The objectives selected for discussion are merely the more important considerations that have been taken into account in the framing of macroeconomic policies. If this book had been written 20 years earlier we would have also selected the balance of payments for attention as a policy objective. The changeover to a system of flexible exchange rates in the early 1970s, however, has meant that balance of payments considerations now play a less important role for their own sake in the formulation of policy. It is rather the effects which the balance of payments has on the exchange rate which are important nowadays. In Chapter 18 we will look at such effects.

All the policy objectives to be discussed in this section are inter-related. In order to have a view on exactly how the objectives are inter-related policy-makers need to have a view as to the way the UK economy works *as a whole*. Several alternative views on the latter are offered by the research programmes discussed in Section I of this book. Which view is taken will have a profound effect on policy-making. At one extreme the New Cambridge Keynesian view of the workings of the UK economy suggests that expansion of *aggregate demand* by fiscal policy inside a wall of tariff barriers is the only feasible means of reducing long-run unemployment and increasing the rate of economic growth. At the other extreme the New Classical Macroeconomics and Supply Side Macroeconomics suggest microeconomic policy measures to stimulate *aggregate supply* as the only feasible means of reducing long-run unemployment and increasing the rate of economic growth.

A distinction is usually drawn between the *objectives* of economic policy and the *instruments* used to achieve such objectives. This distinction, however, is not clear-cut because the dividing line between objectives and instruments will depend on the problem in hand. Thus a central bank may see a target for the rate of monetary expansion as its objective and use open-market operations and interest rates as instruments to achieve this objective. The Chancellor of the Exchequer, however, may see the target for the rate of monetary expansion as an instrument to achieve the objective of reducing the rate of inflation. Further, the Cabinet may see reducing the rate of inflation not as an objective in its own right but as an instrument of achieving a higher rate of economic growth. Thus we can think of a hierarchy of objectives and instruments of economic policy with the distinction between the two depending on the particular problem of economic policy-making at which we are looking.

Traditional approach

The traditional approach to the making of economic policy is the Theil–Tinbergen fixed objectives, fixed instruments approach.[1] This approach assumes that policy objectives are independent of each other, and that policy instruments can be varied independently of each other. The main conclusion reached by this approach is that to achieve a given number of policy objectives, policy-makers will need at least as many policy instruments as there are policy objectives. The two-objectives, two-instruments case is illustrated in Figure 11.1. The line O_1 indicates the combinations of values of policy instruments A and B which would serve to achieve policy objective I; and similarly with the line O_2. Thus if policy-makers were to have sufficient knowledge of the economy, and hence of the positions of lines O_1 and O_2, they could set the policy instruments at A^* and B^* and achieve *simultaneously* both policy objectives. Even with this simpliste approach, however, there are several cases in which policy-makers will not be able to achieve their objectives *simultaneously*. Figure 11.2(a) illustrates the case where the number of objectives is greater than the number of policy instruments available. Figure 11.2(b) illustrates the case where policy objectives are influenced by instruments in such a similar manner that the two objectives cannot be reached simultaneously. Figure 11.2(c) illustrates the case where

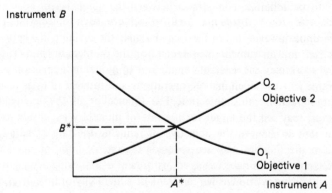

Figure 11.1. Objectives and instruments

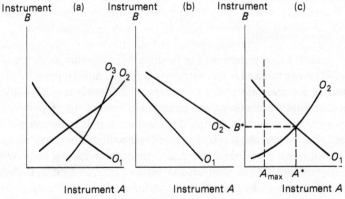

Figure 11.2. Unattainable policy objectives

there is some constraint on the use of policy instruments – there might be a political constraint on raising interest rates above a certain level, for example – and thus policy objectives again cannot be achieved simultaneously.

Problems with traditional approach

There are more important objections, however, to this approach to the formulation of macroeconomic policy. A first problem is that both policy objectives and policy instruments are *interdependent*. As far as policy objectives are concerned it might be the case that a reduction in the rate of inflation could be achieved only by increasing the level of unemployment; this implied reduction in the level of employment would imply a reduction in the rate of economic growth realized in the short run; and so on. An important aspect of such *trade-offs* between policy objectives concerns the short and long run. With the 1979–84 government, for example, the rationale for policy is that raising unemployment in the short run will produce a reduction in the rate of inflation; this will stimulate a higher rate of economic growth; this higher rate of economic growth will allow unemployment to be lower in the long run. Similar interdependence arises with policy instruments. For example, an expansionary fiscal policy will be accompanied by higher government borrowing, which will mean either a higher rate of growth of the money supply if the government increases its borrowing from the banking system, or higher interest rates if the government increases its borrowing from outside the banking system.

A second problem is that governments will formulate economic policy in a state of uncertainty as to (a) which economic theory best explains how the economy works; (b) the trade-offs between policy objectives; (c) the relationships between policy instruments and policy objectives; (d) the trade-offs between policy instruments; (e) the recent history and current state of the economy; and (f) whether the political constraints on economic policy-making will become binding if policy objectives or instruments are varied beyond some 'politically acceptable' values. The debate about whether economic policy is best guided by a set of *rules* which are only allowed to change slowly, or best pursued by the *discretionary* action of policy-makers is in large part a debate about how policy-makers should react to the uncertainty surrounding their decision-taking.

A third problem is that policy-makers are in large part political animals who are responsible not only to their own political party colleagues but also to the electorate as a whole for their actions. Attempts by politicians to gain re-election by pursuing expansionary policies just before a general election, with deflationary policies being pursued in the post-election period to reverse the inflationary impulses arising from such pre-election policies, can result in a *political business cycle*.[2] It would be naive not to see the political survival of policy-makers as a major factor underlying the making of macroeconomic policy. On the other hand it would be equally naive to think that the electorate would not eventually see through macroeconomic policies which were motivated purely by political opportunism.

A fourth problem is that policy-makers will have only limited control over what happens to the UK economy. Forces of an international nature, such as the rise in the world rate of inflation in the late 1960s or the oil price increases of 1973-74 and 1979-80, will often have severe effects on the UK economy, and the task of UK policy-makers will be to try and minimize the adverse effects of such shocks. Such international forces are double-edged in that some, such as the massive increase in world trade in the 1950s and 1960s, have beneficial effects on the UK economy. Policy-makers have an unhappy habit of referring to international factors to explain what is happening to the UK economy only when they wish to have a scapegoat for their own policies.[3]

Policy formulation in the UK

Thus the formulation of macroeconomic policy not only has to deal with complex interrelationships between policy objectives and instruments but also is fraught with uncertainty as to what these relationships are and where the UK economy has been, is, and is going. The formal aspect of macroeconomic policy-making in the UK involves the use of:

(a) an econometric model which attempts to describe the interrelationships between policy objectives and instruments in the UK economy;[4] and

(b) information derived from the government of the day as to their priorities as far as policy objectives are concerned.

Given that it is not possible to capture satisfactorily in a formal model the uncertainties surrounding policy-making, such formal methods can offer only limited guidance to policy-makers. As far as (a), econometric models, are concerned, there is room for improvement:

> ... while care is needed in the use and interpretation of econometric analysis, it is an important tool in the design and testing of policy which has not been used efficiently in the design of ... economic policy ... we are not satisfied that present arrangements produce the most useful model-based evidence for Parliament or for the public.[5]

As far as (b), the preferences of the government, are concerned, there are severe difficulties in

> ... constructing a set of preferences that could be said adequately to reflect the values of the population at large, or even the political party in power ... the unwillingness of Ministers to commit themselves in advance of events or to answer hypothetical questions – and the problems that arise as a result of Ministers changing their minds.[6]

The conclusion of a committee of academic economists appointed by HM Treasury to consider how to derive 'optimum' macroeconomic policies was:

> ... the assessment of economic policy making is not a simple matter ... one cannot ascribe all apparent failures of policy to any single cause such as bad forecasting, bad theory or the undue influence of party political considerations at the expense of the economic realities of life.[7]

Given all this it is wise to beware of those who suggest that there are macroeconomic policy prescriptions which are certain to have the desired effects.

12   Unemployment

Unemployed men (and women) are not simply units of employ-ability who can be put in cold storage and taken out again immedi-ately they are needed. (*Men Out of Work*, Pilgrim Trust (Cambridge: Cambridge University Press, 1938).)

Unemployment in history

According to the *Oxford English Dictionary* the word 'unemployment' first came into use in the late 1880s. Alfred Marshall's classic work *Principles of Economics*, published in 1890, still used the phrase 'inconstancy of employment' to refer to what we nowadays term 'unemployment'. Other economists referred to a 'want of employment'.[1] Karl Marx's *Das Kapital*, published in 1867, in his theory of a disposable *industrial reserve army*, had earlier described how

> ... the increase in the variable part of capital, and therefore the number of labourers employed by it, is always connected with violent fluctuations and transitory production of surplus-popula-tion ... the whole form of the movement of modern industry depends ... upon the constant transformation of a part of the labouring population into unemployed or half employed hands.[2]

Marx, however, had not come to be widely read among English-speaking economists by the late nineteenth century. The treatment of the new term 'unemployment' by 'classical' economists in the 1890s is well described by John Hobson.

'Unemployment' is perhaps the most illusive term which confronts the student of modern industrial society. ... Well-meaning but some-what hasty social reformers stretch the term and bloat it out to gigantic proportions; professional economists and statisticians, provoked by this unwarranted exaggeration, are tempted to a corresponding excess of extenuation, and are almost driven to deny the reality of any 'unemployed' question, over and above that of the mere temporary leakages and displacements due to the character of certain trades, and to changes in industrial methods.[3]

The tendency in 'classical' economics was to ascribe the state of 'unemployment' to moral or productive deficiencies in the individuals concerned. If unemployment could be shown to be a cause for concern, the cure was seen as involving measures to correct for the moral or productive deficiencies in the individuals concerned, and not in collective action to correct for deficiencies in the workings of the economic system as a whole. A first major challenge to this view from 'classical' economists came from John Hobson in his theory of unemployment as *involuntary idleness*.

The fallacy ... that the only thorough treatment of unemployment ... consists in the treatment of individual character ... is necessary to all individualist views of society. A depression of the staple trade in one town throws out of employment 10 per cent of those who are normally employed ... a close investigation of each 'case' discloses in most of this 10 per cent some moral or economic defect: there is drink, laziness, inefficiency or some other personal vice discernible in, or imputed to, most of these 'unemployed' ... our investigator ... reaches the conclusion that unemployment is due to individual causes. Such a conclusion is, of course, wholly fallacious. Personal causes, no doubt, explain in large measure who are the individuals that shall represent the 10 per cent 'unemployment', but they are in no true sense even contributory causes of the 'unemployment'. When economic causes lower the demand for labour, competition will tend to squeeze out of unemployment those individuals who, for reasons sometimes moral, sometimes industrial, are less valuable workers than their fellows. If these individuals had not been morally or industrially defective they would have kept their work, but necessarily by pushing out another 10 per cent. Personal causes do not to any appreciable extent cause 'unemployment', but largely determine who shall be unemployed. ... Moral and technical inefficiency are not the causes of 'unemployment', as may be proved by the fact that in periods of good trade these very individuals who seem defective are for the most part in regular work.[4]

The interwar period

By 1914 a leading 'classical' economist had come to accept the existence of *involuntary* unemployment. 'Unemployment clearly does not include all the idleness of wage earners, but only that part of it which is, from their point of view and in their existing conditions at that time, involuntary'.[5] It was, however, the sheer force of circumstances in interwar Britain and elsewhere which was as responsible as anything else for the emergence of the view that capitalist economies could experience large-scale *involuntary* unemployment. In the period 1860-1913 Britain experienced an average rate of unemployment of around 4-6 per cent of the unionized labour force, unemployment reaching around 10 per cent in the deep depressions of 1879 and 1886.[6] During the period 1920-38 unemployment averaged around 14 per cent of the unionized labour force, with 22 per cent unemployment being experienced in the depression of 1932. Table 12.1 outlines the unemployment experience of interwar Britain.

Table 12.1. Unemployment in interwar Britain

Year	Unemployment rate (U%)	Year	Unemployment rate (U%)
1920	3.9	1930	16.1
1921	17.0	1931	21.3
1922	14.3	1932	22.1
1923	11.7	1933	19.9
1924	10.3	1934	16.7
1925	11.3	1935	15.5
1926	12.5	1936	13.1
1927	9.7	1937	10.8
1928	10.8	1938	12.9
1929	10.4		

Source: D. K. Benjamin and L. A. Kochin (1979), 'Unemployment in interwar Britain', *Journal of Political Economy*, June, 87, pp. 441–78 (Table I).

Also influential, of course, in this changed perspective of unemployment, was Keynes' *General Theory*. Here we have the definition that:

> Men are involuntarily unemployed if, in the event of a small rise in the price of wage-goods relatively to the money-wage, both the aggregate supply of labour willing to work for the current money-wage and the aggregate demand for it at that wage would be greater than the existing volume of unemployment.[7]

Or, more succinctly:

> There is involuntary unemployment to the extent that, at the current money wage and with the current price-level, the number of men desiring to work exceeds the number of men for whose labour there is a demand.[8]

The assumption that Keynes saw all of the unemployment in interwar Britain as being involuntary, and that all of the unemployment could be cured by increasing aggregate demand, however, is far from the truth. In three articles published in *The Times* in January 1937[9] when the unemployment rate was 12 per cent, Keynes pointed to the dangers of inflation arising if unemployment were to be reduced below this rate by measures to increase *aggregate* demand rather than by measures to change the *distribution* of demand. On the basis of these articles it has been argued that Keynes saw 12 per cent unemployment as the level of unemployment which could be sustained without increasing inflation at that date.[10] The counter-argument places Keynes' estimate of the non-inflationary level of unemployment in 1937 at 6-7 per cent.[11] Even this lower figure places Keynes' estimate of the extent to which unemployment could be cured by *aggregate* demand measures alone at a far lower figure than the popular conception of Keynes would have us believe. Even an unemployment rate of 6-7 per cent is certainly a lot higher than the estimates of 'full' employment at around 1-3 per cent of the labour force which came to be the received wisdom of Orthodox Keynesian economics in the 1940s, 1950s and 1960s. Thus it is not entirely obvious that the analysis of unemployment attributed to Keynes by Orthodox Keynesianism accurately represents Keynes' own view on the extent to which unemployment in the interwar period could be attributed solely to deficiencies in aggregate demand.

A far more radical re-evaluation of unemployment in interwar Britain has come from two American economists. Using the Supply

Side Macroeconomics hypothesis – see Chapter 10 of this book – that workers will choose longer spells of unemployment if the ratio of unemployment benefits to wages rises, they estimate that:

> ... the unemployment rate [in interwar Britain] would have averaged more than a third lower, and ... in 1927–1929 and 1936–1938 ... would have been at near normal levels, if the dole had been no more generous than it was when first set up in 1913 ... in the absence of the system [of unemployment insurance] unemployment would have been at normal levels for much of the period ... the army of the unemployed standing watch in Britain at the publication of the *General Theory* was largely a volunteer army.[12]

This argument, however, is inconsistent with many aspects of the UK economy in the interwar period. It implies, for example, that workers in certain parts of the country – such as Clydeside and the north of England – and workers in certain industries – such as coal and shipbuilding – who experienced substantially higher than average unemployment rates, did so because they had a higher propensity to choose unemployment rather than work compared to workers who experienced lower unemployment rates. Try telling that to the retired coalminer from Wigan who was unemployed in the 1920s or 1930s! The argument also flies in the face of the rigorous application of the 'genuinely seeking work' and 'means' tests to disqualify claimants from unemployment benefit.[13] Further doubt can be cast on the argument by pointing to the low number of job vacancies posted for much of period. Finally the argument does not explain why voluntary unemployment was lower in Britain in the late 1940s, 1950s and 1960s, when for much of this period the ratio of unemployment benefits to wages was higher than in interwar Britain.[14]

The postwar period

Whatever view is taken as to why unemployment was so high in interwar Britain, there is no doubting the change in attitude of politicians to unemployment during the 1939–45 war. In January 1944 Winston Churchill was warned by his adviser, Lord Cherwell, that 'the British people will not tolerate a return to the old [unemployed] figures. They will demand that the Government produce a programme for achieving comparable results in peace'.[15] This change in political attitudes to unemployment is documented in the opening sentence in the 1944 Government White Paper on *Employment Policy*: 'The Government accept as one of their primary aims and responsibilities the maintenance of a high and stable level of employment after the war'.[16] From that period up '... until the late 1960s, 500,000 unemployed was a crisis level in the U.K. leading to policy reversals and the sacking of Cabinet Ministers'.[17] Unemployment touched the 1-million mark in the Winter of 1971–72 and sparked off the unprecedented expansionary measures announced in the Spring Budget of 1972.

A major change in the attitude of politicians to unemployment took place in the mid-1970s. Not only did inflation come to be seen as a greater social problem or 'threat to democracy', but unemployment came to be seen as arising from workers 'pricing themselves out of jobs', and the cure for this problem to lie in pursuing measures to reduce real wages rather than measures to stimulate aggregate demand.[17] This change in attitude was expressed clearly by the then Prime Minister, James Callaghan, in his address to the 1976 Labour Party Conference.

> We used to think that you could spend your way out of a recession and increase employment by cutting taxes and boosting government spending. I tell you in all candour that that option no longer exists. It only worked, on each occasion since the war, by injecting a bigger dose of inflation into the economy, followed by a higher level of unemployment at the next step. That's the history of the last twenty years.[18]

Similar sentiments were expressed by Sir Keith Joseph, one of the architects of the 1979–84 Conservative government's economic policies: 'Full employment is not in the gift of governments. It should not be promised and it cannot be provided'.[19] The culmination of this line of thought is that unemployment is likely to breach the 3 million mark in the winter of 1981–82 without the government taking steps to stimulate aggregate demand in the UK economy. This state of affairs is similar in some respects to the response of many politicians to the mass unemployment of 1931. Unemployment reached 21 per cent in 1931 – see Table 12.1 – and the response of the Ramsey MacDonald National government, supported by Conservatives and Liberals, was to cut unemployment benefit by 10 per cent, teachers' salaries by 15 per cent, raise the rate of income tax to 5 shillings in the pound, and increase taxes on beer, tobacco and petrol – though the cuts of 10 per cent and

5 per cent in armed forces and police salaries respectively, announced in September 1931, are the opposite of what has occurred 50 years later.

A picture of UK unemployment

In Table 12.2 we outline some of the main features of UK unemployment over the period 1964-81. Column (1) illustrates how UK unemployment has increased to nearly six times the 500,000 figure which up until the mid-1960s was seen as the maximum level which could be tolerated. The most dramatic increase has occurred in 1979-81 when unemployment, already standing at a high level by postwar standards in excess of 1 million, more than doubled in the space of 2 years. In the UK a person is registered as unemployed if he or she is registered at a government employment exchange as looking for work. Many people who are unemployed do not register as such at official employment exchanges either because there is no financial incentive to do so – as in the case of married women whose husbands have a job and so would not be eligible for unemployment or social security benefits – or because the most effective way to find a job is through other means such as private employment exchanges – secretarial agencies for instance. The 1971 Census revealed around 300,000 people as looking for work but not registered as unemployed at government employment exchanges. The fact that employment fell by 500,000 more than unemployment rose in the period September 1979 to March 1981 suggests that there are more than half a million 'hidden' unemployed people in the UK economy. Column (3) indicates what has happened to job vacancies declared to government employment agencies during this period. Again not all vacancies are declared to government employment agencies, many jobs being filled through word of mouth or notices posted at places of work. The government estimate is that only about 30 per cent of total vacancies are notified to government employment agencies.[20] The number of job vacancies has changed little compared to unemployment, the main change in this series occurring in 1981 when the number of notified vacancies fell below the 100,000 mark.

The change in total unemployment in any one month reflects the balance between those joining the unemployment register and those leaving. In May 1981 in Britain, for example, 334,000 people joined the register, 274,000 left the register, implying an increase in total unemployment of 60,000. Columns (6) and (7) in Table 12.2 indicate

Table 12.2. *Unemployment in the UK, 1964–81*

			U>52 weeks	U>26 weeks	I/E	O/E	BN/E	BA/E
U Unemployment in UK (000s) (1)	*U%* U as a percentage of the working population (2)	*U* Job vacancies in the UK (000s) (3)	Numbers unemployed for longer than 52 weeks. Averages of monthly figures (000s) (4)	Numbers unemployed for longer than 26 weeks. Averages of monthly figures (000s) (5)	Inflow into unemployment per month divided by total employment. Averages of monthly figures G.B. ×100. (6)	Outflow from unemployment per month divided by total unemployment. Averages of monthly figures. G.B. (7)	Ratio of unemployment benefit to average post-tax income if working for married man with two children (8)	Average actual unemployment benefit received over average post-tax earnings (9)
1964	404	1.7	222	60	95	1.43	0.81	45	31
1965	347	1.5	267	47	75	1.34	0.81	49	35
1966	361	1.5	257	41	68	1.48	0.76	69	37
1967	559	2.3	175	62	127	1.74	0.57	73	39
1968	586	2.5	190	85	161	1.70	0.52	73	42
1969	581	2.5	202	92	163	1.79	0.54	71	42
1970	618	2.6	188	99	171	1.84	0.52	73	41
1971	799	3.4	131	116	213	2.09	0.40	78	39
1972	886	3.9	147	160	300	1.89	0.39	74	37
1973	630	2.7	307	160	249	1.44	0.48	71	37
1974	622	2.6	303	128	199	1.57	0.43	70	45
1975	978	4.1	150	147	280	1.81	0.28	67	38
1976	1359	5.7	121	222	455	1.73	0.23	67	36
1977	1484	6.2	158	303	552	1.71	0.23	68	37
1978	1475	6.1	200	332	588	1.67	0.25	66	37
1979	1391	5.8	241	340	566	1.21	0.21	mid-60s†	late 30s†
1980	1795	7.4	143	348	619	1.45	0.16	mid-60s†	late 30s†
1981*	2681	11.1	83	516	1136	1.56	0.11	early 60s†	mid-30s†

Source: Employment Gazette and its predecessors, Department of Employment Gazette and Department of Employment and Productivity Gazette.

* 1981 figures are those for the most recent month available in the July 1981 Employment Gazette.

clearly how the rate of *inflow* into unemployment has changed little over the last 20 years, while the rate of *outflow* from unemployment has declined dramatically. The implication of this is that the average *duration* of unemployment has increased substantially over the last 20 years. Calculations of the average duration of unemployment are difficult to make given that we can never be sure how long people who are unemployed at the moment are going to remain unemployed. One of the more sophisticated studies estimates the average duration of unemployment in Britain in 1979 at about 90 weeks.[21]

The long-term unemployed

The increase in the average duration of unemployment is reflected in the massive increase in the numbers who have been unemployed longer than 6 months or longer than a year – see Columns (4) and (5) in Table 12.2. In 1981 more than half a million of the unemployed had been so for longer than a year, and more than 1 million for longer than 6 months, the latter being the conventional definition of long-term unemployment. This return to mass long-term unemployment brings with it massive social consequences. Evidence that the long-term unemployed experience severe difficulties in regaining employment has been available since the studies of interwar unemployment in the UK. The Pilgrim Trust, for example, reported that

> ... unemployed men are not simply units of employability who can be put into cold storage and taken out again immediately they are needed ... [they experience] a subtle undermining of the constitution through lack of physical exertion and the absence of physical stimuli ... and the emergence of abnormal psychological conditions characterised by disabling fears, anxiety and sympathetic physical conditions, functional disorders and the like.[22]

Similarly two psychologists identified three stages in the experience of long-term unemployment:

> ... first there is a shock, which is followed by an active hunt for a job, during which the individual is still optimistic and unresigned; he still maintains an unbroken attitude. Second, when all efforts fail, the individual becomes pessimistic, anxious and suffers active disstress; this is the most crucial state of all. And third, the individual

becomes fatalistic and adapts himself to his new state but with a narrower scope. He now has a broken attitude.[23]

More recent studies of long-term unemployment in the UK have produced similar results.[24] Such studies indicate that the probability of regaining employment declines markedly after 6 months of unemployment, and that this result remains after taking into account factors such as health, age, skill and location which might be expected to affect the probability of re-gaining employment: '... the conditional probability of an individual obtaining work declines after six months of a spell [of unemployment], falling to a rather low level'.[25] Another aspect of the poor employment prospects of the long-term unemployed is that such people show a high propensity to suffer a *recurrence* of unemployment in the future should they initially regain employment. Evidence of such recurrence is contained in a DHSS longitudinal study of a sample of people who were unemployed in August 1978. In the year prior to 1978 half of the sample of the unemployed had experienced an earlier spell of unemployment. In the prior 5 years 78 per cent had experienced at least one spell of unemployment, over 40 per cent at least two spells and 25 per cent three or more spells of registered unemployment.[26] Follow-up interviews in November/December 1978 of those who had been unemployed in August 1978 revealed that only 13 per cent of those who had spent 9 months of the year before registering as unemployed in registered unemployment were back in full-time employment.[27] Thus not only do the long-term unemployed have a significantly lower probability of regaining employment, but they also have a significantly higher propensity to experience a recurrence of unemployment after they have completed their initial spell of unemployment. All this suggests that it will be extremely difficult to place in steady employment the more than 1 million people who in 1981 had been unemployed for longer than 6 months.

The puzzle to be explained here is that the re-employment probability is so low despite the fact that long-term unemployment spells poverty for most of the people concerned. Not only will any personal savings dwindle as the length of the unemployment spell increases, but also earnings-related unemployment benefit ceases to be paid after 6 months of unemployment, and flat-rate unemployment benefit ceases to be paid after 1 year of unemployment. This puzzle can be explained by mutually reinforcing factors at work on the supply and demand sides of the labour market. On the supply side, '... prolonged unemployment is for most people a profoundly corrosive experience, undermining personality and atrophying work capacities'.[28] Most of the long-term unemployed experience a loss of confidence and self-esteem, this often leading to feelings of hopelessness in relation to finding work and a reduction in the efforts made to find work. The capacity to work depreciates along with any skills previously acquired in work. Government retraining schemes have been remarkably unsuccessful with the long-term unemployed: the latter display a low level of awareness of such schemes, and of those initially embarking on a retraining course, only a small proportion complete the course, the difficulty of readjusting to a work routine being a major problem.[29] Thus long-term unemployment reduces the capacity to work of most of those concerned. On the demand side of the labour market employers often see a curriculum vitae containing a recent spell of long-term unemployment as implying unsuitability for work. Thus employers' perceptions of the work capacities of the long-term unemployed reinforce the depreciation of the actual capacity to work, producing a trap from which it is extremely difficult for the long-term unemployed to emerge and regain employment. This means that the legacy of the re-emergence of mass long-term unemployment in the UK in 1981 is likely to remain with us for a long time.

While one side of the unemployment register is characterized by the same faces being in the unemployment figures month after month, the other side of the register is characterized by a very rapid turnover of faces. In 1972, for example, 26% of those registering as unemployed on a particular day left the register within 4 days; 49% within 2 weeks; 60% within 4 weeks; and 80% within 13 weeks.[30] Thus the picture is one of rapid flows of short-term unemployed on and off the register, and extremely sluggish flows of long-term unemployed on and off the register.

The inequality of unemployment

Amongst the population there is a massive inequality in the incidence of unemployment. A figure which captures the degree of inequality in unemployment experience is that 3% of the UK labour force experience around 70% of the unemployment weeks in a year.[31] A first aspect of this inequality is that unskilled and semi-skilled manual workers are twice as likely as skilled manual workers to be unemployed. Manual workers as a whole are twice as likely as non-manual workers to be unemployed. The professions, managers and employers experience extremely low rates of unemployment compared to other jobs.[32] A second aspect to this inequality is the regional distribution of unemployment. Thus in June 1981 when the UK average rate of unemployment was 11.1%, Northern Ireland had 18% unemployment, the North of England 14.9%, Wales 13.9%, Scotland and the North West of England 13.5%, the West Midlands 13.2%, Yorkshire 11.9%, the East Midlands 10.3%, South West England 9.5%, East Anglia 8.8%, South East England 7.7% and Greater London 7.3%.Thirdly, unemployment is heavily concentrated amongst the 16-25 and 50-65 age groups, though much of the 16-25 age group unemployment is of the short-term variety, whereas much of the unemployment in the 50-65 age group is of the long-term variety. Finally unemployment is also a lot higher amongst certain ethnic minorities, women, those in poor health, those with little education and other social disadvantages.[33]

Diagnosis

Diagnoses of the reasons why unemployment has risen so dramatically in the UK since the mid 1960s differ markedly, reflecting the differences of view that exist regarding the way the economy works. Thus the Orthodox Keynesian explanation runs in terms of deficiency of aggregate demand; the Disequilibrium Keynesian explanation in terms of trading at disequilibrium prices; the Fundamental Keynesian explanation in terms of shifts in expectations formed in the face of intractable uncertainty regarding the future; the New Cambridge explanation in terms of deficiency of aggregate demand arising in part from demand leakages abroad; the Orthodox Monetarist explanation in terms of the natural rate of unemployment having risen and/or the actual having been raised above the natural rate of unemployment; the New Classical Macroeconomics explanation in terms of errors in expectations and/or a decline in aggregate supply; and the Supply Side Macroeconomics explanation runs in terms of a decline in aggregate supply. Thus the research programmes differ in the emphasis placed on (1) demand side factors, (2) supply side factors and (3) co-ordination failures in the economy as a whole in their explanation of unemployment. None of the research programmes has so far produced a completely satisfactory explanation for the massive rise in UK unemployment from the mid-1960s to the early 1980s. Most of the research programmes can explain some of the rise in unemployment for some of this period by invoking the method of explaining unemployment pre-stated in their *positive heuristics*. To explain more than this, however, most of the research programmes have invoked special factors not derived from a pre-planned *positive heuristic* as to how to explain unemployment. In other words the rise in UK unemployment from the mid-1960s to the early 1980s has at least in part been inconsistent with the economic content or predictions of the various research programmes.

At the risk of being compared with the drunk who insisted on looking for his wallet underneath the lamp-post because it was the only part of the street which was lit, we will organize our diagnosis of the reasons for the rise in UK unemployment around the natural rate of unemployment theory put forward by Orthodox Monetarism. We will, however, amend this theory to allow aggregate demand to partly determine the natural rate of unemployment. Before doing this it might be useful to illustrate the different explanations of UK unemployment that have been put forward by outlining two of the more extreme positions.

At one extreme New Cambridge Keynesian economists explain unemployment as arising from a deficiency in aggregate demand for UK output, a large part of the problem being postulated to be the foreign leakage of aggregate demand – see Chapter 7 of this book. This explanation involves a comparison of the growth rate in the working population with the growth rate in the demand for labour implied by the growth rate for aggregate demand: if the former exceeds the latter, unemployment will rise. In 1980, for example, New Cambridge were forecasting that on the basis of unchanged government policies

> ... in the period up to 1985 ... the conjunction of ... job market and demographic changes would cause a rise of 3.7 million in the population of working age without a job, of which three million would appear on the unemployment register .... [34]

In this 'hydraulic' conception of the workings of the UK economy market forces play virtually no role in the determination of unemployment, and supply factors are not mentioned explicitly. The prescription to reduce unemployment is that aggregate demand be expanded inside a wall of import tariffs erected around the UK economy.

At the other extreme comes the New Classical Macroeconomics explanation that the equilibrium rate of unemployment in the UK has risen because of a decline in aggregate supply. Thus, for example, the

Liverpool group estimate the equilibrium level of unemployment to have risen from $1\frac{1}{2}$ per cent in the early 1960s, to $2\frac{1}{2}$ per cent in the late 1960s, 6 per cent in the late 1970s and $8\frac{1}{2}$ per cent in the early 1980s, reflecting the disincentive effects of higher taxation and unemployment and social security benefits, and the effects of trade unions in raising real wages.[35] In this conception markets clear continuously so as to keep the UK economy in a rational expectations equilibrium, and aggregate demand factors only affect unemployment in so far as errors in expectations arise therefrom. The prescription to reduce unemployment is that taxes and unemployment and social security benefits be cut, and that legislative action be taken to curb the power of trade unions.

Neither of the above research programmes has generated sufficient corroborated empirical content for us to be able to place great confidence either in their explanations of UK unemployment, or in their programmes of political action to reduce UK unemployment. In what follows we outline an explanation of UK unemployment based on an amended version of the natural rate of unemployment theory.

Hysteresis and the natural rate of unemployment

The natural rate of unemployment can be defined as the level of unemployment which will be consistent with an unchanging rate of inflation. The conventional formulation of this theory suggests that it will be largely the microeconomic factors which determine aggregate supply, which will determine the natural rate of unemployment.[36] In principle, however, there is no reason why aggregate demand factors should not also affect the natural rate of unemployment, given that this concept merely defines the unemployment level which is consistent with an unchanging rate of inflation. A first channel of influence for aggregate demand arises from the costs of *anticipated* inflation. As outlined in greater detail in Chapter 13, even inflation which is perfectly anticipated will impose costs, in that less efficient methods of exchange will be used, and in that distortions to aggregate supply will arise from such as the non-indexation of the tax system to the rate of inflation. Thus a higher rate of expansion of the money supply will lead to a higher rate of expansion of money demand, a higher rate of inflation and higher costs of anticipated inflation. Such higher costs of anticipated inflation will reduce the output and employment levels which can be sustained without generating a change in the rate of inflation, and thus increase the natural rate of unemployment. This positive relationship between the rate of inflation and the natural rate of unemployment is illustrated in Figure 12.1.

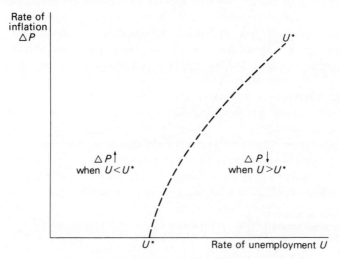

Figure 12.1. The costs of anticipated inflation and U^*

Secondly, if the relationship between *unanticipated* inflation and unemployment is such that the rate of inflation rises more rapidly when the actual rate is below the natural rate of unemployment than it falls when the actual is above the natural rate – as most empirical studies suggest – this means that the natural rate will increase if the *variance* of actual unemployment increases. To see this consider Figure 12.2(a) where we illustrate a short-run Phillips curve relationship between unanticipated inflation and unemployment for a zero expected rate of inflation $\Delta P^e = 0$. If the economy spends all its time at U^* such inflation expectations could be realized, that is $\Delta P = \Delta P^e = 0$. If, however, the economy only *on average* spends its time at U^*, actual unemployment being U_P for half of the time and U_T for the other half, then the actual rate of inflation will be $\frac{1}{2}[\Delta P_P + \Delta P_T] > \Delta P^e = 0$. Thus operating the economy on average at U^* would lead to $\Delta P > \Delta P^e = 0$, so inflation expectations would be revised upwards and U^* would not be consistent with an unchanging rate of inflation. To achieve an unchanging rate of inflation the economy would have to experience on average U^{**} in order to have $\Delta P = \Delta P^e = 0$. The obvious result of this line of

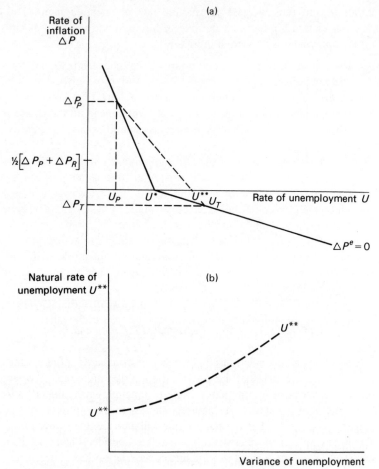

Figure 12.2. (a) The effect of variance on U^*; (b) the variance of U and U^{**}

reasoning is that the higher the variation in actual unemployment around its average value, the higher will be the U^{**} natural rate consistent with unchanging inflation. This relationship is illustrated in Figure 12.2(b).

A third influence for aggregate demand arises once we accept that the history of actual unemployment is likely to shape the natural rate of unemployment. Edmund Phelps, who along with Milton Friedman brought the natural rate of unemployment concept to prominence just after the mid-1960s,[37] used the term *hysteresis* to describe this process.

> The transition from one equilibrium to the other tends to have long-lingering effects on the labour force, and those effects may be discernible in the equilibrium rate for a long time. The natural unemployment rate at any future date will depend on the course of history in the interim. Such a property is sometimes called hysteresis.[38]

Thus if the recent history of the UK economy were to be characterized by low unemployment we would expect to have a more skilled and productive labour force than if the recent history was one of high unemployment, because the labour force would on average have received more on-the-job training and have learned more by doing, given that more people were employed. This means that low actual rates of unemployment will breed low natural rates of unemployment, and high actual rates of unemployment will breed high natural rates of unemployment.

Of particular interest here is the way the history of actual unemployment shapes the number of long-term unemployed in the labour force. As we discussed earlier in this chapter, the increase in actual unemployment in the UK since the mid-1960s has mainly arisen from a fall in the rate of outflow from unemployment and a rise in the average duration of unemployment. There has been a massive concomitant increase in the number of long-term unemployed in the labour force. In the mid-1960s there were under 100,000 people on the unemployment register who had been unemployed for longer than 6 months. In 1981 this number had risen to over 1 million of the unemployed. As we also saw earlier in this chapter, such long-term unemployed people have a low probability of regaining employment, which arises from the actual or perceived decline in productivity or capacity to work associated with a prolonged spell of unemployment. All this means that the increases in unemployment since the mid-1960s have shaped a labour force characterized by an increasing number of the long-term unemployed and hence by an increasing number of people whose actual or perceived productivities are lower as a result of their unemployment experience. Potential output and employment has fallen as a result, and hence a *hysteresis* process transmitted through the unwilling medium of the long-term unemployed has increased the natural rate of unemployment in the UK. Thus bygones are not bygones, and the natural rate of unemployment bears the legacy of the recent experience of actual unemployment, and more specifically of the experience of long-term unemployment. Figure 12.3 illustrates this relationship.

Figure 12.3. The effect of long-term unemployment on U^*

We are now equipped to use of our hysteresis-augmented version of the natural rate of unemployment to offer an explanation for the rise in UK unemployment from the mid-1960s to the early 1980s. Our theory suggests five sets of factors which will determine the actual rate of unemployment:

(a) microeconomic factors such as 'the actual structural characteristics of the labour and commodity markets, market imperfections ... the cost of gathering information about job vacancies and labour availabilities, the costs of mobility and so on ...'[39] which determine the natural rate of unemployment as conventionally defined;
(b) the anticipated rate of inflation – see Figure 12.1;
(c) the variance of unemployment – see Figure 12.2;
(d) the number of long-term unemployed in the labour force – see Figure 12.3; and
(e) the difference between the actual and natural rates of unemployment arising from demand shocks, supply shocks and government macroeconomic policies.

Microeconomic factors

As discussed in Chapter 10 of this book, 'supply side' microeconomic factors appear to be able to explain some of the rise in UK unemployment from the mid-1960s to the early 1980s. We would argue that the following factors have had some noticeable effect:

(a) *legislation* such as that contained in the Redundancy Payments Act of 1965, the Industrial Relations Act of 1972 and the Employment Protection Act of 1975;

(b) the *poverty trap* disincentive effects on unemployment arising from the high marginal tax rates levied on income from low-paid jobs;

(c) the effects of *incomes policies* in first distorting wage relativities and then stimulating an increase in real wages as workers attempt to restore their real wages after wage controls are abandoned, as in 1979–80;

(d) *structural changes* associated with such as the oil price increases of 1973–74 and 1979–80, and any effects of North Sea Oil on the real sterling exchange rate; and

(e) *housing market* distortions arising from rent controls and the tax concessions given to owner occupiers, which have served to reduce the mobility of labour.[40]

We would argue that *unemployment benefits* have not raised unemployment substantially during this period: as Table 12.2 column (8) indicates, the *notional* rate of unemployment benefit relative to wages did increase in the mid-1960s and early 1970s, but has since fallen; and as column (9) indicates the *actual* benefits received relative to wages has not increased much since the mid-1960s. We would also argue that *trade unions* have not raised unemployment substantially during this period; it is not obvious that actual real wages have been pushed in excess of equilibrium real wages during this period; trade unions have only a once-off power to raise the relative real wages of their members and not real wages in the economy as a whole; and as we saw in Chapter 5, unemployment is just as consistent with real wages being too low as real wages being too high. Finally, as we saw in Chapter 10, the evidence on changes in the size of the *black economy* does not provide clear support for the hypothesis that there has been a compensating increase in 'black' employment during this period.

The costs of anticipated inflation

The average rate of inflation, as measured by the Retail Price Index, increased from 3.5 per cent in 1961–65 to 4.6 per cent in 1966–70, 13.2 per cent in 1971–75 and 14.4 per cent in 1976–80. Thus, on the basis of the costs of anticipated inflation analysis outlined in Chapter 13, we would expect the natural rate of unemployment to have risen since the mid-1960s.

The variance of unemployment

As Table 12.2 column (1) clearly indicates, UK unemployment has displayed an increasing variance around its moving average since the mid-1960s, and on this count we would expect the natural rate to have risen.

Hysteresis and the long-term unemployed

To begin with the increase in actual unemployment from the mid-1960s to the early 1980s has meant that fewer people have received the on-the-job training and learning-by-doing that arises from employment. Secondly, the ten-fold increase in the number of people who have been unemployed for longer than 6 months and longer than a year – see Table 12.2 columns (4) and (5) – means that hysteresis effects arising from long-term unemployment have also raised the natural rate of unemployment during this period. We would argue that the latter effect has been substantial and has served to embody in the natural rate of unemployment the effects of the supposed temporary deviations of the actual from the natural rate of unemployment discussed in the next section.

Difference between the actual and natural rate of unemployment

The HM Treasury estimate of the natural rate of unemployment which would be consistent with an unchanging rate of inflation was 1,200,000 unemployed for 1981, or about 5 per cent of the labour force.[41] This figure is almost exactly equal to the number of long-term unemployed in the labour force in 1981. The implication that long-term unemployment is the only component of the natural rate of unemployment, and the implication that unemployment could be reduced by nearly 2 million without increasing the rate of inflation, make it hard to believe this estimate. Presumably the natural rate of unemployment is nearer 2 million unemployed in 1981, or about 8 per cent of the labour force. During the 1970s *supply shocks* such as the oil price increases of 1973–74 and 1979–80 have served to raise the actual above the natural rate of unemployment. *Demand shocks* arising from the decline in the rate of growth of world trade since the mid-1970s have similarly raised unemployment above the natural rate. Similarly the *government* aggregate demand policy measures taken in 1974–75 and 1979–81 to reduce the rate of inflation have raised the actual above the natural rate of unemployment with the expansionary measures of 1972–73 having had the opposite effect of reducing the actual below the natural rate of unemployment. Given the hysteresis effects outlined earlier, such shocks will not be of the once-off variety commonly alleged, but will have served to increase the natural rate of unemployment in the UK. With the exception of the 1972–73 expansionary policy measures, all the shocks referred to above have served to increase the natural rate of unemployment.

Policy action to reduce unemployment

Given the analysis of UK unemployment outlined above, policy action could be geared to any of the five sets of factors which we discerned to have been at work in increasing UK unemployment. Here there would be some conflicts in the suggestions given to policy-makers, given that expansionary policy measures to reduce the difference between actual and natural rate of unemployment would produce beneficial hysteresis effects on the unemployment rate but would also mean that the UK economy would end up with a higher rate of inflation and hence detrimental effects on unemployment arising from the costs of anticipated inflation.

Two main sets of policy measures would seem to be required to reduce the sustainable rate of unemployment in the UK. First of all fiscal and monetary policies need to be relaxed in order to permit actual unemployment to fall if an upswing in economic activity takes place. Only by reducing actual unemployment can the *hysteresis* effects which have served to increase UK unemployment be set in reverse. Such relaxation of fiscal and monetary policies would mean a higher rate of inflation than otherwise would be the case, so our argument here is based on the judgement that the hysteresis effects on the natural rate of unemployment are stronger than the effects of anticipated inflation.

Secondly, *microeconomic* policy measures are suggested to correct for such as the supply disincentives arising from the poverty trap and the barriers to labour mobility arising from housing policies. Job subsidy schemes of the partly cosmetic type pursued by UK governments in the 1970s and 1980s[42] are only likely to provide a temporary palliative to the problem. In the long run we would agree that:

> ... a strategy for full employment in today's circumstances has to concentrate heavily on matters such as education, apprenticeship, regional policy, the work of official job placement centres, the detail of work contracts and pension arrangements. ...[43]

We would add that a strategy for full employment has also to concentrate heavily on avoiding the hysteresis effects on equilibrium unemployment which have arisen from the deflationary macroeconomic policies pursued in 1974–75 and, more particularly, in 1979–81. Bygones are not bygones, and the most imaginative microeconomic policy measures in the world will find it difficult to reverse the effects of the dramatic increases in long-term unemployment experienced in 1979–81.

13 Inflation

> The more volatile the general rate of inflation, the harder it becomes to extract the signal about relative prices from the absolute prices, the broadcast about relative prices ... being jammed by the noise coming from the inflation broadcast (Milton Friedman, *Nobel Prize Lecture*, 1976).

The rate of inflation measures the change in the purchasing power of money, or more formally, 'how much more money you would have to have this year when faced with this year's prices to be as well off as you were last year when faced with last year's prices'.[1] Most people would accept that a lower rate of inflation is desirable, other things being equal, but the problem is precisely that other things will not remain equal if steps are taken to reduce the rate of inflation. There has been much controversy as to whether it is worth bearing the costs associated with policies to reduce the rate of inflation in view of the gains to be had from a lower rate of inflation. At one extreme the 1979-84 Conservative government has argued that '... overriding priority must be given to reducing inflation, which impairs economic efficiency and discourages investment ...'.[2] At the other extreme it has been argued that we should

> ... seriously examine the possibilities of 'living with inflation' ... the government's priorities are hard to understand in the light of their own professed theory of how the economy works. On that theory one would look for a stable rate of inflation and not aim at reducing it at great real costs.[3]

The point at issue here is how high are the costs of inflation compared to the costs of lower output and higher unemployment which will be incurred by policies to reduce inflation. Discussions of the costs of inflation usually distinguish between the costs arising from *anticipated inflation*, and the costs arising from *unanticipated inflation*.

Costs of anticipated inflation

The first item here is the costs that arise from the lower holdings of cash and current accounts at banks at higher rates of inflation. The higher the rate of inflation the greater will be the opportunity cost of holding money balances. The implied economizing on money balances is illustrated in Figure 13.1. At the rate of inflation ΔP_1 people hold real money balances of M_1, at the higher rate of inflation ΔP_2 real money balances are reduced to M_2. If people hold lower real money balances this means that less monetary, and hence usually less efficient, transactions methods will be used; and more trips will be made to banks in order to make more frequent transactions.

With means of payment – currency plus demand deposits – equal currently to 20% of GNP, an extra percentage point of anticipated inflation – produces in principle a social cost of $\frac{2}{10}$ of 1% of GNP per year. This is an outside estimate ... I suspect that intelligent laymen would be utterly astounded if they realised that this is the great evil

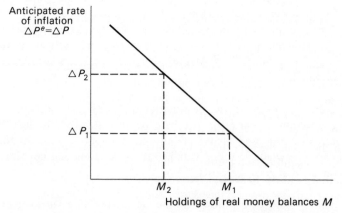

Figure 13.1. Inflation and real money balances

economists are talking about. They have imagined a much more devastating cataclysm, with Vesuvius vengefully punishing the sinners below. Extra trips between savings banks and commercial banks? What an anti-climax![4]

Other costs associated with perfectly anticipated inflation include those arising from changing prices more frequently; those arising from the distortions if taxes, social security benefits, pensions and so on are not indexed to the rate of inflation; those arising from adjusting accounts for inflation; and the fact that higher payments have to be made in the early years of repaying a loan to take account of the higher money interest rates which will be attached to loans to compensate for inflation – this is sometimes known as a *front-loading* problem.[5]

Costs of unanticipated inflation

If the costs outlined above were the only costs arising from inflation it would be hard to understand what all the fuss over inflation is about. A more important set of costs, however, arises from inflation which is not foreseen correctly. Given that the more variable the rate of inflation the more difficult it will be to foresee correctly the rate of inflation, it can be argued that the main costs of inflation arise from *variations* in the rate of inflation rather from the *level* of the rate of inflation. A first issue here is that a varying rate of inflation makes it more difficult to distinguish *relative* price changes from changes in the *general* price level. Thus workers and firms will find it more difficult to organize their economic activities because it is more difficult to tell whether a rise in their money wage rates or output prices indicates that there is a greater demand for their labour services or output, or whether all that is happening is that the general level of prices is rising at a faster rate. Such confusion will increase the uncertainty surrounding economic activities and we would expect output and employment to be lower as a result. A second issue is the redistribution of income and wealth which arises from unanticipated inflation. For example, creditors are likely to lose out to debtors if the actual rate of inflation turns out to be higher than the expected rate of inflation embodied in the contracts between creditors and debtors.[6] A third issue here is that unanticipated inflation is likely to lead people to spend more time and resources in taking steps to protect themselves from inflation, and less in more productive activities.

Diagnosis

As Table 13.1 indicates, the UK rate of inflation has risen for much of the period 1964-81, the main exceptions being the periods of decline in 1977-78 and 1981. The average rate of inflation was 3.5 per cent in 1961-65, 4.6 per cent in 1966-70, 13.2 per cent in 1971-75 and 14.4 per cent in 1976-80. The Keynesian explanation of the rate of inflation stresses institutional features of the labour market, particularly trade unions, as determinants of the rate of inflation - see Chapters 4 and 7 of this book - and sees incomes policies as the main means whereby political action can be taken to reduce the rate of inflation.[7] The

Table 13.1. UK Rate of inflation, 1964–81

Year	Annual percentage change in retail price index	Year	Annual percentage change in retail price index
1964	3.2	1973	9.2
1965	4.8	1974	16.1
1966	3.9	1975	24.2
1967	2.5	1976	16.5
1968	4.7	1977	15.8
1969	5.4	1978	8.3
1970	6.4	1979	13.4
1971	9.4	1980	18.0
1972	7.1	1981	12.0 (est.)

Source: Economic Trends.

monetarist explanation sees the UK rate of inflation as being determined by the rate of expansion of the *world* money supply if the foreign exchange rate if fixed, and by the rate of expansion of the *UK* money supply if the foreign exchange rate if flexible - see Chapter 8 of this book. Orthodox Monetarism suggests a *gradual* reduction in the rate of monetary expansion under flexible exchange rates if the authorities wish to reduce the rate of inflation, so as to minimize the output and unemployment costs of reducing the rate of inflation.[8] New Classical Macroeconomics suggests a *sharp* reduction in the rate of monetary expansion, arguing that the private sector's 'rational' expectations of the rate of inflation will adjust quickly to a lower rate of monetary expansion, and hence that the output and unemployment costs of reducing the rate of inflation will be small in magnitude.[9]

As argued in Section I of this book, the Orthodox Monetarist theory of the rate of inflation has greater corroborated empirical content than the Keynesian and New Classical Macroeconomics theories. The time-lags before a reduction in the rate of monetary expansion feeds through to prices depend on such factors as how quickly expectations adjust, how much confidence the private sector has in the declared policy intentions of the authorities, and so on. Thus we would not expect to see an extremely close correlation between the rate of inflation and the lagged value of the rate of monetary expansion, but rather a broad correlation between the moving annual average rate of the rate of inflation and the moving annual average of the lagged rate of monetary expansion. In this broad sense the Monetarist theory explains the UK experience reasonably well.[10] The institutional features of wage-bargaining invoked by the Keynesian theories of inflation do seem to be able to explain some of the short-run movements in the rate of inflation, but only explain the long-run path of the rate of inflation by reference to exogenous factors not explained within the theory such as the target growth in real wages desired by workers or trade unions. Inflation expectations, particularly those of workers, do not appear to adjust quickly enough to the rate of monetary expansion to support the New Classical Macroeconomics theory.

Political action

The conclusion we would draw as far as political action is concerned is that the rate of monetary expansion should be reduced slowly if the authorities desire to reduce the rate of inflation, but that it is not obvious for inflation rates of around 10 per cent that the benefits to be derived from reducing the rate of inflation exeed the unemployment and output costs of reducing the rate of inflation. In particular, the *hysteresis* effects outlined in Chapter 12 of this book suggest that the rate of inflation can only be reduced at the cost of raising the equilibrium or natural rate of unemployment. Thus even if the UK economy returns reasonably quickly to equilibrium after experiencing the higher unemployment and lower output levels arising from the 1979–84 Conservative government's anti-inflation policies, this new equilibrium will be characterized by a higher rate of unemployment because more people will have experienced long-term unemployment during the process of reducing the rate of inflation. We would argue in this case that the benefits to be gained from a reduction in the rate of inflation are less than the costs associated with an increase in both the transitional and equilibrium or natural rate of unemployment.[11]

14 Economic growth and business cycles

If you hit a wooden rocking-horse with a club, the movement of the horse will be very different to that of the club (Knut Wicksell, Norwegian Economic Society Lecture, 1907).

Economic growth refers to the trend rate of growth of aggregate output whereas the business cycle refers to fluctuations of actual output around its trend value. The level of actual output Y can be divided up into a component Y^* representing the trend value which will increase over time if economic growth is positive; and a component $y = Y - Y^*$ which represents the deviation from trend output associated with the business cycle. The relationship between the economic growth and business cycle components of changes in output is illustrated in Figure 14.1.

Economic growth

The higher the rate of economic growth in an economy the higher are the levels of average consumption per head which can be sustained now or in the future. There is a trade-off between consuming more income now, saving less and hence having less consumption in the future, and consuming less income now, saving more and hence having more income to consume in the future. Figure 14.2 illustrates the inter-temporal choice decision regarding consumption. If preferences are as described in indifference curve I_2 the economy will have a current level of consumption C_{P_2} which is greater than the current income level Y_P, and thus the economy will be able to consume only C_{F_2} in the future. If preferences are as described in indifference curve I_1, the economy has the current level of consumption C_{P_1}, which is less than the current

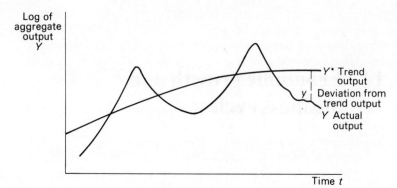

Figure 14.1. Growth and the business cycle

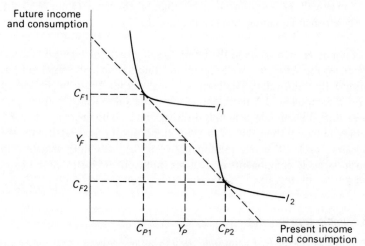

Figure 14.2. Choice between present and future consumption

income level Y_P, thus permitting the consumption of C_{F_1} in the future, that is more than the expected future income level Y_F.

The benefits of economic growth in permitting higher consumption per head over time have been stressed widely. The tendency has been to see '... total economic advance as individual economic advance writ large ...'[1] and to associate 'individual economic advance' with higher levels of consumption per head over time, there being arguments as to the desirable distribution of income, wealth and consumption; as to the desirable division of consumption between public and private goods and so on. This position has been criticized by those who stress the costs associated with economic growth;[2] those who stress the finite nature of raw materials and other basic economic resources;[3] and those who stress that economic growth can merely result in increased pressure on goods whose scarcity is social in nature, such as enjoyable or prestigious jobs, car journeys unmolested by traffic jams or outstanding educational achievement.[4] The conventional position has been defended by pointing out that economic growth allows governments to take measures to make poorer people better off without making richer people worse off, and makes it easier for governments to finance their social policies in the fields of health provision, education and so on.[5] All UK governments since the war have had the professed aim of increasing the rate of economic growth, though the emphasis has changed over recent years from using *demand side* policies to using *supply side* policies to pursue this end.

Keynesian research programmes have assigned a major role to aggregate demand policies in promoting economic growth. Although the equilibrium growth path for output is seen as being determined by the growth in factors of production, and changes in their productivity or efficiency of use, the view taken is that governments need to ensure that a sufficient level of aggregate demand is forthcoming for the potential equilibrium rate of growth to be realized. Aggregate demand policies have not been notably successful in promoting economic growth in the UK. Expansions of aggregate demand have never been sustained. In the fixed exchange period up until 1972 expansionary policies were invariably reversed in response to the balance of payments 'crises' arising from such policies. The floating exchange period from 1972 onwards saw the expansionary fiscal measures of 1972 being reversed in 1973-74 in response to the 'crisis' arising from the sharp increase in the rate of inflation stimulated in large part by the expansionary measures. The verdict of a group of Keynesian economists in 1974 on the record of expansionary fiscal policies to promote economic growth was:

> Throughout [the last 20 years] fiscal policy has been operated in alternating directions to produce periods of strong demand expansion, followed by periods of reversal in crisis conditions. Thus in 1953-54, 1958-59, 1962-63 and most notoriously in 1971-72 demand expansionary policies were introduced. ... Then always, just two years later, the direction was reversed, demand-deflationary

policies being initiated in 1955–56, 1960–61, 1964–65 and now again in 1973–74. ... Demand, output and the balance of payments might have been more stable than they were had some simple rule been followed through thick and thin, such as that ... [the] tax yield ... cover ... some fixed proportion of public expenditure.[6]

The response of UK Keynesian economists to the fact that expansionary fiscal policies have not been sustained long enough to stimulate a higher rate of growth has been to advocate devaluation of the foreign exchange rate;[7] incomes policies;[8] or import controls[9] to deal with the constraints which have led to the reversal of expansionary measures in the past.

An influential sophistication of the Orthodox Keynesian position involves a relationship known as *Verdoorn's law*. This law states that productivity growth is positively related to output growth, and thus that if aggregate demand policy measures manage to sustain an increase in output growth they will also increase the rate of growth of productivity.[10] This line of thought has been one of the inspirations behind the New Cambridge Keynesian research programme – see Chapter 7 of this book. Here import controls are advocated to allow a sustained expansion of aggregate demand. There is, however, considerable doubt over whether Verdoorn's law holds and over the size of the productivity gains which might be engendered by a faster rate of output growth.[11, 12]

In contrast Orthodox Monetarism has seen attempts to stimulate economic growth by *discretionary* aggregate demand policy measures as being more likely to reduce the rate of economic growth because of the disruptive effects of the 'go-stop' reversals of policy. Such policy reversals are seen as disrupting the environment in which firms and workers plan their economic activities and thus as serving to reduce the realizable rate of economic growth. The prescription is rather that aggregate demand policy measures be guided by *rules* which should be changed only slowly over time so as not to disrupt the economic activities of the private sector. An extreme version of this line of thought is to be found in the New Classical Macroeconomics and Supply Side Macroeconomics, where aggregate supply factors are seen as the sole determinants of the rate of economic growth. Thus political action to increase the rate of economic growth in the UK would have to take the form of *microeconomic* policy measures to encourage aggregate supply – see Chapter 10 of this book for an appraisal of the 'supply side' policy measures suggested. The use of 'supply side' policy measures to stimulate economic growth has been the second main component of the 1979–84 Conservative government's economic strategy. If the first priority of this government has been to reduce the rate of inflation, the second priority has been to

> ... strengthen the supply side of the economy ... by encouraging market forces to work as freely and flexibly as possible ... [by] restoring incentives so that hard work pays, success is rewarded and genuine new jobs are created in an expanding economy ... [by cutting] income tax at all levels ... and by ensuring that the standard rate of income tax in the long-term is no more than 25%.[13]

The lesson of 1979–81, however, is that even if the aggregate supply measures undertaken could be effective in increasing the rate of economic growth in the UK the benefits of such measures are not likely to be realized if policies to reduce aggregate demand are pursued at the same time.

Business cycles

Business cycle fluctuations around the trend growth in aggregate output can be classified according to the size of the deviations from trend output involved. In the course of a *mild* business cycle aggregate output would vary by no more than about 5 per cent from the peak of the cycle to the trough. In a *severe* business cycle the decline in output from peak to trough would be more than about 5 per cent. As far as the costs of a *mild* business cycle are concerned it is useful to draw an analogy with the provision of insurance. In private life many individuals are prepared to pay positive sums of money in the form of insurance premiums to insure themselves against eventualities which would generate an uneven flow of income or consumption were they to occur. Extending this analogy to social life we would expect that collectively we would be prepared to devote resources to policy measures which would reduce the fluctuations in output, income and employment experienced between the peaks and troughs of business cycles, and so reduce the disruptions to economic activity arising from such cycles. The question here is whether there is a set of policy measures which could be successful in reducing cyclical fluctuations.

The costs of a *severe* business cycle are far more substantial. If the upswing phase of the cycle gets out of control, *hyperinflation* can result, with dramatic repercussions on output and employment once money no longer serves as an efficient method of exchange in the face of inflation rates in excess of around 50 per cent per annum. Such *hyperinflations* can serve to threaten the survival of states and provide at least the necessary conditions for the overthrow of a particular system of government, as with the Weimar Republic in Germany in the 1920s. If the downswing of the cycle gets out of control, *depressions* will result, with dramatic repercussions on output and employment arising from a cumulative downward movement in tandem of effective demand and effective supply. At the very least great human suffering will be experienced by many people during such depressions, and the reaction to such suffering can again threaten the survival of states or existing systems of government. It has often taken a long time for economies to recover from severe depressions. In the UK, for example, unemployment remained high at 12.9 per cent of the labour force as long as 6 years after the 'Great Depression' of 1930-32.

'Mild' cycles

Figure 14.3 illustrates the cyclical fluctuations in the UK economy over the last 20 years. During the course of the business cycle not all economic activities move together, some variables lagging behind, some variables leading the main business cycle. The main business cycle is indicated in Figure 14.3 as the *coincident* indicator of cycles in economic activity. The Central Statistical Office in the UK uses six variables to arrive at an index of the main or coincident business cycle: the expenditure, income and output estimates of GDP, the index of manufacturing production, the index of the volume of retail sales and CBI Industrial Trends Survey information regarding the number of firms working at below capacity and changes in stocks of materials used in production. From 1963 to the early 1980s the UK experienced four business cycles. Measuring the length of the cycle from trough to trough the cycles have measured 50, 59 and 42 months. Measured from peak to peak the cycles have measured 52, 48 and 72 months. At the time of writing (August 1981) there is considerable doubt as to whether the trough of the current trade cycle has been yet reached. Official statistics used to measure the cycle are subject to revision, month-to-month comparisons can be misleading because of special factors affecting the figures for particular months, and hence it is difficult to pinpoint a turning point until some time after the event. If, in retrospect, the trough of the

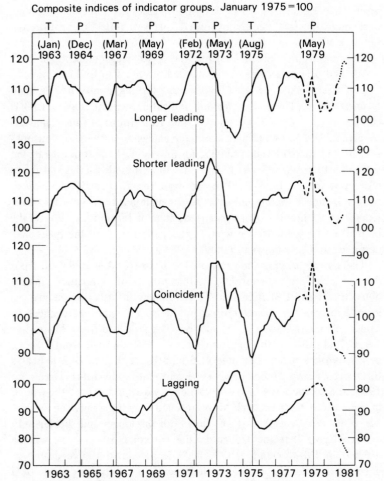

Figure 14.3. *Cyclical indicators for the UK economy (taken from* Economic Trends, *July 1981, p. 69)*

current trade cycle were to be timed at August 1981, this would indicate that the most recent cycle lasted for 72 months. Thus in the last 20 years the UK would have experienced business cycles of 4–6 years in length. In terms of the severity of the fall in output from peak to trough of the business cycle the last two downswings in the UK economy beginning in May 1973 and May 1979 have been far more severe than earlier postwar cycles. In both cases the coincident business cycle indicator has fallen by just over 25 per cent, reflecting a substantial fall in 'real' economic activity.

The importance of the business cycle to decision-taking in both public and private sectors has stimulated attempts to find leading indicators which could be used to forecast turning points in the main business cycle. The *longer leading* indicator series in Figure 14.3 is composed from the *FT* share index, net acquisitions of financial assets by companies, house-building starts, the change in business optimism as reflected in the CBI Industrial Trends Survey, and the interest rate on three-month bank bills. As Figure 14.3 indicates, this series started to move upwards in June 1980 in the most recent cycle. The time lead from this *longer leading* indicator to the main business cycle has varied from 7 to 21 months with a mean lead time of 13 months. Thus on the basis of past experience we would expect the trough in the main business cycle to occur between January 1981 and April 1982.

The *shorter leading* indicator of the business cycle is derived from data on new car registrations, trading profits of companies, finance house credit and CBI Industrial Trends Survey information on changes in new orders for manufactured products and expected changes in stocks of materials used in production. The time lead from this *shorter leading* indicator to the main business cycle has varied from 0 to 12 months with a mean lead time of 5 months. As Figure 14.3 indicates this *shorter leading* indicator series began to move upwards in December 1980, and so the basis of past experience we would expect the trough in the current business cycle to be reached some time between December 1980 and December 1981. Thus both the longer and shorter indicators suggest that the trough in the current business cycle will be reached in 1981 or early 1982. There is of course a large degree of uncertainty attached to any such forecast of the turning point of a business cycle, given that the past does not necessarily repeat itself. There again, even if the turning point is reached in 1981 output and employment could remain low for quite some time afterwards. During the course of 1981 there has been much discussion as to whether output will describe the classical U shape in the upswing from the current trough or whether an L shape prolonged depression or the short-lived recovery associated with a W shape is more likely.

Finally comes a set of indices of economic activity which lag the main business cycle. The indices used to derive the lagging indicator series illustrated in Figure 14.3 are manufacturing investment in plant and machinery, the level of stocks in manufacturing, orders in the engineering industry, unemployment and job vacancies. The average *lag* time for this *lagging indicator* series has been 10 months, the variation being from 3 to 17 months. Of particular interest here is the fact that unemployment lags around 6-12 months behind the main business cycle. Thus even if the main business cycle reaches its trough in 1981 we would expect unemployment to stop rising only 6-12 months later. This time lag with unemployment is of particular importance to the framing of macroeconomic policies. If expansionary aggregate demand policies are pursued most vigorously when unemployment is at its peak, such policies will be mistimed in the sense that they will only be put into effect 6-12 months after the economy has come to recover from the trough in the business cycle. Thus although unemployment reached a then postwar high of 1 million unemployed in the winter of 1971/72, we know with hindsight that the main business cycle reached its trough in February 1972, that is before the massive stimulus to aggregate demand announced in the March 1972 Budget. Thus the expansionary fiscal policy measures of March 1972 were heaped on to expansionary pressures which already existed in the economy at that time.

Orthodox Keynesian view

The Orthodox Keynesian view has been that government aggregate demand policies could be used successfully to reduce the size of business cycle fluctuations. Here a distinction is drawn between *automatic stabilizers* which lead aggregate demand to rise in the downswing of the cycle and fall in the upswing of the cycle, and *discretionary stabilization* policies which involve a more activist attempt to reduce fluctuations in the business cycle. Until the 1979-84 Conservative government's reign of office, policy-makers were agreed that *automatic stabilizers* should be allowed free rein to reduce cyclical fluctuations. Thus income tax receipts would be allowed to fall during the downswing of the business cycle, government spending on such items as unemployment and social security benefits would be allowed to rise and the fiscal deficit to rise. The attempt of the 1979-84 government to reduce the fiscal deficit during the cyclical downswing of 1979-81 constitutes a major departure in that it involves reducing the power of automatic stabilizers to reduce cyclical fluctuations. Figure 14.4 illustrates that on the basis of an unchanged fiscal stance indicated by the line F_1 we would have expected the fiscal deficit to have increased from $(T - G)_1$

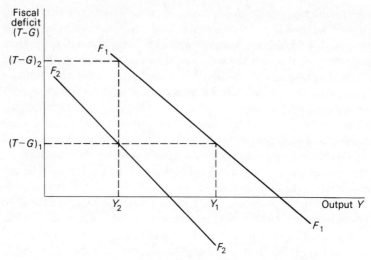

Figure 14.4. Fiscal deficit and the trade cycle

to $(T-G)_2$ as output fell from Y_1 to Y_2 during the period 1979-81. The government, however, has changed its spending and taxation policies so as to aim at containing the fiscal deficit at around $(T-G)_1$, the changed stance of fiscal policy being indicated by the line F_2. The government's argument has been that government spending *crowds out* private sector spending – see Chapter 15 on Fiscal Policy – so that if the fiscal deficit were to have been allowed to increase automatically during the downswing of 1979-81, private spending would have been discouraged because, given the monetary target – see Chapter 16 on Monetary Policy – interest rates would have had to have been higher in order to finance the increase in the fiscal deficit.

The record of *discretionary stabilization* or fine-tuning policies aimed at reducing the size of cyclical fluctuations has been poor: 'it cannot be denied that government policy did differ considerably from what it ought to have been if the objective had been to maintain activity at a stable and consistent level ...';[14] 'as far as internal conditions are concerned ... budgetary and fiscal policy failed to be stabilising and must on the contrary be regarded as destabilising'.[15] Similar judgement was passed in 1974 by the House of Commons Expenditure Committee, which advised governments against the use of countercyclical policies of the fine-tuning variety.[16] The main reason for the failure of such *discretionary stabilization* policies has been that policy measures have taken effect at the wrong time. In July 1974, for example, a witness to the House of Commons Expenditure Committee mentioned 'stories, for example, that work is being done in St. James's Park at the moment and it is because there was a recession in 1971–72 which one is trying to put right by increased public expenditure'.[17] Time lags lie at the heart of the problem, there being a *recognition lag* before the authorities come to have reliable information about the present state or recent history of the business cycle; an *implementation lag* while the authorities organize and put into effect the required policy measures; and *behavioural lags* while the private sector adjusts its behaviour to the new policy measures. Such time lags together imply that something like 2 or 3 years might pass before a stabilization policy comes to take full effect, and by that time the cyclical position of the economy could well have been reversed.

Given such time lags it can be easily demonstrated that a *proportional* stabilization policy which makes aggregate demand most expansionary at the trough of the business cycle, and most restrictive at the peak of the cycle, is likely to correct for the deviation from trend output only at the expense of increasing the size of cyclical fluctuations in the economy.[18] This tendency for *discretionary stabilization* policy to exacerbate fluctuations in output can be reduced only by incorporating a 'common-nonsense' element into stabilization policy. This *derivative* element involves expanding aggregate demand when output is declining and reducing aggregate demand when output is rising. The counter-intuitive implication is that policy be made restrictive just after the trough of the cycle has been passed, and made expansionary just after the peak has been passed. This is illustrated in Figure 14.5 where the *derivative* element in stabilization policy implies restrictive policies when $\Delta Y > 0$ in the upswing of the cycle, and expansionary policies when $\Delta Y < 0$ in the downswing of the cycle. A *proportional* stabilization policy on its own, however, would make policy most expansionary when y took on its greatest negative value at the trough of the cycle, and most restrictive when y took on its greatest positive value at the peak of the cycle. Both *proportional* and *derivative* stabilization policies would have to be used in tandem, because *proportional* policies can correct for a shortfall in output only at the cost of increasing the size of cyclical fluctuations, and *derivative* policies on their own cannot correct for the shortfall in output. The problem with *derivative* elements in stabilization policy is that they would imply the implementation of restrictive policies as soon as output comes to rise from the

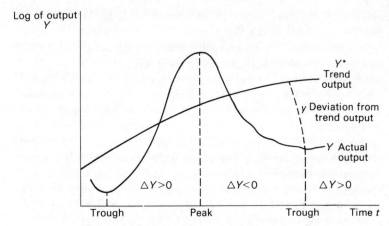

Figure 14.5. Discretionary stabilization policy

trough of the business cycle. As we have seen, unemployment continues to rise for around 6-12 months after the trough in the main business cycle has been reached. So, for example, if the trough in the current business cycle is reached in 1981, unemployment will continue to rise into 1982. *Derivative* stabilization policies would thus imply that restrictive aggregate demand policies be pursued while unemployment is still rising. Ironically enough this implies that there is almost an Orthodox Keynesian rationale for the electorally unpopular policies of the government in pursuing deflationary measures in 1981. The reason why this is only 'almost' a rationale is that the government has not been simultaneously pursuing *proportional* stabilization policies to correct for the shortfall in output in 1981.

Criticisms of Orthodox Keynesian view

The New Cambridge critique of discretionary stabilization policies of the fine-tuning variety is derived from the hypothesis that changes in the fiscal deficit are reflected in changes in the balance of payments deficit. Thus UK 'fine-tuning' policies would serve mainly to affect output in the rest of the world rather than the UK. The prescription is rather that the authorities aim for a *sustained* expansion of aggregate demand behind a wall of import tariffs. The Orthodox Monetarist critique points to the problem of time lags discussed above, argues that discretionary stabilization policies are more likely to exacerbate rather than smooth cyclical fluctuations, and recommends instead that aggregate demand policy be guided by *rules* which should be changed only slowly over time. In particular *rules* should be set for the rate of growth of the money supply. Such *rules* have been used in the UK since 1976 and will be discussed in Chapter 16 on Monetary Policy. The New Classical Macroeconomics critique of discretionary stabilization policy is that fluctuations in output arise from errors in 'rationally' formed expectations regarding the rate of inflation, and that pre-announced policy measures will be incorporated into rational expectations and not have any effects on real output – see Chapter 9 of this book. Thus pre-announced policy measures will have no effects on the business cycle and governments will be powerless to change the course of the business cycle through pre-announced policy measures. Only the *unanticipated* component of policy measures will lead to errors in rational expectations and fluctuations in output. Thus governments are advised merely to make sure that their pre-announced policies are adhered to in order that the unanticipated component of policy measures does not lead to avoidable fluctuations in output.[19]

'Severe' business cycles in interwar Britain

Severe business cycles are those associated with a decline of output of more than about 5 per cent between the peak and the trough of the business cycle. In the interwar period in the UK output fell sharply in 1921–22 and 1930–31 and unemployment remained in excess of 10 per cent of the labour force for nearly the whole of the 1921–38 period, dipping below the 10 per cent rate only for a short spell in 1927. As far as the 1921–22 episode is concerned there is not much dispute that the deflationary policies pursued to return to the gold standard at the pre-1914–18 war parity of \$4.86 were responsible for the fall in output and rise in unemployment.[20] The controversial issue is why unemployment remained so high for the rest of the 1920s. As far as the 1930–31 episode is concerned there is little doubt that the source of the deflationary shock to the UK and many other countries was the Great Crash of the US stock market in 1929 and its aftermath. There is substantial controversy, however, as to what extent the Great Depression in the US 1929–33 was (a) initiated and (b) prolonged by a decline in the money supply as opposed to a decline in aggregate spending.[21] Further controversy surrounds the question of why unemployment again remained high in the UK after the shock of 1930–31.

The Orthodox Keynesian interpretation of the severe business cycles in interwar Britain is that economies left to their own devices are likely to experience sustained depressions in the aftermath of deflationary shocks such as experienced in 1921-22 and 1930-31, the private sector not reacting to such shocks in such a way as to generate a speedy return to 'full' employment. A major role for political action is seen in pursuing expansionary fiscal policies to avoid the onset of such depressions, or to stimulate recovery from such depressions. The key assumption here is that capitalist economies are likely to react in an unstable manner to shocks unless the government intervenes to correct for the unstable behaviour of the private sector. As we saw in Chapter 4, however, not even Keynes thought that the 12 per cent unemployment rate of 1937 could be reduced to any great extent simply by government measures to increase aggregate demand.

The Orthodox Monetarist interpretation of the interwar depressions has been able to explain monetary impulses underlying the deflationary shocks of 1921-22 and 1930-31 but not to explain why unemployment remained so high later on in the 1920s and 1930s. We would suggest that hysteresis effects such as those arising from the long-term unemployment experienced in 1921-22 and 1930-31, can help to explain why the natural rate of unemployment was so high for much of this period – see Chapter 12 of this book. Otherwise the sustained high unemployment in the interwar period remains a puzzle for Orthodox Monetarism. Given this puzzle it is difficult for monetarists to deny that anti-depression discretionary stimuli to aggregate demand might be required in certain circumstances. The view here, however, is that if governments organize their aggregate demand policies inside a set of slowly changing rules, there will not be the destabilizing monetary shocks to create the problem in the first place.

The New Classical Macroeconomics interpretation is that the interwar British economy regained a rational expectations equilibrium quickly after the shocks of 1921-22 and 1930-31, unemployment remaining high for the rest of the 1920s and 1930s because people chose to be unemployed because of the 'generosity' of the unemployment insurance system.[22] As we saw in Chapter 12, this 'supply side' explanation does not appear to provide a satisfactory explanation for the sustained high unemployment in interwar Britain, though the explanation is consistent with the output growth experienced in the 'employed' sector of the British economy during this period.

'Severe' business cycles in postwar Britain

In postwar Britain it has only been in the rapid declines of output from May 1973 to August 1975 and from May 1979 to 1981 or 1982 that the business cycle has approached the severity of the depressions experienced in interwar Britain – see Figure 14.3. The Orthodox Keynesian explanation for the lack of anything approaching severe depressions in the UK economy up until the 1970s has been '... without thinking very much, that it is because we have had a full employment policy – we have had the Keynesian revolution'.[23] This explanation implies that the UK economy avoided the depressions associated with demand deficiency in the interwar period because government fiscal policy action ensured a sufficiently high level of aggregate demand for 'full' employment to be maintained during this period. This explanation flies in the face of the fact that '... throughout the postwar period the government, so far from injecting demand into the system, has persistently had a large current account surplus ... this surplus has varied ... but government saving has averaged about 3% of national income ...'.[24] Rather, it is argued, '... part of the reason for low unemployment in the postwar period has been the trend increase in the scarcity of labour relative to capital. This is non-Keynesian ... and has has little or nothing to do with government policy'.[25] The other part of the reason for low unemployment in the postwar period has been 'an increase in effective demand that was not due in any direct way to government actions, but which was generated principally by private investment and exports'.[26] Thus it is by no means obvious that Keynesian aggregate demand policies were responsible for the UK economy avoiding severe depressions in the postwar period up until the early 1970s.[27]

Since the early 1970s fears that the UK economy might once again experience severe depressions of the type experienced in interwar Britain have been expressed. The dramatic fall in output and rise in unemployment during the period May 1979 to 1981 in particular has given rise to such fears. An extreme expression of such fears is given in the New Cambridge forecast that the 1979-81 downswing will move the economy into a severe depression which is likely to continue until well into the 1980s unless government policies are changed to pursue a programme of massive fiscal expansion inside a wall of tariff barriers. At the other extreme such fears are discounted in the New Classical Macroeconomics view that output will recover and subsequently unemployment will fall once (a) the actual rate of inflation falls below the expected rate of inflation in response to the government's policy of reducing the rate of expansion of the money supply, and (b) the policies to 'strengthen the supply side of the economy' take effect.

We would argue that both extreme views are wrong and that an *hysteresis-augmented* version of Orthodox Monetarism provides a better explanation for the current cyclical experience of the UK economy. This explanation sees the UK natural rate of unemployment – the rate consistent with an unchanging rate of inflation – as having risen since the early 1970s in response to the sharp declines in output of 1973–75 and 1979–81. In particular this increase in the natural unemployment rate can be attributed in large part to the increase in the number of long-term unemployed since the early 1970s – see Chapter 12 of this book. We would argue that unemployment is likely to remain high at around the 3 million mark on the basis of unchanged policies.

To reduce unemployment below this mark, and avoid a severe depression, we would suggest two types of policy. The first would be to increase the target rate of monetary expansion to stimulate aggregate demand so that the actual rate falls below the natural rate of unemployment. Only in this way could the hysteresis effects of the 1979–81 downswing, particularly those on the number of long-term unemployed, be reversed quickly. Such a policy would reduce the natural rate of unemployment. The costs of this policy would be those associated with a higher rate of inflation once the economy adjusts to a higher target rate of expansion of the money supply. Such costs, we would argue, would be worth bearing in return for a reasonably speedy reduction in the sustainable natural rate of unemployment. The second type of policy would involve the *microeconomic* measures to reduce unemployment discussed in Chapter 12 of this book. The point here is that aggregate demand and aggregate supply policies would be used in tandem, and in the same direction, to reduce the sustainable or natural rate of unemployment. We do not see the sense in having aggregate supply and demand policies work in opposite directions, as in 1979–81, if one of the main objectives of policy is to avoid a severe depression.

Section III

Instruments of macroeconomic policy

15 Fiscal policy

Leopards break into the temple and drink the sacrificial chalices dry;
this occurs repeatedly again and again; finally it can be reckoned on
beforehand and becomes a part of the ceremony (Franz Kafka,
Reflections on Sin, Pain, Hope and the True Way).

This policy instrument can be defined as '... any change in the level,
composition or timing of government expenditure, or any change in the
rate of taxation or the timing and composition of fiscal receipts...'.[1] In
the 1940s, 1950s and 1960s fiscal policy was seen as the main instrument to be used by governments in managing the level of aggregate
demand in the economy. Since the early 1970s severe doubts on the
effectiveness of fiscal and demand management policies have been
expressed.

In the interwar years a doctrine which came to be known as the
Treasury View dominated official opinion for much of the period. In
the Treasury View an increase in the fiscal deficit to finance public
works programmes would succeed merely in 'crowding out' private
spending which would otherwise have taken place, and thus not result
in any net change in output or employment. The argument here was
that

> ... increased government borrowing for public works would result
> in higher interest rates, if savings were to be attracted to gilt-edged
> stock so that the borrowing would not be inflationary, and that this
> would tend to divert money which otherwise would have gone to
> home industry or to overseas investment (and thus indirectly, to
> export industry).[2]

In supporting the Lloyd George platform in the general election of
1929 Keynes rebutted the Treasury View and provided reasons why an

129

expansionary fiscal policy of public works programmes would, in the circumstances of that time, serve to increase total output and employment.[3] The Treasury View was rather more flexible than commonly believed: Keynes complained that '... it bends so much that I find difficulty in getting hold of it ...'.[4] After examining the relevant official documents of the period, a recent work concluded that, after 1931, the Treasury showed a '... willingness to consider Keynes' views seriously and sympathetically'.[5] Thus it can be argued that the Treasury had come to be at least in small part converted to Keynes' views on fiscal policy before the publication of the *General Theory*. Also, as we saw in Chapter 12 of this book, Keynes took a less sanguine view of the extent to which unemployment could be reduced by aggregate demand measures alone than the popular interpretation of Keynes would have us believe. All this means that Keynes and the Treasury did not have as diametrically opposed views on the ability of expansionary fiscal policies to reduce unemployment as is commonly alleged. In particular, our present-day preoccupation with the extent to which expansionary fiscal policies serve more to increase the rate of inflation rather than reduce unemployment, was also very much a preoccupation of the debate about fiscal policy in the 1930s.

It was, however, the cruder view of fiscal policy enshrined in Orthodox Keynesianism which came to dominate official thinking in the 1940s, 1950s and 1960s in the UK. This Orthodox Keynesian view is that governments can achieve objectives such as avoiding depressions, reducing the size of business cycle fluctuations and, most of all, 'full' employment, by managing aggregate demand by way of government expenditure and taxation policy: government expenditure policies have direct effects on aggregate demand; and taxation policies affect aggregate demand indirectly by changing private sector income or expenditure. Since the early 1970s severe doubts have been cast on this view of fiscal policy and on the demand management policies suggested by this view. Before discussing such doubts about the workings of fiscal policy as a whole, it is useful to consider some of the considerations which apply separately to the use of government expenditure and taxation as policy instruments.

Government spending

The public spending of central government, local government and nationalized industries accounted for just over 45 per cent of GDP in

1981 if we define public spending as that which has to be financed by taxation, national insurance contributions or government borrowing.[6] According to whether we define public spending at market prices or factor cost, use net or gross figures for debt interest, and so on, we could reduce this figure to a percentage in the late 30s, or increase this figure to a percentage in the late 50s.[7] In the early 1960s total public spending as defined earlier accounted for just over 30 per cent of GDP, so it would appear that public spending has grown dramatically over the last 20 years. Here appearances are deceptive because most of the growth in public spending has taken the form of higher *transfer payments* to the private sector in the form of such items as unemployment and social security benefits. As far as *current spending on goods and services* by central and local government is concerned there has been virtually no growth over the last 20 years: such spending accounts for just over 20 per cent of GDP in 1981 which is virtually the same as in the early 1960s. As far as *public investment* spending is concerned the 1981 figure of around 3 per cent of GDP is lower than the 4–5 per cent figure for the early 1960s. Thus the proportion of public spending on real goods and services has changed little over the last 20 years. It is transfer payments which account for most of the increase in public spending. Such payments in turn have risen in large part because of the increase in unemployment over the last 20 years.[8]

Government spending plans are reviewed annually in the UK, each spending department submitting expenditure plans for the coming 4 years which are reviewed by the interdepartmental Public Expenditure Survey Committee (PESC). Ministers then rejoin the debate about priorities and, after usually Cabinet level discussions, the government publishes its plans in an expenditure White Paper at the beginning of the calendar year. The process culminates in the presentation of detailed 'Supply Estimates' to Parliament by the Government on the March/April Budget day. Besides detailed expenditure estimates the government also announces a 'Contingency Reserve' fund which is designed to allow for any unanticipated increases in the cost of expenditure programmes while at the same time keeping the total level of public spending within the amount planned. Over recent years governments have often revised their expenditure plans between annual Budgets, making somewhat anachronistic the idea of having the economic judgements of governments visited on mankind but once a year.

Spending is initially planned in real terms (numbers of teachers, for example), such plans being then converted to money equivalents at survey prices pertaining usually to the autumn of the preceding year. The higher rates of inflation of recent years have created problems in terms of keeping actual money spending under control, *vide* the substantial over-spending in the mid-1970s. To cope with this problem 'cash limits' for certain building programmes were introduced in 1974/75, the system being extended to cover most of public spending in 1975/76, transfer payments excepted. The 'cash limit' involves embedding an allowance for inflation into each spending programme which implies a ceiling on money spending. The April 1976 White Paper on 'cash limits' (Cmnd 6440) was not clear as to what would happen should the actual inflation rate turn out to be substantially higher than that involved in the 'cash limit', stating that the government would have to take stock of the position in the light of circumstances. The public pronouncements of the 1979–84 Conservative administration, however, imply that such ceilings are rigid and that increases in the money costs of public spending over and above those allowed for in the cash limits have to be met by a cut in the volume of spending. Here the aversion of treasurers in charge of public projects to the risk of breaching the expenditure ceiling has to be taken into account. The substantial underspending in 1977–78 was in large part due to such risk aversion. The severe downswing of 1979–81 has seen transfer payments rise by much more than anticipated in government plans. In response, the government has repeatedly revised downwards its spending plans, seeking additional cuts in spending on real goods and services to compensate for the rise in transfer payments. In spite of such cuts, total public spending has continued to rise.

A first point regarding the use of government spending as a policy instrument is that it is not purely a macropolicy instrument. Public spending is geared to the provision of public services and the achievement of social objectives via transfer payments. It is not obvious that any gains from varying public spending as an instrument of demand management outweigh the costs involved in varying public provision. Secondly, changes in different items of government spending can be expected to have different effects on the economy. The marginal consumption, tax and import ratios for different items of expenditure will usually be different. Thirdly, not all changes in public spending will occur as a result of active policy choices. Transfer payments to the unemployed, for example, will vary with the level of economic activity. There is a presumption that government spending will be higher in the trough and lower at the peak of the trade cycle. Finally, because of the time lags involved, changes in public spending will affect aggregate demand only after a period of time. As we saw in Chapter 14 of this book, this particularly raises problems for policies designed to smooth the trade cycle. If the government pursues a *proportional* stabilization policy, whereby public spending is actively increased most at the trough of the trade cycle, such measures will only take effect once economic activity has already picked up. To avoid such problems a *derivative* element needs to be incorporated into such countercyclical policies, whereby public spending is actively increased (reduced) most the faster economic activity is falling (rising). Such a policy, however, would politically be difficult to introduce given that it would imply an active reduction in public spending immediately the economy comes to recover from a depression, economic activity and employment being still low in this phase of the cycle.

The shift of opinion away from using public spending as a discretionary instrument of demand management is reflected in the 1974 report of the Expenditure Committee of the House of Commons: 'We recommend that therefore in managing the economy ... changes in public spending should only be used in the last resort ... short term demand management by fiscal means should primarily be carried out by changes in taxation'.[9] The 1979–84 Conservative government have attempted to reduce public spending in order to (a) stimulate the 'supply side' of the economy – see Chapter 10 of this book, and (b) reduce the public sector borrowing requirement – see below. In the face of the dramatic rise in unemployment and fall in output from 1979 to 1981 there has thus been a remarkable retreat from the role of public spending as an instrument of demand management.

Taxation

Taxation policy influences aggregate demand indirectly either by changing private sector disposable income through taxes or national insurance contributions levied on income; or by changing the costs of producing and consuming commodities, the division of the tax burden between consumers and producers depending on the relevant elasticities of demand and supply. The influence is indirect, in contrast to that of public spending, reliance being made on the private sector changing its behaviour in a reasonably stable way in response to tax changes. In recent years the effects of the tax level and structure on aggregate supply have come to be emphasized. On the academic side this emphasis has been evident in the arguments for taxing expenditure rather than income.[10] In terms of policy practice the incoming Conservative government of 1979–84 committed itself to reducing income tax rates and the overall level of taxation with a view to creating incentives for an increase in private sector productive effort; and raised the rate of VAT to 15 per cent in an attempt to shift the tax burden towards indirect taxes.

The level and structure of taxes has come to be seen by many commentators as being at least partly responsible for the UK's relatively poor growth performance. The idea here is that the private sector is the mainspring of economic growth and that its productive efforts have been overburdened by high UK tax levels and rates. International comparisons, however, suggest that the UK is not out of line with most other Western industrial countries. In terms of the percentage of GNP at factor cost associated with taxes and social security contributions, the UK tax take was 40% in 1977, which placed the UK below France (44%), West Germany (45%), Belgium (46%), the Netherlands (52%) and Sweden (62%); and above the USA (33%), Switzerland (32%) and Japan (25%).[11] Thus the link between UK taxation policy and its poor growth performance is by no means an obvious one.

A further important role for taxation policy is often involved in the Keynesian analysis of inflation. The idea here is that trade unions respond to any change in direct or indirect taxes by demanding higher money wages in order to maintain the real wages of their members after tax, the idea sometimes being referred to as the real wage resistance hypothesis.[12] Providing the effect is symmetric, taxation policy could thus be used as an instrument to reduce inflation, lower income tax rates leading to lower money wage demands, and lower average costs for prices to be marked up over. This instrument formed part of the 1974–79 Labour government's anti-inflation policy. Here trade unions were told that income taxes would be reduced if they accepted lower wage settlements. In August 1979 the government introduced a new Tax and Price Index (TPI) designed to adjust the Retail Price Index (RPI) to take account of changes in income tax or national insurance contributions.[13] Speaking on 17 August 1979 the Financial Secretary to the Treasury said: '... if you want a general guide to the changes in total costs facing taxpayers, look at the TPI, not the RPI. It is a much truer guide'.[14] It is, however, by no means obvious that taxes should be included in a measure of the cost of living. Ultimately taxes are used to finance the provision of public goods and services. To say that the cost of living increases whenever taxation increases is to imply that no value is placed on public goods and services. It is also interesting that the government has made little or no mention of the TPI in 1980–81 when the TPI has risen faster than the RPI.

The Inland Revenue and Customs and Excise are responsible for the collection of direct and indirect taxes respectively. Whereas indirect taxes and taxes on capital are permanent, income taxes need to be renewed annually. The latter is achieved by the Chancellor tabling Ways and Means Resolutions immediately after the Budget speech, new taxes or changes in permanent taxes also being introduced by such a method. Such Resolutions provide the government with the temporary authority to collect taxes until the Finance Bill based on them becomes a Finance Act. The particular tax rates and allowances are decided by the Chancellor in consultation with his colleagues, part of the background advice being provided by the February forecast from the Treasury macroeconometric model as to what the likely course of the economy will be on the basis of unchanged policy, and on the basis of the contemplated changes in policy.

The qualifying remarks made with regard to public spending also apply to taxation policy: it is not purely a macro-policy instrument; different tax changes can be expected to have different effects; total tax receipts will depend on the level of economic activity, so not all tax changes will occur as a result of active policy choices; and there are profound timing problems faced by any attempt to frame a successful countercyclical policy. Worthy of particular note is the way different tax revenues vary with inflation. Given unchanged tax rates income tax revenue will rise faster than the rate of inflation given the progressive rate structure; VAT revenue at the same rate; and tobacco, alcohol and petroleum taxes at a lower rate than the rate of inflation, given the 'pence per physical unit' nature of the latter taxes. Thus in the absence of changes in the tax rates and allowances, the proportion of total tax revenue contributed by direct taxes would rise in the face of continuing inflation. This problem of 'fiscal drag' has been to a certain extent ameliorated by the commitment placed on governments to increase income tax allowances to take into account inflation, unless the government specifically overrides this commitment in its legislation. This commitment was introduced by a backbench 'Rooker-Wise' amendment to the 1977 Finance Act (see Finance Act 1977, Section 22).

Besides the movement to shift the burden of total taxation from direct to indirect taxes, the main change in policy practice over the last few years has concerned an increased reluctance to make large changes in the total tax take in any one year. This can be partly traced back to the effects of the 1972 Budget, where tax cuts to the almost unprecedented value of £1200 million were introduced at a time when economic activity was already showing strong signs of recovering from the trough which had seen unemployment hover around its then highest post-1945 level of 1 million. This policy succeeded in stimulating a high rate of output growth in the succeeding 18 months, and in reducing unemployment to around half a million by the end of 1973, but only at the cost of exerting strong upward pressure on the rate of inflation and turning the balance of payments round from a current account surplus to deficit. It can be argued that the latter problems stimulated subsequent reversals in policy which imposed losses through higher unemployment and lower output which more than outweighed the earlier gains. Such doubts about the use of taxation policy as an instrument of demand management were expressed in 1978 by the Permanent Secretary to the Treasury:

> ... if the brunt of short-term fiscal policy falls on the tax side, the burden of adjustment falls on the private sector. The consequent costs of disruption may well be as great as the costs of disruption in the public sector [had public spending changes been used].[15]

The June 1979 Budget measures completely overturned the traditional role of taxation as an instrument of demand management.

> This new strategy is based on the strengthening of incentives, particularly through tax cuts, allowing people to keep more of their earnings in their own hands, so that hard work, ability and success are rewarded ... in the government's view excessive rates of taxation take much of the blame for Britain's unsatisfactory performance.[16]

The basic rate of income tax was cut from 33 to 30 per cent, the highest rate of income tax was reduced from 83 to 60 per cent, and tax allowances and tax bands were increased. This was seen as the first instalment of a set of reductions in income tax which would eventually see the basic rate of income tax down to 25 per cent. Thus taxation policy was seen as an instrument for stimulating *aggregate supply* rather than aggregate demand. During the period 1979-81, however, output and employment have fallen dramatically in the UK and unemployment has more than doubled. If the use of taxation as an instrument to stimulate aggregate supply by 'strengthening incentives' has worked it requires a remarkably imaginative mind to be able to discern such effects at work in the period 1979–81. Less imagination is required to see that the reduction in the higher rates of income tax has increased the post-tax incomes of those already on high incomes.

Fiscal policy as a whole

To summarize the effects of public spending and taxation as a whole it might be thought useful to use figures for the fiscal deficit or *public sector borrowing requirement* (PSBR) which measures the difference between public spending and taxation $(G - T)$. A time series for the

Table 15.1. *Nominal and real public sector borrowing requirement (PSBR)*

	Nominal PSBR (£ million annual) (1)	Real PSBR (annual estimates) (2)
1964	990	
1965	1,208	
1966	964	
1967	1,860	*Four-year averages*
1968	1,295	Nominal PSBR Real PSBR
1969	−445	0.6 −2.0
1970	4	
1971	1,382	
1972	2,054	
1973	4,209	5.8 −1.7
1974	6,437	
1975	10,480	
1976	9,128	0.6
1977	5,995	−3.5
1978	8,331	1.5
1979	12,594	−1.5
1980	12,301	−2.6

Sources: Central Statistical Office, April 1981; Treasury and Civil Service Committee Report on Monetary Policy, vol. HC161-I (London: HMSO), 1981.

PSBR is given in column (1) of Table 15.1, and seems to indicate that the thrust of fiscal policy overall has been expansionary over the last 20 years. This is quite misleading for two reasons. The first is that the PSBR will vary automatically with the level of economic activity and thus the PSBR will tend to rise when economic activity falls even though the underlying fiscal stance is unchanged. As far as public spending is concerned, a fall in economic activity will tend to increase payments of unemployment and social security benefits, Redundancy Fund payments, the take-up of special measures to subsidize employment and the loan finance requirements of nationalized industries. As far as taxation receipts are concerned, income tax receipts and national insurance contributions will fall because fewer people are employed, company tax receipts will fall as corporate profits fall, and expenditure tax receipts will be lower because of the lower volume of sales. This endogeneity of the PSBR to the level of economic activity is illustrated in Figure 15.1(a). The line F_1 indicates a given stance of fiscal policy in terms of the provision of a particular level of public goods and services and a particular level and structure of tax rates. If unemployment rises from U_1 to U_2 the PSBR will rise from $PSBR_1$ to $PSBR_2$ purely as a result of the change in economic activity and not as a result of a change in fiscal stance. If the government wishes to maintain $PSBR_1$ in the face of a fall in economic activity, as in the case of 1979–81, this can only be done by adopting a more restrictive fiscal stance involving a reduction in the level of provision of public goods and services or an increase in tax rates. Such a more restrictive fiscal stance is illustrated in Figure 15.1(a) by the line F_2.

To distinguish between changes in the PSBR which arise automatically from changes in the level of economic activity, and changes which arise from an active change in the fiscal stance adopted by the government, a *full employment fiscal deficit* figure is sometimes used. Such a figure attempts to estimate what the PSBR would have been on the basis of the current fiscal stance if the economy had been at 'full' employment, and will obviously be arbitrary to the extent that it relies on some estimate of 'full' employment and requires a difficult line to be drawn between automatic and non-automatic changes in public spending and taxation.[17] An idea of the size of the automatic changes in the PSBR with the level of economic activity can be gained from the Treasury estimate that the PSBR in 1980–81 was £2–4 billion higher because of the 4 per cent fall in aggregate output in 1980–81; or from the Treasury estimate that an additional 100,000 unemployed raises the

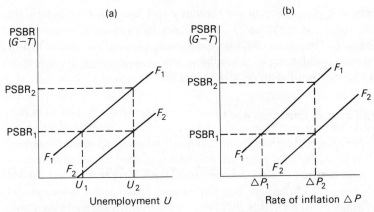

Figure 15.1. Effects of economic activity and inflation on the PSBR

PSBR by £340 million.[18] Thus a large component of the £12 billion PSBR in 1980 can be attributed to the low level of economic activity in 1980 rather than to an expansionary fiscal stance.[19]

A second, and possibly more important, problem with the use of the nominal PSBR as a measure of the stance of fiscal policy is that it does not take account of inflation. Most of public sector debt, such as gilt-edged securities, is denominated in nominal terms. That means that its real value falls with the rate of inflation. Holders of public sector debt, such as pension funds, are concerned with the real purchasing power of their assets. As inflation erodes the real value of holdings of public sector debt, holders of public sector debt are likely to increase their money savings and purchase more public sector debt so as to maintain the real purchasing power of such asset holdings. This means that a higher rate of inflation is going to require a higher PSBR to allow holders of public sector debt to maintain the real value of such holdings.[20] This process is illustrated in Figure 15.1(b), where a rise in the rate of inflation from ΔP_1 to ΔP_2 sees the PSBR rise from $PSBR_1$ to $PSBR_2$ on the basis of the unchanged fiscal stance indicated by the line F_1. If the authorities wish to maintain an unchanged $PSBR_1$, a more restrictive fiscal stance indicated by the line F_2 will be required.[21] In column (2) of Table 15.1 we list figures for the real PSBR which adjust the nominal PSBR for the effects of the rate of inflation. Such real PSBR figures suggest that there has been a real fiscal *surplus* for most of the 1970s despite the fact that the nominal PSBR figures listed in column (1) of Table 15.1 indicate extremely high nominal fiscal *deficits* for this period. A comparison of the nominal **PSBR** figures for 1980 and 1979 indicates little change in the fiscal stance between these years, whereas the real **PSBR** figures indicate a tightening of the fiscal stance. Thus it is grossly misleading to assess the stance of fiscal policy by looking at figures for the nominal fiscal deficit or **PSBR**.

Public sector financing identity

This can be written as:

$$P(G - T) \equiv \Delta M_G + P_D \Delta B + \Delta OD \qquad (1)$$

where $P(G - T)$ is the nominal fiscal deficit or PSBR; ΔM_G is the increase in government borrowing from the banking system; ΔB is the increase in government borrowing from outside the banking system; P_D is the price of the public sector assets sold outside the banking system; and ΔOD is the increase in government borrowing overseas. The term ΔM_G constitutes one component of the change in the money supply, the total change in the money supply being

$$\Delta M = \Delta M_G + \Delta M_P + \Delta NC \qquad (2)$$

where ΔM_G is the increase in government borrowing from the banking system as in (1) above; ΔM_P is the increase in bank lending to the private sector; and ΔNC is the increase in notes and coins held by the non-bank public.

The above financing identity means that the effects of any given fiscal deficit will vary according to how the deficit is financed. An increase in G, for example, could be financed by an increase in T, in which case effects of the balanced budget multiplier type would follow; by an increase in ΔM_G, in which case an increase in the money supply and downward pressure on interest rates would follow; by an increase in ΔB, in which case there would be upward pressure on interest rates in order to sell more public sector debt such as gilt-edged securities outside the banking system; or by an increase in ΔOD, in which case overseas indebtedness would rise. Much of the debate in recent years about the effects of fiscal policy has centred on the implications of how fiscal deficits are financed. In what follows we will discuss the positions taken up by the different research programmes regarding what is some-times known as the *crowding out* question: does an increase in govern-

ment spending net of taxation merely crowd out private sector spending
that otherwise would have taken place?

Crowding out

It is possible to distinguish between *direct* crowding out, where public
spending simply replaces private spending which otherwise would have
taken place – as, for example, in the case of public postal services
replacing private postal services; and indirect crowding out, where it is
the financing implications of the increase in public spending which discourage private spending – as, for example, in the case of an increase in
public spending financed by an increase in borrowing from outside
the banking system, which increases interest rates and hence discourages
private investment spending. It is *indirect* crowding out effects which
have dominated the debate in the last decade about the effectiveness of
fiscal policy. The issues at stake in this debate are similar to those
involved in the arguments about the Treasury View in the interwar
period. The main differences are that:

(a) the orthodoxy under attack since the early 1970s has been the
view that additional public spending *does not* merely crowd out
private spending which otherwise would have taken place; and
(b) the debate in the 1970s has been conducted using the language of
Keynesian models of the *IS–LM* type.[22]

Figure 15.2(a) illustrates the way crowding out arises in the conventional *IS–LM* model. Government spending increases, shifting the *IS*
curve from IS_1 to IS_2. The fiscal deficit arising from this expansion of
spending is financed by selling public sector debt outside the banking
system, so raising the level of interest rates from i_1 to i_2. If the financing
implications of the higher government spending had not increased
interest rates, equilibrium output would have increased from Y_1 to Y_3.
Instead equilibrium output increases only from Y_1 to Y_2 because of the
effects of higher interest rates in discouraging private sector investment.
The distance Y_2-Y_3 measures the indirect crowding out effects which
arises in the context of the orthodox *IS–LM* model.

Wealth effects

The crowding out debate of the 1970s was fuelled by four main exten-
sions to the orthodox *IS–LM* model. The first concerns the incorpora-

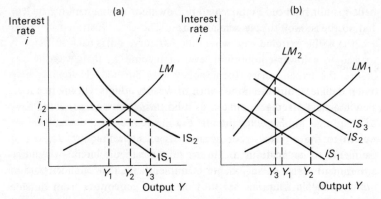

Figure 15.2. (a) Partial crowding out; (b) more than 100 per cent crowding out

tion of wealth effects into the determinants of private sector behaviour. Private sector wealth can be defined as:

$$W = \frac{M}{P} + \frac{B}{P} + K \tag{3}$$

where M/P is holdings of real money balances, B/P is holdings of interesting bearing government debt, and K is the real value of the privately owned capital stock. The relevance of wealth to the crowding out debate arises from the fact that the financing implications of changes in fiscal policy will lead to changes in the private sector's wealth holdings. If private sector wealth increases as a result of the financing of a fiscal deficit we would expect:

(a) that the private sector would consume some of this increase in wealth – if this did not happen the implication would be that the private sector was prepared to accumulate wealth indefinitely without changing its consumption; and

(b) that the private sector would allocate part of the increase in wealth to higher holdings of money balances.

Figure 15.2(b) illustrates such wealth effects at work in response to an increase in private sector holdings of interest-bearing public sector debt arising from a fiscal deficit. The wealth effect on consumption shifts the IS curve further out to IS_3; the wealth effect on the demand for money shifts the LM curve back from LM_1 to LM_2, given that the deficit is not financed by increased borrowing from the banking system, and so the money supply remains fixed. The case illustrated in Figure 15.2(b) is the extreme case where the *LM* curve shifts back sufficiently to lead to a lower equilibrium level of income Y_3 than was the case before the expansionary fiscal policy was pursued. There has been much debate about the importance of wealth effects. On the one hand New Classical Macroeconomics has used the *ultrarationality* hypothesis to argue that public sector interest-bearing debt does not constitute net wealth to the private sector because its existence requires higher tax payments to be made in the future to finance the interest payments governments make on such debt.[23] On the other hand it has been pointed out that the institutional features of actual economies are such as to generate positive wealth effects from government interest-bearing debt.[24]

Long-run effects

A second extension to the orthodox *IS–LM* model involves distinguishing between the short- and long-run effects of fiscal policy. In the short run there is no dispute that fiscal deficits financed by borrowing from the banking system, that is by monetary expansion, will be more expansionary than deficits financed by borrowing outside the banking system, that is by bond finance. Monetary expansion places downward pressure on interest rates, bond finance places upward pressure on interest rates, and so there will be more indirect crowding out with bond finance. In the long run, however, bond-financed deficits can be more expansionary than money-financed deficits.[25] Such a result can arise if we investigate the long-run equilibrium conditions for economies. The equilibrium positions described in the *IS–LM* model are only temporary equilibria, given that the increase in income arising from an expansionary fiscal policy is unlikely to be sufficient to raise tax revenues sufficiently to close the gap between government spending and taxation. Thus in the next period there will still be a fiscal deficit to be financed, and the financing implications will lead to a further change in the level of equilibrium income. Given that bond-financed deficits

(a) lead to lower increases in equilibrium income in the short run because of the indirect crowding out which arises from the higher interest rates involved if governments sell more bonds; and

(b) involve increased government spending in the future in the form of higher interest payments on public sector debt;

this means that the fiscal deficit will stay larger for a longer period of time under bond-finance than under money-finance. This in turn means that any expansionary pressures on income arising from fiscal deficits will be more long-lived under bond-finance than under money-finance, and so bond-financed deficits will be more expansionary in the long run than money-financed deficits.

Rate of inflation effects

A third extension to the orthodox *IS–LM* model involves looking at the effects of fiscal deficits on the rate of inflation. If we accept the Orthodox Monetarist hypothesis that the rate of inflation is determined by the rate of monetary expansion, and that the long-run equilibrium or natural levels of output and unemployment are independent of aggregate demand, this means that expansionary fiscal policies financed by monetary expansion will have only short-run expansionary effects on output and unemployment, the long-run effects being felt in higher rates of inflation – see Chapter 8 of this book. Here crowding out will occur in the long run through a higher rate of inflation.

An extreme version of this crowding out effect occurs in New Classical Macroeconomics where equilibrium output is determined by aggregate supply and economies are postulated to be a continuous state of rational expectations equilibrium in which all markets clear. Figure 15.3 illustrates this hypothesis. An expansionary fiscal policy shifts upwards

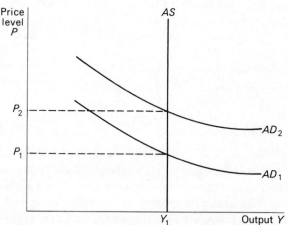

Figure 15.3. Full crowding out and the rate of inflation

the aggregate demand schedule from AD_1 to AD_2 but succeeds only in raising the price level from P_1 to P_2, output remaining unchanged at Y_1.

Open economy effects

A fourth modification of the orthodox *IS–LM* model takes account of the way changes in domestic aggregate demand generated by fiscal policies can be exported through the trade or capital accounts of the balance of payments, resulting in increases in overseas rather than domestic output. The New Cambridge Keynesian analysis suggests that an increase in the fiscal deficit will be matched by an increase in the balance of payments deficit, so fiscal policy effects are not so much crowded out as exported to the rest of the world. Import tariffs are recommended to contain domestically the expansionary effects of fiscal policy – see Chapter 7 of this book. In the fixed exchange rate case Orthodox Monetarism suggests that the expansionary effects of money-financed fiscal policies will result in balance of payments deficits and the export of money balances to the rest of the world.[26] The analysis for the flexible exchange rate case suggests that money-financed fiscal deficits will result in higher output in the short run as the exchange rate depreciates, but no change in output in the long-run equilibrium position which will be characterized by a higher rate of inflation[27] – see Chapter 8 of this book.

Diagnosis

Discussions of whether expansionary fiscal policies will merely crowd out private sector spending which would otherwise have taken place have been plagued by a failure to distinguish between conditions in which output is constrained by (a) aggregate supply and (b) aggregate demand. If output is constrained by aggregate supply then of course full crowding out will occur: by definition fiscal policy-induced increases in aggregate demand cannot increase output because output is already at its maximum level. Thus the New Classical Macroeconomics and Supply Side Macroeconomics proposition that full crowding out occurs is nothing more than a re-statement of their view that output is determined by aggregate supply. As we saw in Chapters 9 and 10 of this book there are good reasons for not believing the proposition that output is *always* determined by aggregate supply. In conditions of reasonably 'full' employment, such as experienced in the 1950s and early 1960s, aggregate supply might well be the main constraint on output and so we would expect full crowding out to occur. In the early 1980s the UK economy has experienced a marked decline in output and a return to mass unemployment. The aggregate supply explanations of this are not very convincing. Thus there is good reason to believe that full crowding out will not occur in the conditions of the early 1980s.

Thus it is difficult to accept the pronouncements of the 1979–84 government that fiscal policy needs to be made more restrictive in order to 'crowd in' private sector spending and economic activity. In particular, the argument that the PSBR needs to be reduced in conditions of high unemployment in order that less public sector debt needs to be sold, interest rates are reduced, and private sector spending is stimulated, does not stand up to close examination. The consequence of this line of thought is that the stance of fiscal policy has been tightened during the 1979–81 downswing in economic activity, the real PSBR having moved into a surplus during this period – see Table 15.1. Thus the government's deflationary fiscal policies have served to turn a downswing in the business cycle into a more severe depression than would otherwise have been experienced. The government's preoccupation with attempting to reduce the nominal PSBR runs the risk of creating a vicious circle whereby attempts to reduce the nominal PSBR increase the deflationary impulses imparted by fiscal policy, unemployment rises further, the nominal PSBR rises as a result and the government reacts by making fiscal policy even more deflationary. Even if the government's attempts to strengthen the supply side of the economy work, the higher potential output is not likely to be realized in the face of a deflationary spiral in aggregate demand arising from such a fiscal strategy.

At the other extreme the Orthodox and New Cambridge Keynesian view that output is determined by aggregate demand, and hence that full crowding out does not occur, can be faulted for not taking into account situations in which output is constrained by aggregate supply. In particular, the New Cambridge view that a massive programme of fiscal measures to expand aggregate demand inside a wall of tariff barriers fails to take account of the at least short-run supply constraints that such a policy would encounter. New firms and industries cannot be established overnight, and unemployed people cannot be transformed into employed people simply by waving a fiscal policy magic wand. Thus a major fiscal stimulus to the UK economy is likely to at least in part result in crowding out effects arising from a higher rate of inflation. Incomes policies could reduce some of the inflation rate crowding out effects in the short run, but there is no evidence that incomes policies are successful in achieving a sustained reduction in the rate of inflation – see Chapter 17 of this book.

Thus it would appear sensible to pursue a gradual programme of expansion of fiscal policy. Government spending on real goods and services should be increased, and taxation, particularly employers' national insurance contributions, reduced in order to convert the present surplus in the real PSBR into a deficit. The resulting increase in the nominal PSBR could be financed in part by an increase in the target rate of monetary expansion. The increase in the rate of inflation arising from such a fiscal policy package would be worth bearing to reverse some of the hysteresis effects on output and unemployment which have arisen from the massive downswing in the UK economy 1979-81. If we accept that the equilibrium or natural levels of output and unemployment are partly determined by aggregate demand by way of the hysteresis effects outlined in Chapter 12 of this book, this means that expansionary fiscal policy measures pursued under conditions when output is not completely supply-constrained will be able to raise the equilibrium or natural level of output, and reduce the equilibrium or natural rate of unemployment. Thus, provided a gradual programme of fiscal expansion is pursued, so as to avoid short-run supply constraints in the economy, an expansionary fiscal policy could succeed in achieving a *sustainable* increase in output and reduction of unemployment in the UK.

16 Monetary policy

The tendency ... of a very great and sudden reduction of the accustomed number of bank notes is to create an *unusual* and *temporary* distress ... [which] would occasion much discouragement of the fabrication of manufactures ... and a fall of price resulting from that distress (Henry Thornton, *Paper Credit*, 1802).

We have the relationships:

$$P(G - T) \equiv \Delta M_G + P_D \Delta B + \Delta OD \tag{1}$$

and

$$\Delta M \equiv \Delta M_G + \Delta M_P + \Delta NC \tag{2}$$

where $P(G - T)$ is the PSBR, M_G is government borrowing from the banks, B government borrowing from the non-bank public, P_D is the price of public sector debt, OD is overseas borrowing, M is the money stock, M_P is bank lending to the private sector and NC is notes and coins in circulation with the non-bank public. This means that monetary policy will be highly interdependent with fiscal policy, given that government borrowing from the banking system M_G is one of the main components of the total stock of money. Thus it does not make sense to talk about monetary policy in complete isolation from fiscal policy. The only fiscal policy which does not have implications for monetary policy is the balanced budget case where $G = T$ and ΔM_G, ΔB and ΔOD are all zero. The only monetary policy which does not have implications for fiscal policy is the open-market operation case where $\Delta M_G = P_D \Delta B$ and $(G - T) = 0$ and $\Delta OD = 0$. Even in the two above cases of pure fiscal policy and pure monetary policy the shocks which affect the economy would make it impossible to hold the other elements in the public sector financing identity constant, and so balanced-budget policies and open-market operations would be accompanied by monetary and fiscal side-effects respectively.

For most of the postwar period monetary policy has been seen as a subsidiary instrument to fiscal policy in the management of the UK economy. Interest rates and the availability of credit were seen as having some influence on aggregate demand in the UK economy, but no importance was attached to the money supply *per se*. During the 1970s this Orthodox Keynesian position was challenged and Orthodox Monetarism has succeeded in at least partly converting policy-makers to the idea that the money supply has important effects on the economy and that it should be controlled lest monetary impulses provide a source of disturbance to the economy. Before considering this yet incomplete conversion to Orthodox Monetarist prescriptions regarding monetary policy it is useful to consider two basic questions: should the authorities control the supply of money or interest rates?; and should the authorities control the supply of money or the exchange rate?

Money supply or interest rate control?

The problem here is that if the authorities control the money supply they will lose control over interest rates; and if they control interest rates they will lose control over the money supply. The reasons for this can be seen by rearranging relationships (1) and (2) above as follows

$$\Delta M_G \equiv P(G - T) - P_D \Delta B - \Delta OD \qquad (3)$$

therefore

$$\Delta M \equiv [P(G - T) - P_D \Delta B - \Delta OD] + \Delta M_P + \Delta NC \qquad (4)$$

Relationship (4) says that the change in the money supply will be equal to that part of the PSBR, $P(G - T)$ which is not financed by an increase in government borrowing from the non-bank public ΔB, or increased borrowing from overseas ΔOD; *plus* the change in bank lending to the private sector ΔM_P; *plus* the increase in notes and coins in circulation with the non-bank public ΔNC. If the authorities control interest rates, the level of interest rates chosen will largely determine the size of ΔB,

ΔOD and ΔM_P, and so the total change in the money supply ΔM will be largely determined by how the private sector reacts to the level of interest rates chosen by the authorities. If, on the other hand, the authorities fix a target for ΔM they will have to accept whatever interest rates are necessary in order that ΔB, ΔOD and ΔM_P are consistent with the target rate of monetary expansion. Thus the authorities are faced with a basic choice between controlling interest rates, and accepting the rate of monetary expansion determined by private sector behaviour; or controlling the rate of monetary expansion, and accepting the level of interest rates determined by private sector behaviour.

The issues involved here can be illustrated by using the *IS–LM* model.[1] In Figure 16.1(a) if the authorities fix the level of interest rates at R^* the *LM* curve becomes LM_{R*}. As the *IS* curve fluctuates between IS_T and IS_P from the trough to the peak of the business cycle, output will fluctuate from Y_1 to Y_5, the private sector being able to determine endogenously the amount of money forthcoming to finance its economic activities. If the authorities control the supply of money, the *LM* curve reverts to its conventional form. The *LM* curve drawn in Figure 16.1(a) is such that on average over the business cycle the interest rate R^* is experienced. This time, however, output fluctuates from Y_2 to Y_4 during the course of the business cycle. The authorities would thus be faced with the choice between having smaller fluctuations in output Y_2-Y_4 and large fluctuations in interest rates R_2-R_4 if the money supply is controlled; or having larger fluctuations in output Y_1-Y_5 and no

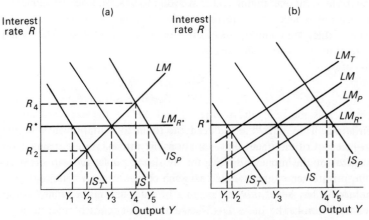

Figure 16.1. Controlling interest rates or the money supply

fluctuation in the interest rate R^* if interest rates are controlled. Even though having larger fluctuations in output over the business cycle might be more damaging to the economy at large, the political sensitivity of interest rates in the UK, arising in large part from the large number of people whose mortgage interest payments are tied to the level of interest rates, might lead policy-makers to control interest rates rather than the money supply.

The analysis outlined in Figure 16.1(a) is somewhat misleading in that we assume that the *LM* curve will always stay in one position if the authorities control the money supply. We would expect (a) that the authorities would only be able to achieve their money supply target on average over the business cycle, and (b) that the *LM* curve would fluctuate with the change in the demand for money over the business cycle. Figure 16.1(b) allows the *LM* curve to fluctuate between LM_P and LM_T during the business cycle. As the diagram is drawn money supply control will still lead to lower fluctuations in output Y_2-Y_4 over the business cycle, as opposed to the fluctuations Y_1-Y_5 implied by interest rate control. It is possible, however, that the position of the *LM* curve varies more than that of the *IS* curve so as to reverse this ranking.

Orthodox Monetarism argues that the money supply rather than interest rates be controlled. The argument is that money supply control will lead to lower fluctuations in output, as discussed above; that it is easier to work out an appropriate rate of monetary expansion than it is to work out an appropriate level of interest rates; and that the costs of higher variations in interest rates incurred if the money supply is controlled can be minimized if a reduction in the rate of monetary expansion reduces the rate of inflation and hence reduces the size of one of the main components of the money rate of interest.[2] The money rate of interest can be defined as

$$R = \pi + \Delta P^e \tag{5}$$

where π is the real rate of interest and ΔP^e is the expected rate of inflation. Thus if ΔP^e is reduced the room for variation in R will be reduced. Critics argue that variations in interest rates arising from control of the money supply severely disrupt investment planning in the private sector, and argue that such costs are not worth bearing in return for any benefits which might arise from having the money supply under control. The issues involved here are not as black or white as the discussion above suggests. If the authorities control the money supply they are likely only to attempt to achieve this target over a period of months rather than day in, day out. Thus short-term control over interest rates can be consistent with long-term control over the money supply. The question then is one of which set of intervention techniques will permit the authorities to achieve the long-run money supply target while minimizing the short-term variations in interest rates.

Money supply or exchange rate control?

The issue here is partly one of whether the authorities should peg the foreign exchange rate for sterling to other currencies – a first step towards this in the 1980s would be to join the European Monetary System (EMS); and partly one of whether in a flexible exchange rate system the authorities should aim at keeping fluctuations in the foreign exchange rate within a certain band. As far as the first issue is concerned we saw in Chapter 8 of this book that if the authorities fix the sterling exchange rate they will lose control over the stock of money that remains in the UK. The definition of the change in the stock of money for a fixed exchange rate open economy is

$$\Delta M = \Delta C + \Delta R \tag{6}$$

where ΔC is domestic credit expansion and ΔR is the balance of payments surplus. Rearranging (6) and using the equilibrium condition $\Delta M^s = \Delta M^d$ implies

$$\Delta R = \Delta M^d - \Delta C \tag{6a}$$

Thus if ΔC is greater than ΔM^d there will be a deficit on the balance of payments and the export of money balances; if ΔC is less than ΔM^d there will be a surplus on the balance of payments and the import of money balances. This means that the authorities will be able to control only ΔC and not ΔM. Thus fixing the price of sterling against other currencies implies losing control over the UK money supply. Since the abandonment of the Bretton Woods fixed exchange rate system in 1971 there has been considerable debate as to whether the UK should join the EMS and thus be part of a European fixed exchange rate system; or whether the UK should pursue concerted action with a wider group of countries to re-establish fixed exchange rates. A major issue here is whether it would be better for the UK to accept the rate of monetary expansion arising from world forces or that determined by the UK authorities.[3]

The second issue turns on what happens in a flexible exchange rate system if the authorities control the rate of monetary expansion. The prediction of the monetary theory of the balance of payments and exchange rate, as discussed in Chapter 8 of this book, is that the exchange rate will appreciate if the UK rate of monetary expansion is lower than that in the rest of the world, and depreciate if the UK rate of monetary expansion is greater than that in the rest of the world. A problem here is that short-term factors, such as 'confidence' or an increase in the oil revenues accruing to the OPEC oil-exporting countries, can lead to highly volatile short-term movements in the sterling exchange rate. The dramatic depreciation of sterling in 1976, and the dramatic appreciation in 1980, are cases in point. The question then is one of whether the authorities should in the short term amend their target for the rate of monetary expansion to correct for any such dramatic movements in the exchange rate. Critics of Orthodox Monetarism point to the undesirable effects such fluctuations in the exchange rate can have on the competitiveness of UK exports, and hence on output and employment in the UK. The prescription is that monetary policy should be geared partly to keeping the sterling exchange rate inside a certain band so as to avoid the undesirable effects that arise from short-term volatility in the exchange rate.[4] Orthodox Monetarists argue that if foreign exchange rate targets are used to guide monetary policy over more than a very short time-period the effect will be to make the longer-term target for the rate of monetary expansion difficult if not impossible to achieve. The prescription is that the authorities only attempt to minimize very short-term fluctuations in the exchange rate – see Chapter 18 of this book for further discussion.

Controlling the money supply

Orthodox Monetarism suggests that targets for the rate of expansion of the money supply should be the centre-piece of the government's monetary policy. Such targets have been in operation in the UK since April 1976. It was the IMF's insistence on a target for domestic credit expansion (DCE) in the IMF loan negotiations of 1976 which triggered off this at least partial conversion to the monetary strategy suggested by Orthodox Monetarism – an earlier but short-lived use of monetary targets occurred in 1969 when the authorities similarly agreed to a DCE

Table 16.1. Monetary targets in the UK since 1976

Date target set	Period of target	£M$_3$ target (Percentage annual growth)	£M$_3$ out-turn (Percentage annual growth)
December 1976	12 months to April 1977	9–13	7.7
March 1977	12 months to April 1978	9–13	16.0
April 1978	12 months to April 1979	8–12	10.9
November 1978	12 months to October 1979	8–12	13.3
June 1979	10 months to April 1980	7–11	10.3
November 1979	16 months to October 1980	7–11	17.8
March 1980	14 months to April 1981	7–11	18.5
March 1981*	12 months to April 1982	6–10	Not known
March 1982*	12 months to April 1983	5–9	Not known
March 1983*	12 months to April 1984	4–8	Not known
Total growth for period April 1976–April 1981		47–77	78

* Indicates targets planned in the medium term financial strategy (MTFS).
Source: Monetary Policy, vol. I of Third Report of Treasury and Civil Service
           Committee 1980–81, HC163-I; *Bank of England Quarterly Bulletin*,
           June 1981; and Financial Statement and Budget Report 1981–82.

target as a condition for an IMF loan. In Table 16.1 we list the various monetary targets that have been in operation in the UK since April 1976. It is interesting to note that despite the actual rates of monetary expansion exceeding the target range in periods such as 1979–81, over the period 1976–81 as a whole the actual growth rate of the money supply has been only just outside the upper limit implied by the monetary targets. Thus the authorities have been more successful on average in achieving their monetary targets than is commonly imagined. A major innovation in the setting of monetary targets was announced in June 1979. Then the Chancellor of the Exchequer said: 'It is crucially important to re-establish sound money. We intend to achieve this through firm monetary discipline ... we are committed to the progressive reduction in the rate of growth of the money supply'. This medium term financial strategy (MTFS) involved announcing targets for the rate of monetary expansion for 3 or 4 years ahead rather than for just 1 year ahead. Thus the target rate for 1979-80 of 7-11 per cent inherited from the Labour government of 1974-79 was to be reduced in successive years to a target of 4-8 per cent in 1983-84.

The Orthodox Monetarist argument for targets for the rate of monetary expansion is that such targets will reduce the uncertainty that otherwise would exist regarding the government's monetary policy. This intention of not allowing monetary factors be a source of disturbance to the economy will be realized only if governments are able consistently to achieve their monetary targets. The question then is one of which method of monetary control will (a) allow the authorities to achieve their monetary targets; and (b) minimize any undesirable side-effects such as interest rate or exchange rate fluctuations which might arise as a result of the pursuit of such targets. To answer these questions we need to look more closely at the factors which determine the money supply.

Determinants of the money stock

The orthodox approach to the determinants of the money stock is the monetary base multiplier approach. Two identities are used in this analysis:

$$M \equiv NC + D \tag{7}$$

and

$$H \equiv R + NC \tag{8}$$

where M is the total money stock; NC is notes and coins held by the non-bank public; D is current and deposit accounts with the banking system; H is the monetary base; R is the cash reserves of the banking system. Manipulating (7) and (8) yields:

$$M \equiv H \left[\frac{1 + NC/D}{R/D + NC/D} \right] \equiv mH \tag{9}$$

where m is the multiplier applied to the monetary base to arrive at the total money stock. This approach suggests that if NC/D and R/D, the ratios of cash to deposits held by the non-bank public and banks respectively, are constant, and if the authorities have tight control over H, then it will be possible to have precise control over the money supply. This approach is not very useful, however, because we know that NC/D and R/D vary over time in response to the behaviour of the non-bank public and banks respectively. If interest rates rise, for example, we would expect the non-bank public and banks to reduce their holdings of cash because the opportunity cost of such holdings has risen.

Monetary base control

To capture such behaviour we need to look at the demand functions of banks and the non-bank public for the assets that constitute the monetary base. Let the assets or asset which constitutes the monetary base be X. The demand functions for X might be

$$X_B^D = X_B^D(i, R, L)D + e_B \qquad (10)$$

and

$$X_P^D = X_P^D(i, W) + e_P \qquad (11)$$

where X_B^D is the demand by banks for asset X; i is the set of interest differentials between the interest rate on asset X and other assets; R is the minimum required ratio for X_B/D imposed by the authorities; L is the demand for bank loans and overdrafts; e_B is the unexplained component of the demand by banks for asset X; X_P^D is the non-bank public demand for asset X; W is the wealth of the non-bank public; and e_P is the unexplained component of the non-bank demand for X. Using the identity $X \equiv X_B + X_P$ which says that the reserve asset X can be held either by the banks or by the non-bank public, and the equilibrium condition $X_B^D + X_P^D = X^S$, we can rearrange (10) and (11) as follows:

$$D = \frac{X^S - X_P^D(\ldots)}{X_B^D(\ldots)} - \frac{(e_B + e_P)}{X_B^D(\ldots)} \qquad (12)$$

Total bank deposits make up most of the total money supply, and so if the authorities were able to control total deposits they would be able to control the money supply. The requirements for this in terms of expression (12) are that:

(1) The authorities have tight control over the supply of asset X;
(2) There is a stable X_B^D function;
(3) There is a stable X_P^D function; and
(4) (a) The disturbances e_B and e_P are small; or
    (b) The disturbances e_B and e_P offset each other so that $e_B \simeq -e_P$.

The asset X which most satisfies conditions (1)–(4) above is cash. The authorities can have tight control over cash because they have a monopoly over the issue of notes and coins in the UK, whereas other assets such as bank loans to the discount houses are created by the private sector. Cash is one of the few assets for which stable X_P^D and X_B^D functions have been found, the demand functions for such as treasury bills or gilt-edged securities not being characterized by such stability.[5] And the unexplained variations in bank and non-bank holdings of cash appear to be small in relation to those for other assets.

A system whereby the authorities control the money supply by controlling the amount of cash issued is usually known as *monetary base control*. So far the authorities have not used such a system for controlling the UK money supply, though the announcement in August 1981 that all UK banks are required to deposit one half of 1 per cent of their liabilities in the form of non-interest-bearing accounts at the Bank of England is a small step towards a monetary base control system. The arguments for monetary base control, however, have been discussed seriously in 1979–81. In 1980 the government produced a Green Paper on the subject,[6] and the Bank of England has discussed the issues involved at great length.[7] The arguments against using a monetary base control system are, firstly, that such a system would lead the banking system to set up offices overseas to avoid any cash shortages that might arise in the UK banking system. Such *disintermediation* would mean that banks could avoid the controls by way of arranging loans for customers through overseas subsidiaries. The Federal Reserve System in the US has experienced rather severe problems with such disintermediation when it has tightened its monetary base. Proponents of monetary base control argue that the problem of disintermediation could be ameliorated by not imposing a required cash ratio on the banking system. Thus it would be left up to the prudence of bankers to determine the cash ratio of the banking system.

Secondly there is a problem sometimes known as Goodhart's law.[8] This law states that the behaviour of the economic system will be quite different, after a new control system is introduced, from what it was before the new control system came into being. Thus even though stable demand functions for cash have been observed in conditions in which the authorities have not been controlling the monetary base, there is no guarantee that similar stability would apply if the authorities were to move to a monetary base control system. As we shall see below, the UK banking system reacted in a quite unexpected manner to the changes in monetary policy associated with the Competition and Credit Control measures announced in 1971. Thus it is feared that there might be similar unexpected and undesired changes in behaviour were a monetary base control system to be introduced. This argument, however, applies to any changes in economic policy and if we were to take the argument to its logical conclusion we would never change the control systems used in the implementation of economic policy.

A third problem with monetary base control is that it would increase the volatility of short-term interest rates. In periods of cash shortage the banks would bid up interest rates in the money markets to try and maintain their cash reserves, and in periods of a glut of cash money market interest rates would fall. The extent of such volatility in interest rates would depend on how tightly the authorities controlled the monetary base. If the latter were to be controlled over a period of months rather than day by day interest rates would vary less. Here it is not obvious that any higher volatility in short-term interest rates need imply a similarly higher volatility in the longer-term interest rates which apply to such items as bank loans, overdrafts and building society mortgages. A problem with the current system is that banks offer customers overdraft facilities which can be used at any time. Thus banks have less control over size of their assets than would be the case if fixed overdraft limits were abolished and all lending to the private sector took the form of loans. The current system implies that banks would not be able to change the size of their assets quickly in response to changes in the monetary base. The outcome would be that banks would try and change their holdings of cash rather than the size of their assets in response to changes in the monetary base, and hence short-term interest rates would move sharply. If all bank lending to the private sector took the form of loans negotiated as and when customers apply for loans, this would allow the banks to have more control over the size of their assets. Given a sophisticated system of financial intermediation it is possible that longer-term rates of interest would be to a large extent cushioned from variations in short-term interest rates.

Fourthly a monetary base control system would mean that the residual financing of the PSBR would have to take place outside the banking system. In the PSBR identity

$$\text{PSBR} \equiv P(G - T) \equiv \Delta M_G + P_D \Delta B + \Delta OD \tag{13}$$

monetary base control would impose tight limits on ΔM_G, the change in government borrowing from the banking system, so the residual financing of the PSBR would have to take place through ΔB, that is, through selling extra government debt to the non-bank public; or through increasing overseas borrowing ΔOD. Financing the residual PSBR outside the banking system would involve reversing the present system whereby any unexpected change in the PSBR is, at least in the first instance, automatically financed inside the banking system. The main type of government debt sold outside the banking system is government bonds, gilt-edged securities being the name commonly used for such bonds in the UK. At present the authorities operate by selling gilt-edged securities through a *tender* system. This involves the government announcing in advance the price at which it is prepared to sell such securities, and then waiting to see if the tenders for securities are greater or less than the amount of securities the authorities wish to sell. This system of selling gilt-edged securities leads inevitably to situations in which the authorities cannot sell all the securities they wish to sell at the price fixed; and situations in which the tender exceeds the amount of securities on offer, implying that the authorities are selling securities at too low a price. Thus the current tender system would not be flexible enough to allow the authorities to finance the residual PSBR outside the banking system. An alternative system of selling securities by *auction* would be required for the authorities to have a more or less automatic source of financing the PSBR outside the banking system. It is not obvious that long-term interest rates would be more volatile under such an auction system than under the present tender system where the authorities operate by raising interest rates substantially to tempt a sufficiently large tender for gilt-edged securities, and then sell securities as their prices rise and their yields fall. Again a sophisticated financial system should be able to arrange 'warehousing' services whereby certain intermediaries buy stocks of gilt-edged securities in the first instance, and then sell such securities off in a more or less steady flow to the major institutional holders of gilt-edged securities, such as pension funds.[9]

A final problem with the monetary base control system is that the authorities would on occasion have to override their plans regarding the monetary base to deal with financial panics and crises of confidence in the banking system. Ultimately a credit money system works only if people have confidence in credit money. Such confidence can be shattered by any fears that banks or other financial institutions might collapse. This happened in December 1973 when property market prices collapsed, threatening the survival of several secondary banks whose assets were heavily tied up in property. Here, however, all systems for controlling the money supply will need to be backed up by some provision for the authorities to act as lender of last resort in crisis conditions.

Flow of funds approach

Since the authorities first announced targets for the rate of monetary expansion in 1976, however, the authorities have not used a market-based system such as monetary base control to achieve their money supply targets. Instead they have intervened in various ways to influence the *flows of funds* which in a definitional sense determine the money supply. Such a system lies half-way between the *market-based* approach to monetary control outlined above, and a *dirigiste* approach whereby the authorities direct the operations of banks by moral suasion, statute or the outright nationalization advocated by the National Executive of the Labour Party. The key to understanding the flow of funds approach to the control of the money stock is the accounting identity which says that

$$\Delta A \equiv \Delta D \tag{14}$$

that is the change in bank assets equals the change in bank liabilities. Thus we could define the change in the money supply as

$$\Delta M \equiv \Delta D + \Delta NC \tag{15}$$

or

$$\Delta M \equiv \Delta A + \Delta NC \tag{16}$$

The change in bank assets will be

$$\Delta A \equiv \Delta M_G + \Delta M_P \tag{17}$$

which is the change in bank lending to the government ΔM_G *plus* the change in bank lending to the private sector ΔM_P. The PSBR tells us that

$$\Delta M_G \equiv P(G - T) - P_D \Delta B - \Delta OD \tag{18}$$

Substituting (18) into (17) gives

$$\Delta A \equiv P(G - T) - P_D \Delta B - \Delta OD + \Delta M_P \tag{19}$$

Substituting (19) into (16) gives

$$\Delta M \equiv P(G - T) - P_D \Delta B - \Delta OD + \Delta M_P + \Delta NC \tag{20}$$

Thus if we look at the determinants of the money stock from the asset side of the balance sheet of the banking system we can define the money stock as the resultant of a series of flows of funds. Attempts to control the money supply to date in the UK have taken the form of attempts to control such flows of funds. Given that the change in notes and coins held by the non-bank public ΔNC is a very small component of the change in the money stock, attempts to control the money supply have involved intervention to change the PSBR, which is $P(G - T)$ in (19) above; intervention to change the sales of public sector debt outside the banking system ΔB; intervention to change bank lending to the private sector ΔM_P; or intervention to change overseas lending to the government ΔOD. In Table 16.2 columns (1)-(5) list such flows of funds in the UK, column (6) lists the growth rates of sterling M_3 which have arisen from such flows, and column (7) lists the short-term interest rates experienced over the last 20 years. The interventions by the authorities to control such flows of funds have taken the form of (a) fiscal policy measures to control the PSBR, (b) changes in interest rates and (c) quantitative controls on the banking system. All this means that there has been a schizophrenic air about monetary policy in the period since 1976 when targets for the rate of monetary expansion have been in operation. On the one hand Orthodox Monetarist ideas have come to hold some sway over policy-makers relating to how

Table 16.2. *Flows of funds, the money supply and interest rates in the UK*

	Public sector borrowing requirement PSBR (1)	Borrowing by government from non-bank private sector ΔB (2)	Borrowing by government from banks in sterling ΔM_G (3)	Borrowing in foreign currency from banks plus direct external borrowing ΔOD (4)	Lending by banks in sterling to private sector ΔM_P (5)	Percentage annual change in sterling M_3 %M (6)	Annual average of bank rate or minimum lending rate R (7)
1964	990	714	−380	656	957	5.8	5.3
1965	1,208	684	428	96	432	7.8	6.4
1966	964	329	220	415	34	3.5	6.5
1967	1,860	788	570	502	511	9.6	6.2
1968	1,295	46	112	1,137	538	7.5	7.4
1969	−445	502	−362	−585	429	2.4	7.9
1970	4	438	893	−1,327	829	6.2	7.2
1971	1,382	2,399	1,648	−2,665	1,625	11.9	5.9
1972	2,054	1,505	−1,030	1,579	5,511	22.5	5.9
1973	4,209	2,308	1,134	767	5,671	25.9	9.9
1974	6,437	4,243	−370	2,564	3,734	15.6	12.0
1975	10,480	6,359	3,096	1,025	−373	8.8	10.8
1976	9,128	6,249	−146	3,025	3,138	8.3	11.7
1977	5,995	9,745	1,696	−5,446	3,492	8.0	8.4
1978	8,331	7,243	123	965	4,710	15.3	9.1
1979	12,594	11,697	1,540	643	8,573	12.7	13.7
1980	12,301	9,904	2,370	27	9,624	15.1	16.3

Sources: Central Statistical Office, April 1981; *Economic Trends; Bank of England Quarterly Bulletin.*

monetary policy should be conducted. On the other hand the policy-makers have used an inherited Orthodox Keynesian system for controlling the availability of credit or interest rates when pursuing their monetary targets.

In this respect the evidence of Milton Friedman to the House of Commons Committee on the Treasury and Civil Service is quite revealing.

Central bankers throughout the world have rendered lip service to the control of monetary aggregates by announcing monetary growth targets. However, few have altered their policies to match their professions of faith. Most have continued to try and ride several horses at once by simultaneously trying to control monetary aggregates, interest rates and exchange rates – in the process introducing excessive variability into all three. And few have altered their operating procedures to make them consistent with the professed goal of controlling monetary growth. I could hardly believe my eyes when I read [in the government's Green Paper on *Monetary Control*[10]]: 'the principal means of controlling the growth of the money supply must be fiscal policy – both public expenditure and tax policy – and interest rates'. Only a Rip Van Winkle who had not read any of the flood of literature during the past decade and more on the money supply process could possibly have written that. ... Direct control of the monetary base is an alternative to fiscal policy and interest rates as a method of controlling monetary growth – there is no necessary relation between the PSBR and monetary growth ... control of the monetary base will affect interest rates ... but that is a very different thing from controlling monetary growth through interest rates ... the attempt to control the money supply through interest rates reflects a longstanding confusion between money and credit.[11]

Policy practice

For most of the period 1950–76 monetary policy in the UK took the form of the authorities using the Bank Rate (renamed Minimum Lending Rate (MLR) in October 1972 and abolished at least temporarily in August 1981) and quantitative controls over bank lending and other forms of credit as policy instruments to influence aggregate demand. On occasion Bank Rate or the MLR was increased sharply to attempt to reverse a balance of payments deficit or reverse a depreciation in the sterling exchange rate. This monetary policy practice reflected the dominance of Orthodox Keynesian ideas which attribute some influence to interest rates and credit availability in the determination of output, unemployment and the balance of payments, but no influence to the money supply *per se*. Since the introduction of targets for the rate of monetary expansion in April 1976 the main change in policy practice has been the use of fiscal policy measures to reduce the PSBR in attempts to keep monetary growth within the targets set. Over the period 1950–81 it is possible to discern four main types of approach to monetary policy which have been adopted by the authorities.[12]

Old approach: 1950–71

Heavy reliance was placed on credit controls, none on the money supply, with interest rates – via Bank Rate – being raised sharply on occasion to deal with balance of payments crises. The view of monetary policy in this period was summarized in the 'Radcliffe Report' of the Committee on the Workings of the Monetary System.[13] Here the 'liquidity' position of the economy was taken to be the monetary magnitude of relevance to policy objectives. Although the Report recommended that a system of Special Deposits be introduced whereby banks be required on occasion to lodge additional balances with the Bank of England – this being enacted in 1961 – this was recommended as a means of controlling bank liquidity and credit availability rather than the money supply. The only major change in policy practice in this period was largely enforced, the IMF requiring that, as a condition for the 1969 loan, the authorities impose a ceiling on DCE. The latter target was achieved by a series of controls on bank lending.

Competition and credit control: June 1971–December 1973

At the heart of this policy change was the philosophy of operating money and credit policy via market means or price rationing rather than by quantitative controls on bank lending and credit.[14] Bank lending was to be controlled by influencing the cost of lending via interest rate policy; the authorities were no longer to intervene to stabilize the prices of gilt-edged securities, such securities composing the large part of public sector debt; the discount houses were no longer to tender for the whole Treasury Bill issue at a common interest rate; and a new reserve ratio system for banks was introduced to replace the old informal 28 per cent liquidity ratio. This new reserve ratio obliged banks to hold assets to the value of at least $12\frac{1}{2}$ per cent of their liabilities in the form of balances with the Bank of England; call money with the discount houses and similar institutions; local authority, Treasury and commercial bills, the latter up to a maximum of 2 per cent of liabilities; tax reserve certificates; and public sector debt instruments with less than 1 year to maturity. Special deposits would be called on occasion, either to ease or impose pressure on the banks' reserve position in order to influence interest rates and bank lending. In addition, the discount houses were required to hold 50 per cent of their assets in the form of public sector debt.

An important point to note regarding the Competition and Credit Control (CCC) changes is that the new $12\frac{1}{2}$ per cent reserve ratio did not involve a move towards a monetary base system of controlling the money supply. The system would have been ill-suited for this purpose given that certain of the qualifying assets, call money being particularly important in this respect, are created by the private sector and thus not under the direct control of the authorities: the effects of a call for Special Deposits for example, could be avoided by extending more call money to the discount houses. Further it was never the avowed intention of the authorities during the CCC period to control the money supply.

The period of CCC saw several developments which eventually led to this approach to monetary policy being largely abandoned in late 1973. Two developments worthy of note here are the massive rates of expansion (around 25 per cent p.a.) of the money supply (M_3) experienced during the period; and the financial crisis surrounding the collapse of several secondary banks in late 1973, this following the collapse of the prices of property in which their assets were tied up. How much the latter developments were due to CCC *per se* is open to question. What is relevant here is the fact that the authorities came to the view that the system did not allow them sufficient control over monetary magnitudes – particularly lending to the private sector.

Post-competition and credit control: 1974–79

This policy involved controlling the banking system by placing a ceiling on bank liabilities, supplementary Special Deposits (SDs) being imposed if the banks exceeded the ceiling. Given that such supplementary SDs bear no interest, this policy involved policing the system by fining the banks if they breached the ceiling (or 'corset' as it was sometimes known). The fines varied with the size of breach, breaches of 0-1 per cent of the ceiling attracting a 5 per cent SD, 1-2 per cent attracting a 25 per cent SD and breaches in excess of 2 per cent attracting a 50 per cent supplementary SD when the policy was introduced. This system was to a certain extent similar to that used before 1971, and as such led to distortions in the banking system and active attempts to avoid the 'corset' controls. The main difference was that bank liabilities rather than bank assets were subjected to quantitative controls. A second main change was a more aggressive approach to the sale of public sector debt. The authorities were prepared to raise interest rates dramatically in order to reduce debt prices sufficiently to attract buyers. Then interest rates would be reduced slowly to encourage continued buying as debt prices rose and so offered the prospect of capital gains. Finally from 1976 onwards the authorities came to use fiscal measures to reduce the PSBR as a means of achieving their monetary targets.

Policy practice since 1979

Several piecemeal changes have been introduced into the practice of monetary policy since 1979, but the authorities have so far resisted committing themselves outright to moving to a new system of controlling the money supply such as monetary base control. A first development was that targets for the rate of monetary expansion 3 or 4 years ahead were announced in the government's medium-term strategy. The idea here is that the commitment of the government to such medium-term targets reduces uncertainty about the government's behaviour more than would be achieved by setting targets for only 1 year ahead. As can be seen in Table 16.1, however, actual monetary growth in the period 1979-81 has been in excess of the target growth by a fairly substantial margin, thus reducing the credibility of such targets. A second development was the abandonment of the supplementary SDs system in 1980. From February 1980 to April 1981 sterling M_3 grew at a rate of $18\frac{1}{2}$ per cent compared with the 7-11 per cent target tate. The Bank of England attribute '... 2-3% [of this excess] to the unwinding of distortions induced by the operation of the supplementary special deposits scheme ...'.[15] A third development was the abolishment of Minimum Lending Rate. Instead of announcing in advance the rate of interest at which it will lend to the market, the Bank of England now seeks to keep short-term interest rates inside an unpublished band.

Fourthly the authorities have created new debt instruments such as partly-paid gilt-edged securities in order to try and achieve a smoother flow of sales of debt to the non-bank public. Fifthly the authorities have established a new cash reserve ratio which requires all banks to deposit one half of 1 per cent of their eligible liabilities in non-interest-bearing accounts at the Bank of England. This move is a small step in the direction of monetary base control.[16] Sixth, the authorities abolished foreign exchange control. Finally the 1979–84 government has seen a reduction in the PSBR as the key to reducing the rate of monetary expansion without crowding out private sector spending by 'excessive' borrowing from outside the banking system. All in all such developments constitute a slow evolutionary change in monetary strategy. Small changes have been made to alleviate the problems arising from the 1974–79 control system and make a gesture in the direction of the monetary base control lobby. The underlying strategy, however, still reflects a flow of funds approach to the determinants of the money stock.

Diagnosis

A problem with assessing the monetary strategy of the government during 1979–81 is that '... it is clear from the evidence that there has been no true "monetarist experiment"'.[17] In large part this has been due to the fact that the government and the monetary policy authorities have not conducted their monetary policy along the lines suggested by Orthodox Monetarism. A first aspect of this confusion in policy-making has been the infatuation of the authorities with attempting to reduce the PSBR in order to attempt to achieve their monetary targets. The judgement of an influential monetarist was:

The key role assigned to targets for the PSBR [is] ... unwise for several reasons: (1) these numbers are highly misleading because of the failure to adjust for the effect of inflation; (2) there is no necessary relation between the size of the PSBR and monetary growth ... there is currently such a relation, but only a loose one, only because of the undesirable techniques to control the money supply; (3) the size of the PSBR does affect the level of interest rates, [but], for a given monetary growth, the major effect on interest rates is exerted by the real PSBR not the nominal PSBR ... in any event, in line with the government's announced ... policy on market mechanisms, interest rates should be left to the market to determine, and not be manipulated by governments.[18]

The government's infatuation with reducing the nominal PSBR reflects the influence of New Classical Macroeconomics rather than Orthodox Monetarism. As we saw in Chapter 15 of this book, attempts to reduce the nominal PSBR in the face of a dramatic downswing of economic activity such as experienced in 1979-81 are more likely to move the economy into a severe depression rather than 'crowd in' private sector economic activity.

A second aspect of this confusion is that authorities have conducted monetary policy by a series of often *ad hoc* interventions in the flows of funds network. At times such interventions have implied that the government has retained interest rate or exchange rate as well as money stock targets. The crude methods used by the authorities to try and achieve their monetary targets make it difficult to assess how much the course taken by the UK economy in 1979-81 has been due to such methods themselves rather than to the stance of monetary policy desired by the authorities. In particular it is not obvious that interest rates would have been so high for so long in 1980 had they been determined by market forces rather than by government policy.

Thus we would conclude that the period 1979-81 has not seen a 'monetarist' revolution in monetary policy but rather an application of policy measures suggested by the New Classical Macroeconomics using an inefficient monetary control system. We would argue that the severe depression experienced by the UK economy in the early 1980s casts severe doubts on the relevance of the hypotheses of New Classical Macroeconomics rather than on the hypotheses of Orthodox Monetarism. On the basis of current policies unemployment appears to be likely to remain at around the 3 million mark well into the 1980s. The Medium Term Financial Strategy money supply targets now appear to be likely to remain below the actual rate of inflation up until 1984. In light of these two assumptions we would suggest that the target rates of monetary expansion be revised upwards so that any recovery in economic activity is not stifled by a restrictive monetary policy. The transition to a higher rate of monetary expansion would be accompanied by an increase in output and a fall in unemployment, given that demand deficiency exists in the UK economy. Given the hysteresis effects outlined in Chapter 12 of this book, some of this transitionally higher output and lower unemployment would be incorporated into higher equilibrium output and lower equilibrium unemployment. Longer-term policies to improve the monetary control system, to find more appropriate magnitudes for monetary control than sterling M_3, to allow for feedback from the real economy on monetary targets and so on would also be required in order to avoid a repeat of the 1979–81 episode when the government's own monetary policy has provided a source of disturbance to the UK economy.

17 Wage and price controls

Players and painted stage took all my love,
And not those things that they were emblems of.
(W. B. Yeats, *The Circus Animals' Desertion*)

Often referred to inappropriately as prices and incomes policy – we would also place fiscal and monetary policies in this category because of their effects – controls on wages and prices have been in operation in the UK for much of the postwar period. Orthodox and New Cambridge Keynesian economists see institutional features of the wage-bargaining process as being the main determinants of the rate of wage and price inflation. Wage and price controls are advocated to deal with such institutional determinants of the rate of inflation, and to avoid having expansionary fiscal policy measures frustrated by an increase in wage and price inflation.[1] Orthodox Monetarism and New Classical Macro-economics, on the other hand, see the rate of inflation as being determined by the rate of monetary expansion. Wage and price controls are seen as undesirable (a) because they do not work; (b) because they divert the attention of policy-makers away from the monetary factors which determine the rate of inflation; and (c) because they distort the allocation of resources in the economy.[2] Between these two polar extreme views of wage and price controls comes the 'pragmatist' view that although monetary factors determine the long-run rate of inflation, wage and price controls still have a useful role to play in reducing the output and unemployment costs of measures to reduce the rate of inflation.[3]

Types of controls

The wage and price controls which have been used in postwar Britain have differed in several respects and so it is wrong to think of wage and

Table 17.1. Summary of wage controls in the UK, 1948-79

Period of policy (1)	Norm for wage increases annual percentage change (2)	Annual percentage change in wage rates		
		(a) Preceding 6 months (3)	(b) During policy (4)	(c) In succeeding 6 months (5)
1958-50	0	3	2.2	10.7
1956	None	7.7	3.4	6.7
1961-62	0	5.4	2.7	
1962-63	2.5		3.9	
1963-64	3.5		4.1	4.9
1965-66	3.5	3.9	5.0	
1966-67	0		4.1	
1968-69	3.5		5.8	
1970	4.5		8.9	13.6
1972-73	0	2.1	2.9	
1973	5.5		13.7	
1973-74	7		18.5	
1974-75	21		25.0	28.3
1975-76	12	32.7	18.6	
1976-77	4.5		4.3	
1977-78	10		19.0	
1978-79	5		12.0	20.3

Source: R. A. Batchelor *et al.* (1980), 'Inflation, unemployment and reform', in Frank Blackaby (ed.) *The Future of Pay Bargaining* (London: Heinemann).

price controls as a homogeneous policy instrument. Table 17.1 summarizes the different norms for wage increases which have been involved. Several other differences between the wage and price controls used can be discerned. First, voluntary controls were in operation in 1948-50, 1956, 1961-64, 1964-66 and in 1974-75; whereas statutory controls were enacted in 1966-70 and 1972-74; and compulsory controls, that is enforced without legal codification, were used in 1975-78. Second, specific enforcing agencies have been used in certain periods: the TUC in 1948-50; the National Incomes Commission in 1962-64; the Prices and Incomes Board in 1964-70; the Pay Board and Price

Commission in 1973-74; but not in the other periods of controls. Third, the specific wage controls involved have varied from the wage freezes of 1961-62, late 1966 and late 1972; to the percentage p.a. wage increase norms of 1962-66, late 1967-70 and 1976-79; to the fixed £ per week increase maximum of 1975-76; to various combinations of percentage p.a. and £ per week increases as in 1973; to indexation of wage controls to the cost of living, as in 1973-75; and, finally, to the 'severe restraint' terminology of the early 1967 controls. Fourth, the different periods have varied widely in terms of the attempts which have been made to control prices as well as wages, this varying from the price freeze of late 1966; the various checks on price increases involved in other periods; through to the silence on prices in the 1961/62 period. Fifth, certain controls have been designed to allow the wages of lower paid workers to rise by a greater percentage than those of other workers; some not. Sixth, the controls have varied widely in their comparative leverage over public and private sector wages, most periods seeing the controls enforced more in the public sector, as might be expected, but the degree differing. Seventh, the initial degree of co-operation of the TUC with the controls operated has varied widely from the active co-operation in 1974-77 through to the hostile compliance of 1972-74. Finally, the reasons for ending the controls have varied widely from the fading away of controls in 1962-64; to the outright hostility to controls in 1979; through to the General Election defeat of February 1974.[4]

The common factor to all the above controls was:

> ... the assumption that there is some connection between the pay bargaining system and inflation ... [some have had the objective] of reducing the rate at which prices rise by reducing the rate at which money earnings rise, and others [the objective] of reducing the unemployment cost an anti-inflationary policy ... the difference is not material.[5]

The controls so far enacted have been but a few of the many sorts of controls which could be used. Since the last period of wage controls was abandoned in 1979, in response to the outright hostility of workers and trade unions to the 5 per cent wage increase norm, several new policies to change the structure of pay bargaining have been advocated. A leading proponent of controls identifies seven such proposals.[6] First is a type of *Social contract* which would add employers and other interested groups to the government-trade union forum used by the

1974–79 Labour government. Second is a *Norm with exceptions* policy which would involve setting up a pay relativities board to arbitrate on which groups of workers should receive less or more than the basic norm increase in wages. Third is a *Synchronization* system where all wage settlements would be conducted simultaneously rather than in a staggered manner, and an economic forum sponsored by the government would produce recommendations as to the wage increases required to achieve national policy objectives. Fourth is a policy for *Public sector* wages alone, with a national review body to arbitrate on public sector wages. Fifth is a *Bargaining power* policy where measures are taken to change the bargaining power of trade unions *vis-à-vis* employers by such as reducing social security benefits to the families of workers on strike. Sixth is a set of *tax-based* policies whereby the government announces that the tax rates faced by employers or workers will be increased if they negotiate wage settlements in excess of those desired by the government. Seventh comes a set of *Radical policies* involving such as workers' self-management or comprehensive planning agreements between the government, firms and workers.

The fact that such a wide array of controls have been used in the past, and that such a wide array of schemes have been suggested for the future, makes it difficult to assess wage and price controls as a whole. A common denominator exists, however, in that proponents of controls have stressed the benefits to be gained in terms of reducing the rate of inflation; and opponents have stressed the costly side-effects of controls. Thus an assessment of controls can be conducted by comparing such benefits and costs.

Costs of controls

The main costs of controls arise from the distortion of the structure of relative wages and prices involved if controls are effective. If firms wishing to attract labour are not allowed to raise wages by as much as they would like, shortages of labour are likely to arise with the disruptions to production involved. Similarly if firms are not allowed to raise prices by as much as they wish, this is likely to introduce uncertainty as to whether new investment projects will be able to generate enough revenue to earn a return sufficient to make them attractive, thus discouraging investment. A common complaint from firms during the operation of wage controls has been that such controls have reduced the differential between the wages of skilled and unskilled workers to the extent that major shortages of skilled workers have arisen. Given the complexities of the price mechanism, it is difficult to think of a system of controls which would not have harmful effects on relative prices with all the resource misallocations and inefficiencies entailed.

Such problems of course arise only to the extent that controls are effective. During most periods of controls, many firms, mainly in the private sector, have avoided the controls by devices such as upgrading particular jobs or workers so as to be able to pay higher wages than those involved in the controls; such as increasing the non-wage remuneration attached to jobs; such as reducing the weights or sizes of goods sold; or simply by overtly breaching the controls, the authorities facing huge problems in finding out about such breaches in the first place, and often not having effective ways of punishing such breaches. Such breaches have often been revealed by official statistics showing higher increases in wage rates than those involved in the controls – see Table 17.1. Such avoidance or evasion of controls will reduce the success of controls in reducing inflation, but will reduce some of the resource misallocation costs attached to controls. Here, however, there has been the particular problem that controls have been more effective in the public sector than in the private sector. A familiar pattern has emerged of public sector wages falling behind private sector wages during the control periods, followed by public sector unions, largely successfully, pushing strongly to restore their relative wages at the end of control periods. Indeed, the pressure of public sector unions to breach the controls has often provided the spark that has led to controls being abandoned, as in late 1969, early 1974, and in the winter of 1978-79. The aftermath of the most recent period of controls was a massive increase in public sector wages in 1979-80. Finally, controls have often been a central factor in industrial disputes and strikes. On several occasions private and public sector firms would have been prepared to offer higher wage increases than those involved in the controls had controls not been in operation, and conforming with government policy has led to disputes and strikes which would not otherwise have taken place.

In response to such arguments proponents of controls tend to stress that the economic world in the absence of controls is a second-best one where distortions already exist, and that it is not obvious in such a world that controls serve to increase resource misallocation. It is also pointed out that controls have not in the long run had much effect on pay relativities in the UK.[7]

Benefits of controls

Here it is useful to distinguish between the effects of controls in reducing the rate of inflation during the period of controls, and the effects following the dismantling of controls. As indicated in columns (3) and (4) of Table 17.1, most of the controls have succeeded in reducing the rate of wage inflation compared to that experienced before the controls were introduced. The figures also indicate, however, that the actual rate of wage inflation during the period of controls has been substantially higher than the norms set. Thus most of the controls imposed have been breached during the period of operation. The most dramatic success achieved by controls was the reduction of the rate of wage inflation to 4.3 per cent in 1976–77 under the *Social contract* wages policy.

Such short-term successes in reducing the rate of wage inflation have never been sustained. The dismantling of controls, often in response to the tensions arising from the application of controls, has always been followed by a sharp increase in the rate of wage inflation – see column (5) of Table 17.1. It is not obvious that the average rate of wage inflation before, during and after controls would have been lower if controls had not been imposed. Here there is the problem of estimating what would have happened in the absence of controls. Proponents of controls tend to argue that the rates of inflation experienced would have been higher in the absence of controls, and that controls succeeded at least in reducing the expectations of workers regarding the rate of inflation. Studies of inflation expectations, however, have discerned little or no effect which could be attributed to the imposition of controls.[8] The main alternative view to what would have happened in the absence of controls is provided by Orthodox Montarism. Here it is argued that sustained variations in the rate of inflation can be explained by prior sustained variations in the rate of monetary expansion, and that wage and price controls have had at most short-term effects which have not been sustained. The Diocletian Edict of A.D. 301 backed up its controls on wages and prices by the death penalty for those violating the controls. Wages and prices still rose, and this has been the case with most if not all controls imposed since then in peacetime.

Diagnosis

The 1979–84 government has so far refrained from using explicit wage and price controls, arguing that wages and prices are best set by market forces. The government, however, is a major employer and so is necessarily involved in at least public sector wage negotiations, and has to take some attitude to pay settlements. This attitude has been formalized in the cash limits applied to public sector spending. In 1981–82, for example, the government has assumed an average 4 per cent increase in the rate of wage inflation in the public sector when setting cash limits. Public sector employees have been told that if they on average breach this wage inflation figure the cash limit will become binding and so employment and the volume of public sector spending will have to fall.

Our judgement is that the 1979–84 government is correct not to use wage and price controls:

(1) because such controls could achieve only a short-run and not a sustained reduction in the rate of inflation;
(2) because such controls direct attention away from monetary policies which are effective with regard to the rate of inflation; and
(3) because of the distortions and industrial tensions which arise from controls.

We would, however, criticize the government for setting its cash limits too low, the actual rate of inflation being nearly treble that implied by the cash limits for 1981–82. Such a policy is likely to achieve only a short-term reduction in the real wages of public sector employees. To the extent that real wages do not fall, such a policy will reduce the public sector provision of real goods and services and increase unemployment at a time when the UK economy is already experiencing mass unemployment. We would advocate not only the raising of cash limits but also the raising of the target rate of monetary expansion and the implied target rate of inflation, as discussed earlier in this book.

18 Balance of payments and exchange rate policies

Nobody ever did anything very foolish except from some strong principle (Lord Melbourne).

Here there is a distinction between the balance of payments and exchange rate outcomes which are implied by the government's fiscal and monetary policies; and the use by governments of policy instruments designed specifically to affect the balance of payments or exchange rate. We have already mentioned some of the implications of the government's fiscal and monetary policies for the balance of payments or exchange rate. In this chapter we will discuss policies which are designed specifically to affect the external transactions of the UK economy through (1) import controls and (2) measures to change the sterling exchange rate.

Import controls

The New Cambridge Keynesian research programme sees import controls as being necessary in order that expansionary fiscal policy measures succeed in increasing output and reducing unemployment in the UK. As we saw in Chapter 7 of this book, the New Cambridge analysis is that under a system of free trade an increase in the fiscal deficit is reflected in an increase in the balance of payments deficit. In order that expansionary fiscal policies stimulate UK rather than world output and employment, a substantial tariff on all imports of manufactured goods is recommended. The devaluation of the sterling exchange rate required to provide the same stimulus to output and employment is seen as being too substantial to be feasible, and thus the use of devaluation as a policy instrument is ruled out. The argument is not that a retreat from free trade is desirable in itself, but that the imposition of import controls is the only feasible way of removing the balance of payments constraint on the expansion of output and employment in the UK economy. The aim would be to see the UK economy importing at least the same level of manufactured imports as before controls were imposed, the argument being that such controls would permit the UK economy to sustain a higher level of output, which would be accompanied by at least the same level of imports as would have been the case without controls.[1]

Experience of import controls

The use of import controls in the postwar era in the UK has been strictly limited, reductions in import tariffs associated with GATT typifying most of the period. The two main periods when such controls were imposed occurred in 1964-66 with the import surcharge scheme; and in 1968-70 with the import deposit scheme. The import surcharge involved a 15 per cent levy on the value of most imports of manufactured goods, this levy being reduced to 10 per cent in 1965. The intention was to reduce imports by more than £550 million, whereas the actual effect is estimated to have been a reduction to the value of around £250 million.[2] The import deposit scheme required importers to deposit with the government for 6 months an amount equal to half the value of imports purchased, the scheme applying largely to manufactured goods. Investigators have found it difficult to discern a significant impact on the balance of payments arising from the scheme.[3] The above schemes, however, were not applied as generally or as permanently as the controls envisaged by New Cambridge, so it is not in order to draw too sceptical a view of the efficacy of import controls from such experience.

Arguments against import controls

The main arguments against import controls are similar to the arguments against wage controls: such controls can be avoided or evaded so it is not obvious that they would have the balance of payments effects postulated; such controls can be harmful in diverting the attention of policy-makers away from such as the monetary factors which determine the balance of payments and exchange rate; and such controls would distort the allocation of resources. Some of the main criticisms of the argument for import controls,[4] together with the New Cambridge response to such criticisms,[5] are as follows.

Central here is the free trade argument that import tariffs restrict world trade and, if they work, only achieve a higher level of employment in the UK at the expense of a loss of jobs in the rest of the world. The New Cambridge (NC) response here is that tariffs would allow the UK to operate at a higher level of demand, income and employment, and thus allow the UK to maintain at least the same level of imports as before the imposition of controls. Second, there is the problem of retaliation by other countries; NC reply that major beneficial effects would remain in the event of retaliation to the extent thought likely. Third, there is the tendency of tariffs to 'featherbed' inefficient UK producers, so casting doubt on the growth gains to be had behind such a tariff wall; the NC reply here is that 'exposure of UK industry to competition makes it bankrupt, not efficient'.[6] Fourth, the imposition of tariffs will increase the prices of imported goods in the UK, thus increasing the price level and costs; the reply here is that the government revenues arising from import tariffs could be used to reduce taxes so as to leave prices and costs unchanged. Fifth, there is the general problem of reducing the choice options open to UK consumers and producers; not important, compared with the growth benefits, is the reply. Sixth, there is the point that any given level of tariff will provide only a temporary degree of protection in the face of UK costs and prices rising faster than elsewhere: the size of such tariffs would have to be increased to provide the same degree of protection in future periods. Seventh, the imposition of import tariffs, to the extent that such a policy was effective in reducing the level of imports in the short run, would add further upward pressure to the sterling exchange rate to that already imparted by North Sea oil. This would reduce output and employment in the UK at least in the short run. Seventh, there is the problem that tariffs can be avoided or evaded by reshipment or even outright smuggling. Eighth, tariffs would discourage multinational companies from operating in the UK to the extent that the protection offered in the UK market does not compensate for the higher prices paid to import intermediary goods used in production. Finally, but by no means exhaustively, it is not obvious that the NC view of UK output and employment as being determined by aggregate demand alone holds much water - see Chapter 7 of this book.

Diagnosis

It is not obvious that import tariffs could afford UK industry the degree of protection alleged by New Cambridge, given that other countries could well retaliate and that tariffs can be, to a certain extent, avoided or evaded. Even if a tariff wall were to give UK industry a measure of protection it is not obvious that the supply response would be such as to generate a sustained increase in economic growth and employment in the UK. There again, even if such a supply response were forthcoming, there would be the long-term danger of a retreat from the system of relatively free trade evolved in the postwar world. The growth in world trade up until the late 1970s was a major factor behind the historically high rates of growth experienced by many western industrial countries including Britain. We would argue that there is a severe risk that the imposition of import controls would be accompanied by very small gains in output and employment, compared to costs incurred in terms of a higher rate of inflation and resource misallocation. Further the analysis does not seem to have much relevance to the depression in the UK economy in the early 1980s. As column (1) of Table 18.1 indicates, the UK economy moved from a deficit in the balance of payments in 1979 to a fairly substantial surplus in 1980. The PSBR changed little over this period, so casting doubt on the tight link between fiscal deficits and the balance of payments postulated by New Cambridge. Furthermore, as column (4) in Table 18.1 indicates, the early 1980s has also seen a substantial appreciation of the sterling exchange rate. To impose import tariffs at such a juncture would serve to place upward pressure on the sterling exchange rate and exacerbate the problems of UK exporters.

Exchange rate policies

On 13 August 1971, the US government announced the abandonment of its commitment to convert dollars into gold at a fixed price as far as inter-central bank transactions were concerned. Up until then the UK had maintained a fixed sterling rate in the post-1945 era, this rate having been devalued by 30 per cent in 1949 and 14 per cent in 1967. The abandonment of the convertability of the dollar into gold at a fixed price signalled the breakdown of the Bretton-Woods fixed exchange rate system. Since then the UK exchange rate has been flexible, the degree of flexibility varying from periods in which the authorities have allowed the rate to move freely in response to market pressures,

Table 18.1. *The UK balance of payments, exchange rate and competitiveness, 1970–81*

	Balance on current account of balance of payments (£ million) (1)	Official financing of balance of payments (£ million) (2)	Terms of trade value of exports as percentage of value of imports (3)	Sterling effective exchange rate[a] (4)	Import price competitiveness[b] (5)	Relative profitability of exports[c] (6)
1970	779	−1420	118.8	128.1	102.8	99.9
1971	1076	−3271	119.8	127.9	107.0	95.5
1972	189	1141	121.1	123.3	108.3	95.1
1973	−1056	771	106.8	111.8	100.6	97.9
1974	−3380	1646	93.1	108.3	96.8	98.0
1975	−1674	1465	100.0	100.0	100.0	100.0
1976	−1060	3628	97.9	85.7	96.3	101.2
1977	−206	−7362	100.2	81.2	97.6	102.7
1978	776	1126	105.8	81.5	99.6	102.9
1979	−1425	−1905	106.1	87.3	104.6	99.8
1980	2763	−1372	103.9	96.1	109.0	97.3
1981			105.1*	93.8*		

Source: Economic Trends May 1980 and July 1981.
* Indicates latest figure available for 1981.
[a] Upward movement indicates appreciation of sterling.
[b] Upward movement indicates imports becoming more competitive.
[c] Upward movement indicates exports becoming more competitive.

to periods in which the authorities have bought or sold foreign exchange reserves in an attempt to achieve the exchange rate desired. IMF rules allowed member countries to change their exchange rates in response to any 'fundamental disequilibria' in their balance of payments in the pre-1971 era, and this degree of freedom has substantially increased in the post-1971 era. Thus the question arises of how, if at all, the exchange rate should be used as a policy instrument.

There have been several developments over the last decade which have stimulated debate about the appropriate policies for the authorities to adopt with regard to the exchange rate.[7] First, the establishment of the European Monetary System (EMS) in March 1979 has stimulated discussion as to whether the UK should join this European group of countries in which member central banks intervene to keep fluctuations in exchange rates between member countries within pre-stated intervention bands.[8] The UK joined the European 'snake' system – a forerunner of the EMS – established in April 1972, but left the 'snake' in June 1972 after the Bank of England had used up a substantial proportion of its foreign exchange reserves in an attempt to keep the sterling exchange rate within the 'snake' bands. Since then the authorities have been non-committal about joining the EMS, not being convinced that the monetary policies required to stay in the EMS would be consistent with domestic policy objectives.[9] A second development to stimulate debate was the massive depreciation of the sterling exchange rate in the spring and summer of 1976 – see column (4) of Table 18.1. The debate here concerned whether monetary factors, confidence factors or the mismanagement of the foreign exchange rate market by the authorities were to blame for the sudden depreciation. This episode attracted attention to the effects of exchange rate depreciation on the UK rate of inflation. The third development of note was the dramatic appreciation of the sterling exchange rate from 1979 to early 1981 – see column (4) of Table 18.1. The debate here concerned whether North Sea oil, monetary policy or confidence factors were behind the sudden appreciation. This time attention was attracted to the effects of exchange rate appreciation on UK output and employment. We now consider the different views that exist regarding the effects of exchange rate changes on the UK economy.

Effects of exchange rate changes

The Orthodox Keynesian view is that a deliberate depreciation or devaluation of the exchange rate will have permanent effects in higher output and employment by allowing UK firms to compete on more favourable price terms in overseas and domestic markets. Whether or not exporters will reduce their foreign currency prices in response to an exchange rate depreciation will depend, *inter alia*, on the elasticity of the demand for their goods: if the elasticity is greater than one a reduction in price will increase total revenue, otherwise not. The main issue here is the size and permanence of the effects of exchange rate changes. A first factor limiting such effects on output and employment is the role of non-price factors in international trade. To the extent that the reliability of products, the ability to meet delivery deadlines and so on are more important than price factors in explaining trade flows, exchange rate changes will have only small effects on output and employment. Here there is also the problem that many UK exporters do not change their foreign currency invoice prices in response to exchange rate changes, thus leaving unexploited any possibilities of increasing export sales. A second factor limiting the response of output and employment is the adjustment of domestic wages and prices to exchange rate changes. If exchange rate changes are matched equally by changes in domestic wages and prices there will be no effect on domestic output and employment. The Treasury, during the course of the 1970s, came to place a far higher weight on the effects of changes in the exchange rate on the rate of inflation, and a far lower weight on the effects on output and employment. The estimate now is that the latter 'real' effects are transitory, lasting for a period of about 5 years after exchange rate changes.[10]

Differences of view exist amongst Keynesian economists as to how long-lived the output and employment effects of exchange rate changes will be. Disequilibrium Keynesians tend to argue that an appreciation in the exchange rate '... may have very long lasting consequences if import substitute industries or export industries are destroyed ...'.[11] Here the consequences of disequilibrium trading arising from exchange rate movements are stressed. In the circumstances of 1981 policies to engender a depreciation of the sterling exchange rate have been advocated to restore the competitiveness of UK industry.[12] On the other hand New Cambridge Keynesians have argued that

... to devalue on a large scale would require some complex combination of official sales of sterling, relaxation of fiscal and monetary policy, and inspired rumour ... the size of the fall engendered could be excessive, threatening severe inflation and risking collapse ... unless real earnings [were] held down by a successful incomes policy, devaluation [would] add to inflation without necessarily restoring full employment ...[13]

Thus import controls are advocated as a preferred alternative to devaluation.

Orthodox Monetarism sees the exchange rate as moving to reflect differences between the domestic and world rates of monetary expansion. Thus once the authorities have fixed the domestic rate of monetary expansion the exchange rate will appreciate if this is less than the rate of monetary expansion in the rest of the world, and depreciate if this rate is greater than the rate of monetary expansion in the rest of the world.[14] As far as commodity markets are concerned, equilibrium requires that *purchasing power parity* holds. This means that the rate of depreciation in the exchange rate will be equal to any excess or any excess or shortfall of the domestic rate of inflation compared to the world rate of inflation. As far as capital markets are concerned, equilibrium requires that the excess or shortfall of domestic interest rates over world interest rates is equal to the rate of depreciation or appreciation of the exchange rate.[15]

Again there is a difference of substance between monetarists as to how long-lived the effects of exchange rate changes will be on domestic output and employment. Orthodox Monetarists tend to argue that although such 'real' effects will not persist in the long run, such effects can persist for some time while wages and prices adjust to the new exchange rate. Thus gradual changes in the rate of monetary expansion are recommended in order that monetary factors do not disturb the real economy by way of the exchange rate.[16] On the other hand the New Classical Macroeconomics sees expectations regarding the rate of inflation and the exchange rate as responding quickly to the announced rate of monetary expansion, and thus sees any 'real' effects of exchange rate changes as being short-lived. Given that the 'real' effects do not last long, it is argued that the authorities might as well change the rate of monetary expansion and hence the exchange rate sharply in order to achieve their objectives regarding the rate of inflation.[17]

Diagnosis

Thus the controversial issue here is one of how long-lived or permanent the effects of exchange rate changes on output and employment are. The evidence for the UK in the 1920s, when the authorities pursued deflationary policies in order to raise the exchange rate and return to the gold standard at the pre-1914–18 war parity, suggests that the 'real' effects of exchange rate changes can be long-lived.[18] As we saw in Chapter 12 of this book, unemployment still remained at above 10 per cent in the late 1920s, 4 years after the return to the gold standard in 1925. We would explain the persistence of the 'real' effects of exchange rate changes through hysteresis effects. Thus a short-run decline in output and increase in unemployment in response to an appreciation of the exchange rate is transformed into a decrease in the long-run or natural level of output, and an increase in the long-run or natural rate of unemployment. The initial exchange rate impulse leading to a fall in output and increase in unemployment may be temporary or once-off in nature, but this impulse will be propagated into the future given that firms made bankrupt cannot be replaced overnight, and people experiencing long-term unemployment cannot regain employment overnight.

The appreciation of sterling, 1979–81

As illustrated in Table 18.2 the sterling exchange rate appreciated dramatically from 1979 to the first quarter of 1982. Columns (4) and (5) of Table 18.1 illustrate how this appreciation made imports into the UK more competitive, and reduced the profitability of UK exports. Many commentators have seen this dramatic appreciation of sterling as the main factor behind the sharp decline in manufactured output and increase in unemployment in the UK 1979–81. The authorities did not envisage that their monetary and fiscal policies would lead to such a sharp appreciation of sterling during this period. The Chief Economic Adviser to the Treasury told a Commons Committee on 1 December 1980:

I do not think it is possible to explain the level of sterling today relative to either its monetary behaviour compared with other countries or its price level relative to other countries satisfactorily.[19]

On 7 July 1980 the Chief Adviser to the Bank of England told the Committee:

It is very difficult to understand why the exchange rate is where it is now. Under any of the main theories of the exchange rate determination it is considerably higher than one might have analytically expected.[20]

*Table 18.2. The sterling exchange
rate, 1979-81*

		Quarterly average of effective exchange rate for sterling (1975 = 100)
1979	1	82.4
	2	87.0
	3	91.3
	4	88.5
1980	1	93.0
	2	94.5
	3	96.7
	4	100.2
1981	1	101.4
	2	97.8

Source: Economic Trends, July 1981.

The subsequent debate has concerned the extent to which the appreciation of sterling reflected the effects of North Sea oil, and the extent to which appreciation arose from a restrictive monetary policy.

North Sea oil

The argument here is that a

> ... rise in the exchange rate is ... the market's mechanism for bringing about ... a contraction of manufacturing absorption of imported manufactures [which is], whether desirable or not, the only means by which the British economy can benefit from the North Sea.[21]

The line of reasoning is that the balance of payments always balances; an inflow of revenues into the UK from North Sea oil thus has to be matched by an opposite outflow of revenues arising elsewhere; the market mechanism achieves this by raising the exchange rate; the rise in the exchange rate reduces UK exports and increases UK imports; manufactured imports and exports are the most sensitive to price; the structure of the UK economy has to change to accommodate North Sea oil; and this will be achieved by a reduction in UK manufactured output. Proponents of the North Sea oil explanation for the appreciation of sterling have estimated that a 22 per cent appreciation of the exchange rate is required to accommodate North Sea oil.[22] Critics of this position have argued that North Sea oil has also generated outflows of revenues in forms such as profits repatriated overseas, thus reducing the appreciation of sterling required to accommodate the inflow of revenues from North Sea oil.[23]

Restrictive monetary policy

On the surface it would appear to be difficult to attribute the appreciation of sterling to a restrictive monetary policy. As Table 16.1 indicates the period January 1979 to April 1981 saw sterling M_3 grow at an annual rate of around 18 per cent compared to the target of 7–11 per cent. Here, however, it is not obvious that sterling M_3 is a good indicator of the thrust of monetary policy. A comprehensive study of monetary policy during this period argues that

> ... sterling M_3 is likely to be a misleading indicator of monetary policy, often showing an expansion when policy is restrictive and vice versa. The main reason is that this aggregate includes interest-bearing short-term assets that are used as substitutes for cash balances, thus increasing as the supply of cash balances is tightened....[24]

As discussed in Chapter 16 of this book, interest rates have been one of the main instruments used to achieve money supply targets in the UK. For much of 1980 short-term interest rates were more than 5 per cent higher than the rate of inflation. This would suggest that monetary policy was far more restrictive than indicated by the sterling M_3 figures. This impression is confirmed by the growth rates for monetary aggregates which do not include short-term interest-bearing deposits. During the period May 1979–October 1980 sterling M_3 grew at an annual rate of 14.4 per cent; whereas M_1, which excludes interest-bearing deposits, grew at only 3.7 per cent; and M_B, the monetary base of notes and coins in circulation and the liabilities of the Banking Department of the Bank of England, grew at only 2.4 per cent.[25] Thus the conclusion to be drawn from money stock figures which exclude interest-bearing deposits is that the period 1979-80 was one of '... abrupt and pronounced monetary restraint...'.[26]

The above analysis is quite persuasive and suggests that although North Sea oil factors may have contributed, the main reason for the dramatic appreciation of sterling from 1979 to early 1981 was a very restrictive monetary policy. Given that prices and wages are slow to adjust to changes in the exchange rate, the appreciation led to a similarly dramatic decline in the competitiveness of manufacturing industry in the UK. The resulting decline in output and increase in unemployment will persist for quite some time because of hysteresis effects.

Lessons for monetary policy

The exchange rate experience of 1979-81 suggests certain lessons for monetary policy. First, monetary targets should be re-phrased in terms of the monetary base, M_1 or some other monetary aggregate or aggregates which exclude interest-bearing deposits. Second, to achieve such targets the authorities should abandon their practice of manipulating the PSBR or interest rates in order to achieve their monetary targets, and move to a system of controlling the monetary base. Third, in order to avoid a repeat of such disastrous episodes as 1979-81 the authorities should announce targets for several measures of the money stock rather than just one. Fourth, the authorities should be prepared to revise their monetary targets gradually in response to signals from the real economy.[27] A man and a woman may agree to a trial marriage of 1 year. If after 3 months the woman stabs the man with a knife, it would be absurd to stick to the original plan of a 1-year trial marriage. Similarly with monetary policy. To maintain the monetary targets announced in the Medium Term Financial Strategy in 1979 when the UK economy has since experienced a massive decline in output and a return to mass unemployment, is a recipe for a prolonged depression in the 1980s. Finally, given that the starting point is the opposite of ideal state of a severe depression, created at least in part by a restrictive monetary policy, priority should be given to attempting to reverse some of the hysteresis effects arising from the 1979-81 episode. To achieve this end the authorities should announce an increase in the target rate of monetary expansion.

19 Policy in the 1980s

We have behaved as though the intermediate 'short periods' of the economist between our [one?] position of equilibrium and another were short, whereas they can be long enough – and have been before now – to encompass the decline and downfall of nations (Maynard Keynes, address to the *Economic Advisory Council*, July 1930)

The thrust of the argument in this book has been that both supply and demand side factors are required to explain how the UK economy works. This means that Orthodox Keynesian and New Cambridge Keynesian views of the UK economy are faulted in that they see output and unemployment as being determined purely by demand factors; and that the New Classical Macroeconomics and Supply Side Macroeconomics views are faulted in that they see output and unemployment as being determined almost purely by supply factors. This also means that programmes of political action geared towards affecting demand factors alone or supply factors alone are not likely to come near to achieving their objectives. The research programme which best explains the way the UK economy works, we have argued, is a hysteresis-augmented version of Orthodox Monetarism. Hysteresis is a process whereby there is a significant time lag between the forces applied to a body being released and the body reverting to its previous shape. Through such a process shocks to aggregate demand or supply came to have lasting effects on the sustainable or natural levels of output and unemployment. Thus demand management as well as supply management policies are required to achieve sustainable objectives of economic policy with regard to output and unemployment.

In the circumstances of the UK economy in 1981 we have argued that first priority should be given to reducing unemployment, and that a stimulus to aggregate demand is required to achieve this because policies to stimulate aggregate supply will only take effect slowly, over a period of years. Further, supply side measures will only achieve an increase in output and employment if a sufficient level of demand is forthcoming. To stimulate an increase in demand the authorities would need to relax the restrictive stance of fiscal policy and increase the target rate of monetary expansion. The idea that an expansionary fiscal policy would merely crowd out private spending does not hold water in the circumstances of 1981. The monetary target should be set in terms of several aggregates rather than just one; monetary targets should be revised in light of what has happened to the 'real' economy; and the authorities should adopt a system of controlling the monetary base of the banking system in order to achieve its monetary targets. The cost of such an expansionary fiscal and monetary policy would be a higher rate of inflation. We would advocate a policy of gradual expansion of aggregate demand to minimize the effects on the rate of inflation, and would argue that the costs of a higher rate of inflation are worth bearing to reverse some of the hysteresis effects on output and unemployment experienced in 1979–81. We would rule out the use of controls over wages, prices or imports because such controls are likely to be ineffective; have costly side-effects on resource allocation; and serve to divert attention from the more fundamental determinants of what happens in the UK economy.

The policies of the present 1979–84 government involve managing aggregate supply alone, with aggregate demand being contained by the monetary targets outlined in the Medium Term Financial Strategy. It is not the lot of humans to know the future, but what we can say is that this strategy runs the severe risk of keeping the UK in its present state of recession well into the 1980s. Even if a sizeable recovery in economic activity occurs the signs are that unemployment will still be at around the $2\frac{1}{2}$ million mark by the mid-1980s. This would mean that the UK population would in effect comprise two groups: one group being employed and experiencing reasonable prosperity, and the other group experiencing the miseries of unemployment. Those who forget the lessons of the 1920s and 1930s are destined to repeat the experience.

Notes and References

Chapter 1: Introduction

1. *Treasury Economic Progress Report* (1979), June supplement.
2. See A. Sharples (1981), 'Alternative economic strategies', *Socialist Economic Review*, pp. 71–92 (London: Merlin Press).
3. See David Cobham (1981), 'The Socialist economic review project', *Politics and Power*, no. 3, pp. 255–67.

Chapter 2: Arguments in macroeconomics

1. Tony Courakis (1981) *Sunday Times*, 5 April 1981. See also Geoffrey E. Wood (1981), 'Can 364 economists be wrong?', *Journal of Economic Affairs*, July 1981, pp. 221–7.
2. See W. D. Hudson (ed.) (1979) *The Is/Ought Question* (London: Macmillan).
3. Compare the memoranda of HM Treasury and Frank Hahn in *Memoranda on monetary policy*, House of Commons Treasury and Civil Service Committee, July 1980, HC720 (London: HMSO).
4. Compare Patrick Minford and David Peel (1981), 'Is the government's economic strategy on course?', *Lloyds Bank Review*, no. 140, April 1981, with Adrian Sinfield (1981), *What Unemployment Means* (Oxford: Martin Robertson).
5. Compare Wilfred Beckerman (1974), *In Defence of Economic Growth* (London: Jonathan Cape) with E. J. Mishan (1967), *The Costs of Economic Growth* (London: Staples Press).
6. John Maynard Keynes (1936), *The General Theory of Employment, Interest and Money*, pp. 383–4 (London: Macmillan).
7. See Richard Lipsey, *An Introduction to Positive Economics* (London: Weidenfeld & Nicolson; various editions).
8. See Karl Popper (1959), *The Logic of Scientific Discovery* (London: Hutchinson); and (1963), *Conjectures and Refutations* (London: Routledge & Kegan Paul).
9. See Thomas Mayer (1980), 'Economics as a hard science: realistic goal or wishful thinking?', *Economic Inquiry*, April 1980, pp. 165–78.

10. See Sandra G. Harding (ed.) (1976), *Can Theories be Refuted?* (Dordrecht: Reidel) for further discussion.
11. See Daniel Benjamin and Levis Kochin (1979), 'Unemployment in interwar Britain', *Journal of Political Economy*, June 1979, pp. 441–78, and Dennis Maki and Z. A. Spindler (1975), 'The effects of unemployment compensation on unemployment in Britain', *Oxford Economic Papers*, November 1975, pp. 440–54.
12. For further discussion of methodological issues in economics, see Mark Blaug (1981), *The Methodology of Economics* (Cambridge: Cambridge University Press), and for further discussion of methodological issues in science as a whole, see A. F. Chalmers (1978), *What Is This Thing Called Science?* (London: Open University Press).

Chapter 3: The schools of thought

1. See M. Blaug (1981), *The Methodology of Economics*, p. 260 Cambridge: Cambridge University Press).
2. Samuel Brittan (1981), *How to End the Monetarist Controversy*, p. 11 (Hobart Paper 90, Institute of Economic Affairs).
3. Frank Hahn (1981), 'Preposterous claims of monetarists', *The Times*, 28 April 1981.

Chapter 4: Orthodox Keynesianism

1. See Donald Winch (1972), *Economics and Policy*, Chapters 8–14 (London: Fontana).
2. Alan Coddington (1976), 'Keynesian economics: the search for first principles', *Journal of Economic Literature*, December 1976, pp. 1258–73 (at p. 1264).
3. Here there is a difference of substance with US orthodox Keynesian economics which has assigned monetary factors a more important role in output determination.
4. And thus the demand for money M^d is infinitely elastic with respect to the level of interest rates.
5. Thus making the supply of money M^s infinitely elastic at the pegged rate of interest.
6. It is for this reason that the term 'fiscalist' is sometimes used to describe the research programme.
7. The term 'hydraulic' is due to Alan Coddington, op. cit., pp. 1263–7. The A. W. Phillips of Phillips Curve fame did indeed build models in the late 1940s where coloured water was pumped through glass pipes, complete with valves and other devices more associated with swimming pools, in order to illustrate this theory of output determination.
8. J. R. Hicks (1937), 'Mr Keynes and the "Classics": a suggested interpretation', *Econometrica*, March, pp. 147–59.

9. Quoted in J. R. Hicks (1973), 'Recollections and Documents', p. 9, *Economica*, February, pp. 2–11.
10. A. W. Phillips (1958), 'The relationship between unemployment and the rate of change of money wage rates in the U.K., 1861–1957', *Economica*, November, pp. 283–99.
11. See David Laidler and Michael Parkin (1975), 'Inflation: a survey', *Economic Journal*, December, pp. 741–809.

Chapter 5: Disequilibrium Keynesianism

1. Axel Leijonhufvud (1968), *On Keynesian Economics and the Economics of Keynes* (Oxford: Oxford University Press); and (1969), *Keynes and the Classics*, Occasional Paper 30 (Institute of Economic Affairs).
2. Robert W. Clower, 'The Keynesian counter-revolution: a theoretical appraisal', in Frank H. Hahn and F. P. R. Brechling (eds) (1965), *The Theory of Interest Rates* (London: Macmillan); reprinted in R. W. Clower (ed.) (1969), *Monetary Theory* (Harmondsworth: Penguin).
3. See E. Roy Weintraub (1974), *General Equilibrium Theory* (Macmillan: London) for discussion of the Walrasian conception of the workings of economic systems.
4. Robert W. Clower, 'The Keynesian counter-revolution . . .', op. cit., p. 290. (my brackets); though see H. I. Grossman (1972), 'Was Keynes a "Keynesian"?', *Journal of Economic Literature*, March 1972, pp. 26–30, for the argument against interpreting Keynes' *General Theory* in such a light.
5. The term 'reconstituted reductionism' has been used by Alan Coddington (1976), 'Keynesianism economics: the search for first principles', *Journal of Economic Literature*, December 1976, pp. 1267–71, to describe this research programme because it 'reduces' or traces aggregate macroeconomic phenomena to the individual choices made by economic agents, and this is a 'reconstituted' disequilibrium trading version of 'classical' Walrasian economics.
6. Remember that a demand schedule is derived on the basis of buyers being able to purchase as much as they want at the going price, and is thus relevant only to equilibrium trading.
7. Again remember that the supply schedule is derived on the assumption of equilibrium trading.
8. This diagram is taken from Edmond Malinvaud (1977), *The Theory of Unemployment Reconsidered*, p. 85 (Oxford: Basil Blackwell) which is good source of a more sophisticated exposition of these ideas.
9. J. M. Keynes (1936), *The General Theory of Employment Interest and Money*, p. 259 (London: Macmillan).
10. For an example, see R. Morley (1980), 'Profit, relative prices and unemployment', *Economic Journal*, September 1980, pp. 582–600.

Chapter 6: Fundamentalist Keynesianism

1. J. M. Keynes (1937), 'The General Theory: fundamental concepts and ideas', *Quarterly Journal of Economics*, February, pp. 209–23, reprinted in R. W. Clower (ed.) (1969), *Monetary Theory* (Harmondsworth: Penguin).
2. Alan Coddington (1976), 'Keynesian economics: the search for first principles', *Journal of Economic Literature*, December, pp. 1258–73 (at p. 1260).
3. See Brian J. Loasby (1976), *Choice, Complexity and Ignorance* (Cambridge: Cambridge University Press).
4. Joan Robinson (1971), *Economic Heresies*, p. ix (London: Macmillan).
5. This research programme has its own journal, *The Journal of Post-Keynesian Economics*, which is a useful source for a fuller exposition of its ideas.

Chapter 7: New Cambridge Keynesianism

1. *Cambridge Economic Policy Review*, April 1980, p. 40.
2. Francis Cripps, Wynne Godley and Martin Fetherston, 'Public expenditure and the management of the economy', p. 1 of *Public Expenditure, Inflation and the Balance of Payments* (1974), Expenditure Committee of the House of Commons, HC328 (London: HMSO).
3. Alan S. Blinder, 'What's "New" and what's "Keynesian" in the "New Cambridge" Keynesianism?', p. 83 of K. Brunner and A. H. Meltzer (eds) (1978), *Public Policies in Open Economies*, vol. 9 of Carnegie–Rochester Conference Series on Public Policy (Amsterdam: North Holland).
4. Relationship (3) is derived from (10 and (2) as follows:

$$PSFA_t = (1-x)\, Y_{D_t} \tag{1}$$

$$C_t + I_t = Y_{D_t} - \Delta PSFA_t \tag{2}$$

Rewrite (1) as

$$\Delta PSFA_t = (1-x)\, \Delta Y_{d_t} \tag{1a}$$

i.e.

$$\Delta PSFA_t = (1-x)\, Y_{D_t} - (1-x)\, Y_{D_{t-1}} \tag{1b}$$

Substitute (1b) into (2) giving)

$$C_t + I_t = Y_{D_t} - (1-x)\, Y_{D_t} + (1-x)\, Y_{D_{t-1}} \tag{2b}$$

i.e.

$$C_t + I_t = x Y_{D_t} + (1 - x) Y_{D_{t-1}} \tag{3}$$

5. *Cambridge Economic Policy Review*, April 1980, p. 39.
6. Francis Cripps and Wynne Godley (1976), 'A formal analysis of the Cambridge Economic Policy Group Model', *Economica*, November 1976, 335–48 (at pp. 336–7).
7. *Cambridge Economic Policy Review*, April 1980, p. 35.
8. See for example M. F. G. Scott (1980), *The Case Against Import Restrictions*, Thames Essay (Trade Policy Research Centre).
9. The New Cambridge group has its own journal, *The Cambridge Economic Policy Review*, which is the main vehicle for publishing its ideas.
10. Alan S. Blinder, op. cit., p. 83 (my brackets).
11. Ibid.
12. See K. A. Chrystal, 'The New Cambridge Aggregate Expenditure Function', *Journal of Monetary Economics*, June 1981, pp. 395–402.

Chapter 8: Orthodox monetarism

1. Karl Brunner (1968), 'The role of money and monetary policy', *Federal Reserve Bank of St Louis Review*, July, pp. 8–24.
2. This is not quite true, but conveys sufficiently the gist of monetarism for our present purposes.
3. In the absence of destabilizing government policy measures – see Milton Friedman (1968), 'The role of monetary policy', *American Economic Review*, March 1968, pp. 1–17.
4. M. Friedman, 'The quantity theory of money – a restatement', in M. Friedman (ed.) (1956), *Studies in the Quantity Theory of Money* (Chicago: University of Chicago Press); reprinted in R. W. Clower (ed.) (1969), *Monetary Theory* (Harmondsworth: Penguin).
5. M. Friedman (1956), op. cit.
6. See Don Patinkin (1969), 'The Chicago tradition, the quantity theory and Friedman', *Journal of Money, Credit and Banking*, February 1969, pp. 46–70 for a detailed account of the Keynesian elements in Friedman's theory.
7. See Milton Friedman (1968), op. cit., and Edmund S. Phelps (1967), 'Phillips curves, expectations of inflation and optimal unemployment over time', *Economica*, August 1967, pp. 254–81.
8. As would happen if the authorities were to ever increase or decrease the rate of monetary expansion.
9. The most influential paper was Harry G. Johnson, 'The monetary approach to balance of payments theory', in H. G. Johnson (ed.) (1973), *Further Essays in Monetary Economics* (London: Allen & Unwin). Johnson's paper circulated widely before this and the

monetary theory of the balance of payments had been 're-discovered' before this by the Dutch Central Bank in the early 1950s, the IMF in the late 1950s, and in the writings of such as Robert Mundell – see J. A. Frenkel and H. G. Johnson (eds) (1976), *The Monetary Approach to Balance of Payments Theory* (London: Allen & Unwin).

10. Note that given $\Delta R = 0$, $\Delta C = \Delta M^s$ and so domestic credit expansion is the only source of UK montary expansion.

11. In the absence of the unstable cases discussed earlier.

12. See David Laidler (1977), *The Demand for Money*, 2nd edn (New York: Dun-Donnelley).

13. Such studies could not *prove* that causality ran from the money stock to nominal income, only demonstrate that the empirical evidence was *consistent* with such a direction of causation.

14. See Hans Genberg (1976), 'A note on inflation rates under fixed exchange rate open economies', in M. Parkin and G. Zis (eds) (1976), *Inflation in the World Economy* (Manchester: Manchester University Press).

15. The ratio of unemployment benefit to wages, for example, has fallen during this period.

16. The paper by David Laidler (1981), 'Monetarism: an interpretation and assessment', *Economic Journal*, March 1981, pp. 1–28, should be consulted for a fuller exposition and appraisal of Orthodox Monetarism.

17. Such a property is often called 'hysteresis', there being a time lag between the tension applied to the economy (the aggregate demand shock) being removed and the economy returning to its previous state: see E. S. Phelps (1972), *Inflation Policy and Unemployment Theory*, pp. xi–xxviii (London: Macmillan).

Chapter 9: New classical macroeconomics

1. Robert E. Lucas, Jr (1972), 'Expectations and the neutrality of money', *Journal of Economic Theory*, 103–24.

2. Originally formulated by John F. Muth (1961), 'Rational expectations and the theory of price movements', *Econometrica*, January, pp. 315–35.

3. James Tobin (1980), 'Are new classical models plausible enough to guide policy?', *Journal of Money, Credit and Banking*, November, Part 2, pp. 788–99 (at p. 789). See also the other papers in this special issue of the *Journal of Money, Credit and Banking*.

4. Robert E. Lucas, Jr (1980), 'Methods and problems in business cycle theory', *Journal of Money, Credit and Banking*, November, Part 2, pp. 710–711.

5. See David Laidler (1981), 'Monetarism: an interpretation and assessment', *Economic Journal*, March, pp. 1–28 for an account of this and other differences between New Classical Macroeconomics and Orthodox Monetarism.

6. This is not quite true, in that certain fiscal policy measures are postulated to have real effects, see F. Kyndland and E. C. Prescott (1980), 'A competitive theory of fluctuations and the desirability of stabilisation policy', in S. Fischer (ed.) (1980), *Rational Expectations and Economic Policy* (Chicago: University of Chicago Press).

7. This is the main point made in Patrick Minford, 'Memorandum', *Memoranda on Monetary Policy*, pp. 131–43. House of Commons Treasury and Civil Service Committee, 1979/80, July 1980, HC720 (London: HMSO); see the memorandum to the same Committee by David Laidler, pp. 48–54, 'Notes on gradualism', for the opposing Orthodox Monetarist view on the costs of reducing the rate of monetary expansion.

8. See Patrick Minford and David Peel (1981), 'Is the government's economic strategy on course', *Lloyds Bank Review*, April, pp. 1–19.

9. See Brian Kantor (1979), 'Rational expectations and economic thought', *Journal of Economic Literature*, December, pp. 545–55; and Willem H. Buiter (1980), 'The macroeconomics of Dr. Pangloss: a critical survey of the New Classical Macroeconomics', *Economic Journal*, March, pp. 34–50.

10. For an account of fix-price and flexi-price markets see J. R. Hicks (1974), *The Crisis in Keynesian Economics* (Oxford: Blackwell).

11. See Robert M. Solow (1980), 'On theories of unemployment', *American Economic Review*, March, pp. 1–11.

12. See Frank Hahn (1980), 'Monetarism and economic theory', *Economica*, February, pp. 1–18; though note that Hahn confuses Monetarism with the New Classical Macroeconomics.

13. See T. J. Sargent (1976), 'A classical macroeconomic model for the US', *Journal of Political Economy*, April, pp. 207–38, and R. J. Barro (1980), 'Unanticipated money, output and the price level in the US', *Journal of Political Economy*, August, pp. 549–81.

14. See the evidence of Patrick Minford to the House of Commons Committee on the Civil Service and Treasury, op. cit., HC720, pp. 131–7.

15. See the papers by David Metcalf, Stephen Nickell and Nicos Floros, David Worswick and Paul Ormerod, and Rodney Cross (1982), in the *Journal of Political Economy*, April, for criticism of the aggregate supply explanation of UK unemployment in the 1920s and 1930s; and A. B. Atkinson, 'Unemployment benefits and incentives' in John Creedy (ed.) (1981), *The Economics of Unemployment in Britain* (London: Butterworths), for criticism of the aggregate supply explanation of UK unemployment in the 1970s.

16. James Tobin (1980), op. cit., p. 791.

Chapter 10: Supply side macroeconomics

1. See the various publications of the Institute of Economic Affairs, including *The Journal of Economic Affairs*, for a detailed exposition of this position. This institute was set up to promote individual or private sector economic activity as opposed to State or public sector economic activity.
2. See R. W. Bacon and W. A. Eltis (1978), *Britain's Economic Problems: Too Few Producers*, 2nd edn (London: Macmillan).
3. See the essays in F. T. Blackaby (ed.) (1978), *Deindustrialisation* (London: Heinemann).
4. See R. Millward (1980), 'The comparative performance of public and private ownership', *Salford Papers in Economics*.
5. See, for example, the arguments employed in B. J. Fine and K. O'Donnell (1981), 'The nationalised industries', *Socialist Economic Review*, pp. 265–86 (London: Merlin Press). The *Socialist Economic Review* is a good source for arguments against the position taken by the Institute of Economic Affairs.
6. N. Stern (1976), 'Taxation and labour supply – a partial survey', *Taxation and Incentives*, p. 9 (Institute for Fiscal Studies).
7. See J. A. Kay, C. N. Morris and N. A. Warren (1980), 'Tax, benefits and the incentive to seek work', *Fiscal Studies*, November, pp. 8–25.
8. Michael Beenstock (1979), 'Taxation and incentives in the U.K.', *Lloyds Bank Review*, October, pp. 1–15 (at p. 12).
9. See Peter Grinyer *et al.* (1980), 'Taxation and incentives in the U.K.', *Lloyds Bank Review*, January, pp. 41–3; and A. B. Atkinson and N. H. Stern (1980), 'Taxation and incentives in the U.K.', *Lloyds Bank Review*, April, pp. 43–66.
10. R. Hemming and J. A. Kay (1980), 'The Laffer curve', *Fiscal Studies*, March, pp. 83–90 (at p. 85).
11. For the 1920s and 1930s see Daniel K. Benjamin and Levis A. Kochin (1979), 'Unemployment in interwar Britain', *Journal of Political Economy*, June, pp. 441–78. For the late 1960s and 1970s see Z. A. Spindler and D. Maki (1975), 'The effects of unemployment compensation on the rate of unemployment in Great Britain', *Oxford Economic Papers*, November, pp. 440–54.
12. Patrick Minford and David Peel (1981), 'Is the government's economic strategy on course?', *Lloyds Bank Review*, April, pp. 1–19 (at pp. 16–17).
13. See A. B. Atkinson, 'Unemployment benefits and incentives', in John Creedy (ed.) (1981), *The Economics of Unemployment in Britain* (London: Butterworths).
14. See Stephen J. Nickell (1979), 'The effect of unemployment and related benefits on the duration of unemployment', *Economic Journal*, March, pp. 34–49.
15. See Alan Deacon (1978), 'The scrounging controversy', *Social and Economic Administration*, vol. 12.
16. See Adrian Sinfield (1980), *What Unemployment Means* (Oxford: Martin Robertson).

17. See A. B. Atkinson (1981), op. cit., Table 5.1, p. 134.
18. See C. J. Parsley (1980), 'Labour, unions and wages', *Journal of Economic Literature*, March, pp. 1–31.
19. Minford and Peel (1981), op. cit., p. 15.
20. Edgar L. Feige (1981), 'The U.K.'s unobserved economy: a preliminary assessment', *Journal of Economic Affairs*, July, pp. 205–12 (esp. p. 205).
21. Taken from Edgar L. Feige (1981), op. cit., p. 207.
22. K. Macafee (1980), 'A glimpse of the hidden economy in the national accounts', *Economic Trends*, February, p. 316.
23. Committee of Public Accounts (1981), Twelfth Report, Session 1980/81, House of Commons, HC318 (London: HMSO).
24. A. Dilnot and C. N. Morris (1981), 'What do we know about the black economy', *Fiscal Studies*, March, pp. 58–73.
25. Edgar L. Feige (1981), op. cit., p. 210.
26. K. Macafee (1980), op. cit.
27. Edgar L. Feige (1981), op. cit.
28. A. Dilnot and C. N. Morris (1981), op. cit., Table 1.
29. See Stephen J. Nickell, 'Unemployment and the structure of labour costs', in K. Brunner and A. Meltzer (eds) (1979), *Policies for Employment, Prices and the Exchange Rate* (Amsterdam: North Holland).
30. See Samuel Brittan (1981), *How to End the 'Monetarist' Controversy*, Chapter VI, Hobart Paper 90 (Institute of Economic Affairs) for further discussion of Supply Side Macroeconomics.

Chapter 11: Formulation of macroeconomic policy

1. See Robert A. Mundell, 'The nature of policy choices', in his *International Economics* (1968) (London: Macmillan).
2. See Edward R. Tufte (1978), *Political Control of the Economy* (Princeton, NJ: Princeton University Press) and J. E. Alt and K. A. Chrystal (1981), 'Public sector behaviour: the status of the political business cycle', in D. Currie, R. Nobay and D. Peel (eds) (1981), *Macroeconomic Analysis* (London: Croom-Helm).
3. For a sophisticated treatment of the problems involved in formulating macroeconomic policies, see Maurice Peston (1974), *Theory of Macroeconomic Policy* (Deddington: Philip Allan).
4. See, for example, HM Treasury (1979), *Macroeconomic Model: Technical Manual 1979*.
5. Treasury and Civil Service Committee (1981), *Monetary Policy*, vol. 1, Session 1980–81, HC163-I, House of Commons (London: HMSO).
6. Committee on Policy Optimisation (1978), *Report*, pp. 102–3, House of Commons Cmnd 7148 (London: HMSO).
7. See footnote 6 of this chapter.

Chapter 12: Unemployment

1. See John A. Garraty (1978), *Unemployment in History*, Chap. 6 (New York: Harper & Row), and J. Harris (1972), *Unemployment and Politics* (Oxford: Oxford University Press).
2. Cited in John A. Garraty (1978), op. cit., p. 105.
3. John A. Hobson (1895), 'The meaning and measure of "unemployment"', *Contemporary Review*, March 1895, pp. 415–32 (at p. 415).
4. John A. Hobson (1895), op. cit., pp. 429–30.
5. A. C. Pigou (1914), *Unemployment*, p. 14 (London: Williams & Northgate).
6. See W. A. Garside (1980), *The Measurement of Unemployment in Great Britain 1850–1979*, p. 20 (Oxford: Blackwell).
7. J. M. Keynes (1936), *The General Theory of Employment, Interest and Money*, p. 15 (London: Macmillan).
8. Richard Kahn, 'Unemployment as seen by the Keynesians', in G. D. N. Worswick (ed.) (1976), *The Concept and Measurement of Involuntary Unemployment*, p. 21 (London: Allen & Unwin).
9. J. M. Keynes (1937), 'How to avoid a slump', *The Times*, January.
10. See T. W. Hutchison (1977), *Keynes v. the 'Keynesians'?*, Hobart Paperback 11 (London: Institute of Economic Affairs).
11. See Richard Kahn, 'A comment', in T. W. Hutchison (1977), op. cit., pp. 48–57. See G. C. Peden (1980), 'Keynes, the Treasury and unemployment in the later nineteen-thirties', *Oxford Economic Papers*, March, pp. 1–18 for a review of this debate.
12. Daniel K. Benjamin and Levis A. Kochin (1979), 'Unemployment in interwar Britain', *Journal of Political Economy*, June, pp. 441–78 (at pp. 465, 442 and 474).
13. See Rodney Cross (1982), 'How much voluntary unemployment in interwar Britain', *Journal of Political Economy*, April.
14. For this and other more technical criticisms of the Benjamin–Kochin thesis, see David Metcalf, Stephen Nickell and Nicos Floros (1982), 'Still searching for an explanation of unemployment in interwar Britain', *Journal of Political Economy*, April.
15. Cited in Alan Deacon, 'Unemployment and politics in Britain since 1945', in Brian Showler and Adrian Sinfield (eds) (1981), *The Workless State*, pp. 61–2 (Oxford: Martin Robertson).
16. Ministry of Reconstruction (1944), *Employment Policy*, Cmnd 6527 (London: HMSO).
17. See Alan Deacon (1981), op. cit., for an account of the changes in political attitudes to unemployment.
18. BBC tape of Labour Party Conference, October 1976. See Labour Party (1976), *Report of 74th Annual Conference*, for further details.
19. Keith Joseph (1978), *Conditions for Fuller Employment*, p. 20 (London: Centre for Policy Studies).
20. See the reply by John Golding (1978), P.U.S.S. in the Department of Employment, Hansard column 265, 4 May 1978, House of Commons. See also Bridget Rosewell and Derek Robinson (1981),

'The reliability of job vacancy statistics', *Bulletin of the Oxford Institute of Economics and Statistics*, February, pp. 1–16.

21. See Brian G. M. Main (1981), 'The length of employment and unemployment in Great Britain', *Scottish Journal of Political Economy*, June, pp. 146–64.

22. Pilgrim Trust (1938), *Men Without Work*, pp. 67, 137 (Cambridge: Cambridge University Press).

23. Philip Eisenburg and Paul F. Lazarsfeld (1938), 'The psychological effects of unemployment', *Psychological Bulletin*, pp. 358–90 – cited in Adrian Sinfield, 'Unemployment in an unequal society', in Adrian Sinfield and Brian Showler (eds) (1981), *The Workless State*, pp. 152–3 (Oxford: Martin Robertson).

24. See Adrian Sinfield (1981), op. cit.; Richard Harrison (1976), 'The demoralising experience of prolonged unemployment', *Department of Employment Gazette*, April, pp. 330–49; and Manpower Services Commission (1980), *A Study of the Long-Term Unemployed*, February (London: MSC).

25. Stephen Nickell (1979), 'Estimating the probability of leaving unemployment', *Econometrica*, September, pp. 1249–66.

26. Sue Moylan and Bob Davies (1980), 'The disadvantages of the unemployed', *Employment Gazette*, August, pp. 830–2.

27. Sue Moylan and Bob Davies (1981), 'The flexibility of the unemployed', *Employment Gazette*, January, pp. 29–33.

28. Richard Harrison (1976), op. cit., p. 347.

29. See Manpower Services Commission (1980), op. cit.

30. C. H. Smee and J. Stern (1978), 'The unemployed in a period of high unemployment', *Government Economic Service Working Paper No. 11*.

31. See David Metcalf (1980), 'Unemployment: history, incidence and prospects', *Policy and Politics*, pp. 21–37 (at p. 24).

32. See Adrian Sinfield (1981), op. cit.

33. See Stephen J. Nickell (1980), 'A picture of male unemployment in Britain', *Economic Journal*, December, pp. 776–94 for further details.

34. *Cambridge Economic Policy Review*, April 1980, p. 23.

35. See *The Economic Outlook* (1981), Liverpool Occasional Papers No. 1.

36. See Milton Friedman (1968), 'The role of monetary policy', *American Economic Review*, March, pp. 1–17.

37. Edmund S. Phelps (1967), 'Phillips curves, expectations of inflation and optimal unemployment over time', *Economica*, August, pp. 254–81.

38. Edmund S. Phelps (1972), *Inflation Policy and Unemployment Theory*, p. xxiii (London: Macmillan).

39. Milton Friedman (1968), op. cit., p. 8.

40. For further discussion see Samuel Brittan (1981), op. cit., Chap. VI.

41. See HM Treasury (1981), p. 27 of *Fifth Report of the Treasury and Civil Service Committee*, 1980–81, House of Commons,

HC232-II (London: HMSO) – though note the scepticism with which the Treasury treats this estimate.

42. See Andrew McIntosh (ed.) (1981), *Employment Policy in the U.K. and the U.S.* (London: John Martin), for an outline of such policies, and P. R. G. Layard and S. J. Nickell (1980), 'The case for subsidising extra jobs', *Economic Journal*, March, pp. 51–73 for the argument for job subsidies.

43. Samuel Brittan (1981), op. cit., p. 121.

Chapter 13: Inflation

1. For discussion of the problems involved in deriving a correct measure of the rate of inflation, see Armen A. Alchian and Benjamin Klein (1973), 'On a correct measure of inflation', *Journal of Money, Credit and Banking*, February, pp. 173–91.

2. Sir Geoffrey Howe, Chancellor of the Exchequer, letter to House of Commons Committee on the Treasury and the Civil Service, 13 February 1980.

3. Frank Hahn (1980), 'Memorandum', *Memoranda on Monetary Policy*, pp. 80–1. House of Commons Treasury and Civil Service Committee, Session 1979–80, HC720 (London: HMSO).

4. James Tobin (1972), 'Inflation and unemployment', *American Economic Review*, March, pp. 1–18.

5. See Samuel Brittan (1981), *How to End the Monetarist Controversy*, pp. 45–47. Hobart Paper 90 (London: Institute of Economic Affairs).

6. For further discussion, see John Foster (1976), 'The redistributive effects of inflation – questions and answers', *Scottish Journal of Political Economy*, February.

7. See Maurice Peston (1981), 'The integration of monetary, fiscal and incomes policy', *Lloyds Bank Review*, April, pp. 1–13.

8. See David Laidler (1980), 'Notes on gradualism', *Memoranda on Monetary Policy*, pp. 48–54. House of Commons Treasury and Civil Service Committee, Session 1979–80, HC720 (London: HMSO).

9. See Patrick Minford (1980), 'Memorandum', in *Memoranda on Monetary Policy* (see note 8), pp. 131–43.

10. See, for example, Simon Wren-Lewis (1981), 'The role of money in determining prices: a reduced form approach', *Government Economic Service Working Paper* No. 42, March.

11. See Edmund S. Phelps (1972), *Inflation Policy and Unemployment Theory: A Cost–Benefit Approach to Monetary Planning* (London: Macmillan) for further discussion of the cost–benefit approach to unemployment and inflation policy.

Chapter 14: Economic growth and business cycles

1. Fred Hirsch (1977), *Social Limits to Growth*, p. 9 (London: Routledge & Kegan Paul).
2. See E. J. Mishan (1967), *The Costs of Economic Growth* (London: Staples Press).
3. See D. H. Meadows *et al.* (1967), *The Limits to Growth* (London: Earth Island Limited).
4. See Fred Hirsch (1977), op. cit.
5. See Wilfred Beckerman (1974), *In Defence of Economic Growth* (London: Jonathan Cape) and Anthony Crosland (1974), *Socialism Now* (London: Jonathan Cape).
6. Francis Cripps, Wynne Godley and Martin Fetherston (1974), 'Public expenditure and the management of the economy', *Public Expenditure, Inflation and the Balance of Payments*, p. 1. Ninth Report of the Expenditure Committee, House of Commons HC328 (London: HMSO).
7. See Nicholas Kaldor (1966), *Causes of the Slow Rate of Economic Growth in the U.K.* (Cambridge: Cambridge University Press).
8. Maurice Peston (1981), 'The integration of monetary, fiscal and incomes policy', *Lloyds Bank Review*, July, pp. 1–13.
9. W. Godley and R. M. May (1977), 'The macroeconomic implications of devaluation and import restriction', *Cambridge Economic Policy Review*, March.
10. See Nicholas Kaldor (1966), op. cit.
11. See R. E. Rowthorn (1975), 'What remains of Kaldor's law?', *Economic Journal*, March, pp. 10–19; and J. S. L. McCombie (1981), 'What still remains of Kaldor's laws?', *Economic Journal*, March, pp. 206–16.
12. For further discussion of demand management in the UK, see Andrew Graham, 'Demand management policy in changing historical circumstances', in David A. Currie and Will Peters (eds) (1980), *Contemporary Economic Analysis*, vol. 2 (London: Croom Helm).
13. Cited in *Cambridge Economic Policy Review*, April 1980, p. 11.
14. R. C. O. Matthews, cited in Samuel Brittan (1969), *Steering the Economy*, p. 264 (London: Secker & Warburg).
15. J. C. R. Dow (1964), *The Management of the British Economy 1945-1960*, p. 384 (Cambridge: Cambridge University Press).
16. See *Public Expenditure, Inflation and the Balance of Payments* (see note 6).
17. Reference as in Chapter 8, note 16.
18. See A. W. Phillips (1962), 'Employment, inflation and growth', *Economica*, February, pp. 1–16 for a non-technical discussion of his 'Stabilisation policy in an open economy', *Economic Journal*, June 1954, pp. 290–323, and 'Stabilisation policy and the time form of lagged responses', *Economic Journal*, June 1957, pp. 265–77.
19. See F. T. Blackaby, 'The economics and politics of demand management', in S. T. Cook and P. M. Jackson (eds) (1981), *Current Issues*

in Fiscal Policy (Oxford: Martin Robertson) for a defence of discretionary stabilization policies.

20. See D. E. Moggridge (1969), *The Return to Gold 1925* (Cambridge: Cambridge University Press).
21. See the papers in Karl Brunner (ed.) (1981), *The Great Depression Revisited* (The Hague: Martinus Nijhoff).
22. See Daniel K. Benjamin and Levis A. Kochin (1979), 'Unemployment in interwar Britain', *Journal of Political Economy*, June, pp. 441–78.
23. R. C. O. Matthews (1968), 'Why has Britain had full employment since the war?', *Economic Journal*, September, pp. 555–69 (at pp. 555–6).
24. Ibid., p. 556.
25. Ibid., 568.
26. Cited in G. B. Stafford (1970), 'Full employment since the war – comment', *Economic Journal*, March, pp. 165–72 (at p. 166); Stafford criticizes this thesis – though see the reply by Matthews in the same issue of the *Economic Journal*.
27. See Andrew Graham (1980), op. cit., for further discussion of why the U.K. economy avoided severe depressions for most of the postwar period.

Chapter 15: Fiscal policy

1. G. K. Shaw (1977), *An Introduction to the Theory of Macroeconomic Policy*, 3rd edn (Oxford: Martin Robertson).
2. G. C. Peden (1980), 'Keynes, the Treasury and unemployment in the later nineteen-thirties', *Oxford Economic Papers*, March, pp. 1–18 (at p. 6).
3. J. M. Keynes (1931) (with H. O. Henderson), 'Can Lloyd George do it?', *Essays in Persuasion* (London: Macmillan).
4. Cited in G. C. Peden (1980), op. cit., p. 7.
5. Susan Howson (1975), *Domestic Monetary Management in Britain 1919–1938*, p. 142 (Cambridge: Cambridge University Press).
6. See, for example, *Financial Statement and Budget Report 1981–1982* (March 1981) (London: HMSO).
7. See David Cobham (1981), 'Monetarism and the expenditure cuts', in *Socialist Economic Review* (London: Merlin Press).
8. See K. A. Chrystal and J. Alt, 'Endogenous government behaviour; Wagner's law or Gotterdamerung?', in S. T. Cook and P. M. Jackson (eds) (1979), *Current Issues in Fiscal Policy* (Oxford: Martin Robertson), for further discussion.
9. *Expenditure Committee: Public Expenditure, Inflation and the Balance of Payments*, p. xi, Ninth Report, Session 1974, House of Commons HC328 (London: HMSO), 1974.

10. See J. E. Meade, Chairman (1978), *The Structure and Reform of Direct Taxation*, Institute for Fiscal Studies (London: Allen & Unwin).
11. *Economic Trends*, p. 112, December 1979 (London: HMSO).
12. See J. D. Sargan, 'A study of wages and prices in the U.K., 1949–1968', in H. G. Johnson and A. R. Nobay (eds) (1971), *The Current Inflation* (London: Macmillan).
13. See 'Tax and price index: sources and methods', *Economic Trends*, August 1979.
14. Cited in HM Treasury, *Economic Progress Report*, September 1979.
15. Douglas Wass (1978), 'The changing problems of economic management', *Economic Trends*, March.
16. HM Treasury (1979), 'The Budget', *Economic Progress Report Supplement*, June.
17. See G. K. Shaw, 'The measurement of fiscal influence', in S. T. Cook and P. M. Jackson (eds) (1979), *Current Issues in Fiscal Policy* (Oxford: Martin Robertson).
18. See HM Treasury (1981), *Economic Progress Report*, February.
19. A re-evaluation of the New Deal fiscal policies in the 1930s in the USA reveals that there really was no 'new deal', the full employment fiscal deficit having been in surplus for the whole of this period: see Herbert Stein (1969), *The Fiscal Revolution in America*, (Chicago: University of Chicago Press).
20. See C. T. Taylor and A. R. Threadgold (1979), ' "Real" national saving and its sectoral composition', *Bank of England Discussion Paper*, No. 6, October.
21. For further discussion here see: Treasury and Civil Service Committee (Session 1980–81), *Monetary Policy*, Annex to Chapter 6, Vol. 1, House of Commons HC163-I (London: HMSO); and M. J. Artis, 'Fiscal policy and crowding out', in Michael Posner (ed.) (1978), *Demand Management* (London: Heinemann).
22. See Alan S. Blinder and Robert M. Solow (1973), 'Does fiscal policy matter?', *Journal of Public Economics*, November, pp. 319–37.
23. See R. J. Barro (1974), 'Are government bonds net wealth?', *Journal of Political Economy*, November, pp. 1095–1117.
24. See James Tobin (1980), *Asset Accumulation and Economic Activity* (Oxford: Blackwell).
25. See Alan S. Blinder and Robert M. Solow' 'Analytical foundations of fiscal policy', in A. S. Blinder *et al.* (eds) (1974), *The Economics of Public Finance* (Washington DC: Brookings).
26. For a comparison of the New Cambridge and Monetarist views, see John McCallum and David Vines (1981), 'Cambridge and Chicago on the balance of payments', *Economic Journal*, June, pp. 439–53.
27. See David A. Currie, 'Macroeconomic policy and government financing', in M. J. Artis and A. R. Nobay (eds) (1978), *Contemporary Economic Analysis* (London: Croom-Helm).

Chapter 16: Monetary policy

1. See William Poole (1970), 'Optimal choice of monetary instruments in a simple stochastic macro model', *Quarterly Journal of Economics*, May.
2. See Milton Friedman (1968), 'The role of monetary policy', *American Economic Review*, March.
3. For discussion of the issues here, see David Laidler (1981), 'Some policy implications of the monetary approach to balance of payments and exchange rate analysis', *Oxford Economic Papers*, July, Supplement.
4. See William Buiter and Marcus Miller (1981), 'Monetary policy and international competitiveness', *Oxford Economic Papers*, July, Supplement; and M. J. Artis and D. A. Currie (1981), 'Monetary targets and the exchange rate', *Oxford Economic Papers*, July, Supplement.
5. See Nigel Duck and David Sheppard (1978), 'A proposal for the control of the U.K. money supply', *Economic Journal*, March.
6. Green Paper, *Monetary Control* (March 1980), Cmnd 7858 (London: HMSO).
7. See for example, 'Monetary base control', *Bank of England Quarterly Bulletin*, June 1979.
8. See Charles Goodhart (1981), 'Problems of monetary management: the U.K. experience', in A. S. Courakis (ed.), *Inflation, Depression and Economic Policy in the West* (Oxford: Alexandrine Press).
9. For further discussion of the gilt-edged market, see 'The gilt-edged market', *Bank of England Quarterly Bulletin*, June 1979.
10. See note 6 for this reference.
11. Milton Friedman (1980), *Memoranda on Monetary Policy*, pp. 56–8. Treasury and Civil Service Committee, Session 1979-1980, House of Commons HC720 (London: HMSO).
12. See David Gowland (1978), *Monetary Policy and Credit Control* (London: Croom-Helm), for further discussion the changes in policy practice.
13. Radcliffe Report (1959), *Committee on the Workings of the Monetary System*, Cmnd 827 (London: HMSO).
14. See *Competition and Credit Control*, Bank of England, April 1971.
15. *Bank of England Quarterly Bulletin*, June 1981, p. 163.
16. See the *Bank of England Quarterly Bulletin* for further information regarding such changes in policy practice.
17. See *Monetary Policy*, p. xcii. Third Report from Treasury and Civil Service Committee, Session 1980-1981, vol. I, HC163-I, House of Commons (London: HMSO, 1981).
18. Milton Friedman (1980), op. cit., pp. 56–7.

Chapter 17: Wage and price controls

1. See F. T. Blackaby (1980), 'An array of proposals', in F. T. Blackaby (ed.), *The Future of Pay Bargaining* (London: Heinemann).

2. See Samuel Brittan and Peter Lilley (1977), *The Delusion of Incomes Policy* (London: Temple Smith).

3. See Maurice Peston (1981), 'The integration of monetary, fiscal and incomes policy', *Lloyds Bank Review*, July, pp. 1–4.

4. For a lucid account of controls over the 1960–74 period, see F. T. Blackaby (1978), in F. T. Blackaby (ed.), *British Economic Policy 1960–1974* (Cambridge: Cambridge University Press). For an account of controls since 1974, see D. Purdy (1981), 'Government–trade union relations', *Socialist Economic Review* (London: Merlin Press).

5. See F. T. Blackaby (1980), op. cit.

6. Ibid.

7. See C. T. Saunders (1980), 'Changes in relative pay in the 1970's', in F. T. Blackaby (ed.), *The Future of Pay Bargaining* (London: Heinemann).

8. J. A. Carlson and J. M. Parkin (1975), 'Inflation expectations', *Economica*, May, pp. 231–38.

Chapter 18: Balance of payments and exchange rate policies

1. See *Cambridge Economic Policy Review*; and T. Ward (1981), 'The case for an import control strategy in the U.K.', *Socialist Economic Review* (London: Merlin Press) for further discussion.

2. See M. J. Artis (1978), 'The import surcharge', and 'The temporary import deposit scheme', in F. T. Blackaby (ed.) (1978), *British Economic Policy 1960–1974*, pp. 344–9 (Cambridge: Cambridge University Press).

3. M. J. Artis (1980), op. cit.

4. For criticism of the argument for import controls see M. F. G. Scott (1980), *The Case Against Import Controls*, Thames Essay (London: Trade Policy Research Centre); and D. Lal (1979), 'Comment', in R. Major (ed.), *Britain's Trade and Exchange Rate Policy* (London: Heinemann).

5. See 'Academic criticisms of the CEPG analysis', *Cambridge Economic Policy Review*, April 1980, pp. 35–42.

6. W. Godley (1976), 'What Britain needs is growth . . .', *The Times*, 1 November.

7. For an account of the recent changes in the international monetary system, see Ronald I. McKinnon (1979), *Money in International Exchange* (Oxford: Oxford University Press).

8. See M. Emerson (1979), 'The U.K. and the European monetary system', in R. Major (ed.), *Britain's Trade and Exchange Rate Policy* (London: Heinemann).

9. See HM Treasury (1978), *The European Monetary System*, Cmnd 7405 (London: HMSO).

10. See HM Treasury (1978), *Economic Progress Report*, March.

11. Frank Hahn (1981), cited in *Monetary Policy*, p. lxi, volume I of Treasury and Civil Service Committee Report, Session 1980–81, House of Commons HC163-I (London: HMSO).

12. See M. F. G. Scott (1981), 'How best to deflate the economy', *Oxford Economic Papers*, July Supplement, pp. 47–69.
13. *Cambridge Economic Policy Review*, April 1980, p. 36.
14. See J. A. Frenkel and H. G. Johnson (1978), *The Economics of Exchange Rates* (Reading: Reading Press).
15. See J. A. Frenkel and M. L. Mussa (1981), 'Monetary and fiscal policy in an open economy', *American Economic Review*, May, pp. 253–8.
16. See David Laidler (1981), 'Some implications of the monetary approach to balance of payments and exchange rate analysis', *Oxford Economic Papers*, July Supplement, pp. 70–84.
17. See Patrick Minford (1981), 'The exchange rate and monetary policy', *Oxford Economic Papers*, July, pp. 120–42.
18. See D. E. Moggridge (1969), *The Return to Gold 1925* (Cambridge: Cambridge University Press).
19. See Hahn (1981), op. cit., p. lxii.
20. Ibid.
21. P. J. Forsyth and J. A. Kay (1980), 'The economic implications of North Sea oil revenues', *Fiscal Studies*, July, pp. 1–28 (at p. 1).
22. Ibid.
23. For further discussion see W. M. Corden (1981), 'The exchange rate, monetary policy and North Sea oil', *Oxford Economic Papers*, July, pp. 23–46.
24. Jürg Niehans (1981), 'The appreciation of sterling – causes, effects, policies', *S.S.R.C. Money Study Group Discussion Paper*, February, p. 28.
25. Jürg Niehans (1980), op. cit., Table 18.2.
26. Ibid., p. 35.
27. See W. H. Buiter and M. Miller (1981), 'Monetary policy and international competitiveness', *Oxford Economic Papers*, July Supplement, pp. 143–75.

Bibliography

Alchian, A. A. and Klein, B. (1973), 'On a correct measure of inflation', *Journal of Money, Credit and Banking*, February, pp. 173–91.

Alt, J. E. and Chrystal, K. A. (1981), 'Public sector behaviour: the status of the political business cycle', in D. Currie, R. Nobay and D. E. Peel (eds), *Macroeconomic Analysis* (London: Croom-Helm).

Artis, M. J. (1978), 'Fiscal policy and crowding out', in M. Posner (ed.), *Demand Management* (London: Heinemann).

Artis, M. J. (1978), 'The import surcharge' and 'The temporary import deposit scheme', in F. T. Blackaby (ed.), *British Economic Policy 1960-1974* (Cambridge: Cambridge University Press).

Artis, M. J. and Currie, D. A. (1981), 'Monetary targets and the exchange rate', *Oxford Economic Papers*, July Supplement.

Atkinson, A. B. (1981), 'Unemployment benefits and incentives', in J. Creedy (ed.), *The Economics of Unemployment in Britain* (London: Butterworths).

Atkinson, A. B. and Stern, N. H. (1980), 'Taxation and incentives in the U.K.', *Lloyds Bank Review*, April, pp. 43–6.

Bacon, R. W. and Eltis, W. A. (1978), *Britain's Economic Problems: Too Few Producers* (2nd edn) (London: Macmillan).

Barro, R. J. (1974), 'Are government bonds net wealth?', *Journal of Political Economy*, November, pp. 1095–117.

Barro, R. J. (1980), 'Unanticipated money, output and the price level in the U.S.', *Journal of Political Economy*, August, pp. 549–81.

Batchelor, R. A. *et al.* (1980), 'Inflation, unemployment and reform', in F. T. Blackaby (ed.), *The Future of Pay Bargaining* (London: Heinemann).

Beckerman, W. (1974), *In Defence of Economic Growth* (London: Jonathan Cape).

Beenstock, M. (1979), 'Taxation and incentives in the U.K.', *Lloyds Bank Review*, October, pp. 1–15.

Benjamin, D. and Kochin, L. (1979), 'Unemployment in interwar Britain', *The Journal of Political Economy*, June, pp. 441–78.

Blackaby, F. T. (1978) (ed.), *British Economic Policy 1960-1974* (Cambridge: Cambridge University Press).

Blackaby, F. T. (ed.) (1978), *Deindustrialisation* (London: Heinemann).

Blackaby, F. T. (1979), 'The economics and politics of demand management', in S. T. Cook and P. M. Jackson (eds), *Current Issues in Fiscal Policy* (Oxford: Martin Robertson).

Blackaby, F. T. (1980), 'An array of proposals', in F. T. Blackaby (ed.), *The Future of Pay Bargaining* (London: Heinemann).

Blaug, M. (1981), *The Methodology of Economics* (Cambridge: Cambridge University Press).

Blinder, A. S. (1978), 'What's "New" and What's 'Keynesian" in the "New Cambridge" Keynesianism?', in K. Brunner and A. H. Meltzer (eds) (1978).

Blinder, A. S. and Solow, R. M. (1973), 'Does fiscal policy matter?', *Journal of Public Economics*, November, pp. 319–37.

Blinder, A. S. and Solow, R. M. (1974), 'Analytical foundations of fiscal policy', in A. S. Blinder *et al.* (1974), *The Economics of Public finance* (Washington DC: Brookings).

Brittan, S. (1969), *Steering the Economy* (London: Secker & Warburg).

Brittan, S. (1981), *How to End the Monetarist Controversy*. Hobart Paper 90 (Institute of Economic Affairs).

Brittan, S. and Lilley, P. (1977), *The Delusion of Incomes Policy* (London: Temple Smith).

Brunner, K. (1968), 'The role of money and monetary policy', *Federal Reserve Bank of St. Louis Review*, July, pp. 8–24.

Brunner, K. (ed.) (1981), *The Great Depression Revisited* (The Hague: Martinus Nijhoff).

Brunner, K. and Meltzer, A. H. (eds) (1978), *Public Policies in Open Economies*; vol. 9 of Carnegie–Rochester Conference Series on Public Policy (Amsterdam: North-Holland).

Buiter, W. H. (1980), 'The macroeconomics of Dr. Pangloss: a critical survey of the New Classical Macroeconomics', *Economic Journal*, March, pp. 34–50.

Buiter, W. H. and Miller, M. (1981), 'Monetary policy and international competitiveness', *Oxford Economic Papers*, July Supplement, pp. 143–75.

Cambridge Economic Policy Review.

Carlson, J. A. and Parkin, J. M. (1975), 'Inflation expectations', *Economica*, May, pp. 123–38.

Chalmers, A. F. (1978), *What is This Thing Called Science?* (London: Open University Press).

Chrystal, K. A. (1981), 'The New Cambridge Aggregate Expenditure Function', *Journal of Monetary Economics*, June, pp. 395–402.

Chrystal, K. A. and Alt, J. (1979), 'Endogenous government behaviour: Wagner's law of Gotterdamerung?', in S. T. Cook and P. M. Jackson (eds) (1979).

Clower, R. W. (1969), 'The Keynesian counter-revolution: a theoretical appraisal', in F. H. Hahn and F. P. R. Brechling (eds), *The Theory of Interest Rates* (London: Macmillan); reprinted in R. W. Clower (ed.) (1969), *Monetary Theory* (Harmondsworth: Penguin).

Cobham, D. P. (1981), 'The Socialist Economic Review project', *Politics and Power*, no. 3, pp. 255–67.

Cobham, D. P. (1981), 'Monetarism and the expenditure cuts', in *Socialist Economic Review* (London: Merlin Press).

Cook, S. T. and Jackson, P. M. (eds) (1979), *Current Issues in Fiscal Policy* (Oxford: Martin Robertson).

Courakis, A. (1981), *Sunday Times*, 5 April.

Coddington, A. (1976), 'Keynesian economics: the search for first principles', *Journal of Economic Literature*, December, pp. 1258–73.

Committee of Public Accounts (1981), *Twelfth Report*, Session 1980/81, House of Commons, HC318 (London: HMSO).

Committee on Policy Optimisation (1978), *Report*, House of Commons, Cmnd 7148 (London: HMSO).

Corden, W. M. (1981), 'The exchange rate, monetary policy and North Sea oil', *Oxford Economic Papers*, July Supplement, pp. 23–46.

Cripps, F. and Godley, W. (1976), 'A formal analysis of the Cambridge Economic Policy Group model', *Economica*, November, pp. 335–48.

Cripps, F., Godley, W. and Fetherston, M. (1974), 'Public expenditure and the management of the economy', in *Public Expenditure, Inflation and the Balance of Payments* (1974), Ninth Report of the Expenditure Committee of the House of Commons, HC328 (London: HMSO).

Crosland, A. (1974), *Socialism Now* (London: Jonathan Cape).

Cross, R. B. (1982), 'How much voluntary unemployment in interwar Britain', *Journal of Political Economy*, April.

Currie, D. A. (1978), 'Macroeconomic policy and government financing', in M. J. Artis and A. R. Nobay (eds), *Contemporary Economic Analysis* (London: Croom-Helm).

Deacon, A. (1978), 'The scrounging controversy', *Social and Economic Administration*, vol. 12.

Deacon, A. (1981), 'Unemployment and politics in Britain since 1945', in B. Showler and A. Sinfield (eds), *The Workless State* (Oxford: Martin Robertson).

Dilnot, A. and Morris, C. N. (1981), 'What do we know about the black economy?', *Fiscal Studies*, March, pp. 58–73.

Dow, J. C. R. (1964), *The Management of the British Economy 1945–1960* (Cambridge: Cambridge University Press).

Duck, N. and Sheppard, D. (1978), 'A proposal for the control of the U.K. money supply', *Economic Journal*, March.

Economic Trends, December 1979 (London: HMSO).

Economic Outlook, The (1981), Liverpool Occasional Paper No. 1.

Eisenburg, P. and Lazarsfeld, P. F. (1938), 'The psychological effects of unemployment', *Psychological Bulletin*, pp. 358–90.

Emerson, M. (1979), 'The U.K. and the European monetary system', in R. Major (ed.), *Britain's Trade and Foreign Exchange Rate Policy* (London: Heinemann).

Feige, E. L. (1981), 'The U.K.'s unobserved economy', *Journal of Economic Affairs*, July, pp. 205–12.

Financial Statement and Budget Report 1981-1982, March 1981 (London: HMSO).

Fine, B. J. and O'Donnel, K. (1981), 'The nationalised industries', *Socialist Economic Review* (London: Merlin Press).

Forsyth, P. J. and Kay, J. A. (1980), 'The economic implications of North Sea oil revenues', *Fiscal Studies*, July, pp. 1–28.

Foster, J. (1976), 'The redistributive effects of inflation – questions and answers', *Scottish Journal of Political Economy*, February.

Frenkel, J. A. and Johnson, H. G. (eds) (1976), *The Monetary Approach to the Balance of Payments Theory* (London: Allen & Unwin).

Frenkel, J. A. and Johnson, H. G. (1978), *The Economics of Exchange Rates* (Reading: Reading Press).

Frenkel, J. A. and Mussa, M. L. (1981), 'Monetary and fiscal policy in an open economy', *American Economic Review*, May, pp. 253–8.

Friedman, M. (ed.) (1956), *Studies in the Quantity Theory of Money* (Chicago: University of Chicago Press).

Friedman, M. (1956), 'The quantity theory of money – a restatement', in M. Friedman (ed.) (1956), op. cit.; reprinted in R. W. Clower (ed.) (1969), *Monetary Theory* (Harmondsworth: Penguin).

Friedman, M. (1968), 'The role of monetary policy', *American Economic Review*, March, pp. 1–17.

Friedman, M. (1980), 'Memorandum' in Treasury and Civil Service Committee, *Memoranda on Monetary Policy*, op. cit., pp. 56–8.

Garraty, J. A. (1978), *Unemployment in History* (New York: Harper & Row).

Garside, W. A. (1980), *The Measurement of Unemployment in Great Britain 1850-1979* (Oxford: Blackwell).

Godley, W. (1976), 'What Britain needs is growth...', *The Times*, 1 November.

Godley, W. and May, R. M. (1977), 'The macroeconomic implications of devaluation and import restriction', *Cambridge Economic Policy Review*, March.

Goodhart, C. (1981), 'Problems of monetary management: the U.K. experience', in A. S. Courakis (ed.), *Inflation, Depression and Economic Policy in the West* (Oxford: Alexandrine Press).

Gowland, D. (1978), *Monetary Policy and Credit Control* (London: Croom-Helm).

Graham, A. (1980), 'Demand management policy in changing historical circumstances', in D. A. Currie and W. Peters (eds), *Contemporary Economic Analysis*, vol. 2 (London: Croom-Helm).

Green Paper, *Monetary Control* (March 1980), Cmnd 7858 (London: HMSO).

Genberg, H. (1976), 'A note on inflation rates under fixed exchange rate open economies', in M. Parkin and G. Zis (eds), *Inflation in the World Economy* (Manchester: Manchester University Press).

Grinyer, P. *et al.* (1980), 'Taxation and incentives in the U.K.', *Lloyds Bank Review*, January, pp. 41–3.

Grossman, H. I. (1972), 'Was Keynes a "Keynesian"?', *Journal of Economic Literature*, March, pp. 26–30.

Hahn, F. (1980), 'Memorandum' in Treasury and Civil Service Committee, *Memoranda on Monetary Policy*, op. cit.

Hahn, F. (1980), 'Monetarism and economic theory', *Economica*, February, pp. 1–18.

Hahn, F. (1981) 'Preposterous claims of monetarists', *The Times*, 28 April.

Harding, S. G. (ed.) (1976), *Can Theories be Refuted?* (Dordrecht: Reidel).

Harris, J. (1972), *Unemployment and Politics* (Oxford: Oxford University Press).

Harrison, R. (1976), 'The demoralising experience of prolonged unemployment', *Department of Employment Gazette*, April, pp. 330–49.

Hemming, R. and Kay, J. A. (1980), 'The Laffer curve', *Fiscal Studies*, March, pp. 83–90.

Hicks, J. R. (1937), 'Mr Keynes and the "Classics": a suggested interpretation', *Econometrica*, March, pp. 147–59.

Hicks, J. R. (1973), 'Recollections and documents', *Economica*, February, pp. 2–11.

Hicks, J. R. (1974), *The Crisis in Keynesian Economics* (Oxford: Blackwell).

Hirsch, F. (1977), *Social Limits to Growth* (London: Routledge & Kegan Paul).

HM Treasury (1979), 'The Budget', *Economic Progress Report Supplement*, June.

HM Treasury (1979), *Macroeconomic Model: Technical Manual 1979*, HM Treasury, October.

HM Treasury (1981), *Fifth Report of The Treasury and Civil Service Committee*, Session 1980/81, House of Commons, HC232-II (London: HMSO).

Hobson, J. A. (1895), 'The meaning and measure of "Unemployment"', *Contemporary Review*, March, pp. 415–32.

Howe, G. (1980), Letter to House of Commons Committee on the Treasury and the Civil Service, 13 February.

Howson, S. (1975), *Domestic Monetary Management in Britain 1919–1938* (Cambridge: Cambridge University Press).

Hudson, W. D. (ed.) (1979), *The Is/Ought Question* (London: Macmillan).

Johnson, H. G. (1973), *Further Essays in Monetary Economics* (London: Allen & Unwin).

Johnson, H. G. (1973) 'The monetary approach to balance of payments theory', in H. G. Johnson (1973).

Joseph, K. (1978), *Conditions for Fuller Employment* (London: Centre for Policy Studies).

Kahn, R. (1976), 'Unemployment as seen by the Keynesians', in G. D. N. Worswick (ed.), *The Concept and Measurement of Involuntary Unemployment* (London: Allen & Unwin).

Kaldor, N. (1966), *Causes of the Slow rate of Economic Growth in the U.K.* (Cambridge: Cambridge University Press).

Kantor, B. (1979), 'Rational expectations and economic thought', *Journal of Economic Literature*, December, pp. 545-55.

Kay, J. A., Morris, C. N. and Warren, N. A. (1980), 'Tax benefits and incentives to seek work', *Fiscal Studies*, November, pp. 8-25.

Keynes, J. M. (1936), *The General Theory of Employment, Interest and Money* (London: Macmillan).

Keynes, J. M. (1937), 'The General Theory: fundamental concepts and ideas', *Quarterly Journal of Economics*, pp. 209-33; reprinted in R. W. Clower (ed.) (1969), *Monetary Theory* (Harmondsworth: Penguin).

Keynes, J. M. (1937), 'How to avoid a slump', *The Times*, January.

Keynes, J. M. (with Henderson, H. O.) (1931), 'Can Lloyd George do it?', in *Essays in Persuasion* (London: Macmillan).

Kyndland, F. and Prescott, E. C. (1980), 'A competitive theory of fluctuations and the desirability of stabilisation policy', in S. Fischer (ed.), *Rational Expectations and Economic Policy* (Chicago: University of Chicago Press).

Labour Party (1976), *Report of 74th Annual Conference*.

Laidler, D. (1977), *The Demand for Money* (2nd edn) (New York: Dun-Donnelley).

Laidler, D. (1980), 'Notes on gradualism', in Treasury and Civil Service Committee (1981), pp. 48-54.

Laidler, D. (1981), 'Some policy implications of the monetary approach to balance of payments and exchange rate analysis', *Oxford Economic Papers*, July.

Laidler, D. (1981), 'Monetarism: an interpretation and assessment', *Economic Journal*, March, pp. 1-28.

Laidler, D. and Parkin, M. (1975) 'Inflation: a survey', *Economic Journal*, December, pp. 741-809.

Lal, D. (1979), 'Comment', in R. Major (ed.), *Britain's Trade and Exchange Rate Policy* (London: Heinemann).

Layard, P. K. G. and Nickell, S. J. (1980), 'The case for subsidising extra jobs', *Economic Journal*, March, pp. 51-73.

Leijonhufvud, A. (1968), *On Keynesian Economics and the Economics of Keynes* (Oxford: Oxford University Press).

Leijonhufvud, A. (1969), *Keynes and the Classics*, Occasional Paper 30 (London: Institute of Economic Affairs).

Lipsey, R. *An Introduction to Positive Economics* (London: Weidenfeld & Nicolson), various editions.

Loasby, B. J. (1976), *Choice, Complexity and Ignorance* (Cambridge: Cambridge University Press).

Lucas, R. E. Jr (1972), 'Expectations and the neutrality of money', *Journal of Economic Theory*, April, pp. 103-24.

Lucas, R. E. Jr (1980), 'Methods and problems in business cycle theory', *Journal of Money, Credit and Banking*, November, pp. 710-11.

Macafee, K. (1980), 'A glimpse of the hidden economy in the national accounts', *Economic Trends*, February.

Main, B. G. M. (1981), 'The length of employment and unemployment in Great Britain', *Scottish Journal of Political Economy*, June, pp. 146-64.

Maki, D. and Spindler, Z. A. (1975), 'The effects of unemployment compensation on unemployment in Britain', *Oxford Economic Papers*, November, pp. 440–54.

Malinvaud, E. (1977), *The Theory of Unemployment Reconsidered* (Oxford: Basil Blackwell).

Mayer, T. (1980), 'Economics as a hard science: realistic goal or wishful thinking?', *Economic Inquiry*, April, pp. 165–78.

Manpower Services Commission (1980), *A Study of the Long-term Unemployed*, February (London: MSC).

Matthews, R. C. O. (1968), 'Why has Britain had full employment since the war?', *Economic Journal*, September, pp. 555–69.

Matthews, R. C. O. (1970), 'Full employment since the war – reply', *Economic Journal*, March, pp. 173–6.

McCallum, J. and Vines, D. (1981), 'Cambridge and Chicago on the balance of payments', *Economic Journal*, June, pp. 439–53.

McCombie, J. S. L. (1981), 'What still remains of Kaldor's laws?', *Economic Journal*, March, pp. 206–16.

McIntosh, A. (ed.) (1981), *Employment Policy in the U.K. and the U.S.* (London: John Martin).

McKinnon, R. I. (1979), *Money in International Exchange* (Oxford: Oxford University Press).

Meade, J. E., Chairman (1978), *The Structure and Reform of Direct Taxation*, Institute for Fiscal Studies (London: Allen & Unwin).

Meadows, D. H. *et al.* (1967), *The Limits to Growth* (London: Earth Island Limited).

Metcalf, D. (1980), 'Unemployment: history, incidence and prospects', *Policy and Politics*, pp. 21–37.

Metcalf, D., Nickell, S. and Floros, N. (1982), 'Still searching for an explanation of unemployment in interwar Britain', *Journal of Political Economy*, April.

Millward, R. (1980), 'The comparative performance of public and private ownership', *Salford Papers in Economics*.

Minford, P. (1980), 'Memorandum', in Treasury and Civil Service Committee (1981), pp. 131–43.

Minford, P. (1981), 'The exchange rate and monetary policy', *Oxford Economic Papers*, July Supplement, pp. 120–42.

Minford, P. and Peel, D. (1981), 'Is the government's economic strategy on course?', *Lloyds Bank Review*, no. 140, April.

Ministry of Reconstruction (1944), *Employment Policy*, Cmnd 6527 (London: HMSO).

Mishan, E. J. (1967), *The Costs of Economic Growth* (London: Staples Press).

Moggridge, D. E. (1969), *The Return to Gold 1925* (Cambridge: Cambridge University Press).

Morley, R. (1980), 'Profit, relative prices and unemployment', *Economic Journal*, September, pp. 582–600.

Moylan, S. and Davies, R. (1981), 'The flexibility of the unemployed', *Employment Gazette*, January, pp. 29–33.

Moylan, S. and Davies, R. (1980), 'The disadvantages of the unemployed', *Employment Gazette*, August, pp. 830–2.

Mundell, R. A. (1968), 'The nature of policy choices', in R. A. Mundell (ed.), *International Economics* (London: Macmillan).

Muth, J. F. (1961), 'Rational expectations and the theory of price movements', *Econometrica*, January, pp. 315-35.

Nickell, S. J. (1979), 'The effect of unemployment and related benefits on the duration of unemployment', *Economic Journal*, March, pp.34-49.

Nickell, S. J. (1979), 'Unemployment and the structure of labour costs', in K. Brunner and A. Meltzer (eds), *Policies for Employment, Prices and the Exchange Rate* (Amsterdam: North-Holland).

Nickell, S. J. (1979), 'Estimating the probability of leaving unemployment', *Econometrica*, September, pp. 1249-66.

Nickell, S. J. (1980), 'A picture of male unemployment in Britain', *Economic Journal*, December, pp. 776-94.

Niehans, J. (1981), 'The appreciation of sterling – causes, effects, policies', *SSRC Money Study Group Discussion Paper*, February.

Parsley, C. J. (1980), 'Labour, unions and wages', *Journal of Economic Literature*, March, pp. 1-31.

Patinkin, D. (1969), 'The Chicago tradition, the quantity theory and Friedman', *Journal of Money, Credit and Banking*, February, pp. 46-70.

Peden, G. C. (1980), 'Keynes, the Treasury and unemployment in the later nineteen-thirties', *Oxford Economic Papers*, March, pp. 1-18.

Peston, M. (1974), *Theory of Macroeconomic Policy* (Deddington: Philip Allan).

Peston, M. (1981), 'The integration of monetary, fiscal and incomes policy', *Lloyds Bank Review*, April, pp. 1-13.

Phelps, E. S. (1967), 'Phillips curves, expectations of inflation and optimal unemployment over time', *Economica*, August, pp. 254-81.

Phelps, E. S. (1972), *Inflation Policy and Unemployment Theory: A Cost Benefit Approach to Monetary Planning* (London: Macmillan).

Phillips, A. W. (1954), 'Stabilisation policy in an open economy', *Economic Journal*, June, pp. 290-323.

Phillips, A. W. (1957), 'Stabilisation policy and the time form of lagged responses', *Economic Journal*, June, pp. 265-77.

Phillips, A. W. (1958), 'The relationship between unemployment and the rate of change of money wage rates in the U.K., 1861-1957', *Economica*, November, pp. 283-99.

Phillips, A. W. (1962), 'Employment, inflation and growth', *Economica*, February, pp. 1-16.

Pigou, A. C. (1914), *Unemployment* (London: Williams & Northgate).

Pilgrim Trust (1938), *Men Without Work* (Cambridge: Cambridge University Press).

Poole, W. (1970), 'Optimal choice of monetary instruments in a simple stochastic macro model', *Quarterly Journal of Economics*, May.

Popper, K. (1959), *The Logic of Scientific Discovery* (London: Hutchinson).

Popper, K. (1963) *Conjectures and Refutations* (London: Routledge & Kegan Paul).

Purdy, D. (1981), 'Government–trade union relations', *Socialist Economic Review* (London: Merlin Press).
Radcliffe Report (1959), *Committee on the Workings of the Monetary System*, Cmnd 827 (London: HMSO).
Robinson, J. (1971), *Economic Heresies* (London: Macmillan).
Rosewall, B. and Robinson, D. (1981), 'The reliability of job vacancy statistics', *Bulletin of the Oxford Institute of Eoncomics and Statistics*, February.
Rowthorn, R. W. (1975), 'What remains of Kaldor's law?', *Economic Journal*, March, pp. 10–19.
Sargan, J. D. (1971), 'A study of wages and prices in the U.K. 1949–1968', in H. G. Johnson and A. R. Nobay (eds), *The Current Inflation* (London: Macmillan).
Sargent, T. J. (1976), 'A classical macroeconomic model for the U.S.', *Journal of Political Economy*, April, pp. 207–38.
Saunders, C. T. (1980), 'Changes in relative pay in the 1970's', in F. T. Blackaby (ed.), *The Future of Pay Bargaining* (London: Heinemann).
Scott, M. F. G. (1980), *The Case Against Import Controls*, Thames Essay (London: Trade Policy Research Centre).
Scott, M. F. G. (1981), 'How best to deflate the economy', *Oxford Economic Papers*, July Supplement, pp. 47–69.
Sharples, A. (1981), 'Alternative economic strategies', in *Socialist Economic Review*, pp. 71–92 (London: Merlin Press).
Shaw, G. K. (1977), *An Introduction to the Theory of Macroeconomic Policy* (3rd edn) (Oxford: Martin Robertson).
Shaw, G. K. (1979), 'The measurement of fiscal influence', in S. T. Cook and P. M. Jackson (eds) (1979).
Sinfield, A. (1981), *What Unemployment Means* (Oxford: Martin Robertson).
Sinfield, A. and Showler, B. (eds) (1981), *The Workless State* (Oxford: Martin Robertson).
Smee, C. H. and Stern, J. (1978), 'The unemployed in a period of high unemployment', *Government Economic Service Working Paper No. 11*.
Solow, R. M. (1980), 'On theories of unemployment', *American Economic Review*, March, pp. 1–11.
Spindler, Z. A. and Maki, D. (1979), 'More on the effects of unemployment compensation on the rate of unemployment in Great Britain', *Oxford Economic Papers*, November, pp. 147–64.
Stafford, G. B. (1970), 'Full employment since the war – comment', *Economic Journal*, March, pp. 165–72.
Stein, H. (1969), *The Fiscal Revolution in America* (Chicago: University of Chicago Press).
Stern, N. (1976), 'Taxation and labour supply – a partial survey', in *Taxation and Incentives* (Institute for Fiscal Studies).
Taylor, C. T. and Threadgold, A. R. (1979), '"Real" National Saving and its Sectoral Composition', *Bank of England Discussion Paper*, No. 6, October.

Tobin, J. (1972), 'Inflation and unemployment', *American Economic Review*, March, pp. 1–18.

Tobin, J. (1980), 'Are new classical moels plausible enough to guide policy?', *Journal of Money, Credit and Banking*, November, Part 2, pp. 788–99.

Tobin, J. (1980), *Asset Accumulation and Economic Activity* (Oxford: Blackwell).

Treasury (1978), *The European Monetary System*, Cmnd 7405 (London: HMSO).

Treasury and Civil Service Committee (1980), Session 1979/80, *Monetary Policy*, vol. I, House of Commons, HC163-I (London: HMSO).

Treasury and Civil Service Committee (1981), Session 1980/81, *Memoranda on Monetary Policy*, House of Commons, HC720 (London: HMSO).

Treasury Economic Progress Report (1979), June Supplement.

Tufte, E. R. (1978), *Political Control of the Economy* (Princeton, NJ: Princeton University Press).

Ward, T. (1981) 'The case for an import control strategy in the U.K.', *Socialist Economic Review*, pp. 93–108 (London: Merlin Press).

Wass, D. (1978), 'The changing problems of economic management', *Economic Trends*, March.

Weintraub, R. E. (1974), *General Equilibrium Theory* (London: Macmillan).

Winch, D. (1972), *Economics and Policy* (London: Fontana).

Wood, G. E. (1981), 'Can 364 economists be wrong?', *The Journal of Economic Affairs*, July, pp. 221–7.

Wren-Lewis, S. (1981), 'The role of money in determining prices: a reduced form approach', *Government Economic Service Working Paper* No. 42, March.

Index